365 DAYS of UFOs

A Year of Alien Encounters

Published by Lisa Hagan Books 2017

Powered by

SHADOW
TEAMS

ISBN: 9781945962011

Cover design and interior layout by Simon Hartshorne

NICK REDFERN

365 DAYS
of UFOs

A Year of
Alien Encounters

CONTENTS

INTRODUCTION

365 Days of UFOs is very different to most of the many other UFO-themed books I have written. I'll explain what I mean by that. The vast majority of all my previous titles have been on specific, stand-alone topics. I'm talking about the likes of the Men in Black, the Women in Black, the Roswell affair of 1947, Bigfoot, Zombies, secret societies, and NASA conspiracies. The book you are now reading, however, is somewhat of a departure. Instead of being focused on one particular aspect of Ufology – such as alien abductions, contactee-type cases, or crashed UFO incidents – the connecting thread here is very different. That thread revolves around dates, rather than subjects.

As the title makes very clear, this book takes a deeply alternative approach to all of my earlier titles: it provides you with a UFO case for each and every day of the year. And, instead of covering just one, or even a handful of phenomena, it covers the entire subject of Ufology.

You will find in the pages of *365 Days of UFOs* fascinating – and, in many cases, never-before-seen – events involving Crop Circles, dead aliens held by the US military, MIB, Black-Eyed Children, radar-based UFO incidents, "black helicopters," Reptilians, Puerto Rico's Chupacabra, and much more.

And, with that said, it's now time to dig deep into what I call the "Cosmic Calendar."

JANUARY

JANUARY 1, 1947

A UFO ON A NATIVE AMERICAN RESERVATION
GLOBE, ARIZONA

Leonard Stringfield recorded the following details:

"WH" was on temporary leave from the Navy, waiting for reassignment, when he and his friend CC, just out of the Army, took a scouting trip in a jeep to look for desert property to homestead. Toward dusk, around 5 p.m., they were following a dirt trail when they came upon a group of Air Force personnel armed with carbines. They were ordered to stop and show identification, then questioned regarding their reason for being in the area.

While stopped for questioning, "WH" could make out other military personnel about a quarter of a mile away, grouped around an object that appeared to be half sunk in the sand. "WH" described the object as disc-shaped with a dome on top, about 30 feet in diameter and 18 feet high. On its outer edge, he said, were two rings that seemed to have windows in between.

In "WH's" opinion, the military had just arrived on the scene. "There was no evidence of an encampment or any heavy equipment," he told Stringfield.

JANUARY 2, 1952

"IT WAS A GOVERNMENT COVER-UP"
200 MILES FROM DENVER, COLORADO

A fascinating but little-known story of a crashed UFO came from the late R.E. Thull, a man who spent most of his career working as an airline pilot. In Thull's own words, written in 2000:

"UFOs are real! The government knows it! Why are they

withholding information? Do you have any idea of how many 'unreported' sightings are made by airline pilots? How long have UFOs been coming here? What is their purpose? Could Ezekiel have made the first recorded sighting, over two thousand years ago? I flew for fifty years, forty-two of them for a living, and have recently retired from a large airline. If I were still working, I wouldn't say what I am going to say now. I will not give exact dates or names in this writing because I do not want to implicate anyone in a controversial matter."

Thull launched into his knowledge of a crashed UFO incident, somewhere near Denver, Colorado, in the early 1950s. He revealed his personal knowledge of this significant affair:

"My first sighting was in the early Fifties, within two hundred miles or so of Denver, Colorado. It was mid-afternoon on a cloudless day when a 'government employed' radio range operator sighted two UFOs. As he watched, one of them crashed on a nearby mountain, then the remaining one circled the site for approximately thirty minutes. In those days, radio range operators were stationed across the country every one or two hundred miles for the purpose of controlling air traffic.

"A commercial airliner passed that particular station shortly after the UFO crashed and made their required position report. Then the excited operator asked the flight crew to verify what he was watching. The flight crew did verify, not the actual crash, but the circling craft. They, too, were quite excited and made a full report to the 'government operated' control tower at Denver. I was a co-pilot on another commercial aircraft in the vicinity at the time and was a 'silent' witness to everything except the initial crash.

"Now, all tower conversations are recorded, but somehow that one seems to have been 'misplaced.' No information about it has ever been released, at least not to the public. The fact that this report was made to a government controlled operations and was 'taken care of' so fast that it never made the newspapers, is definite proof, in my mind, and in many others, that it was a government cover-up."

A UFOLOGICAL THEORY
WORLD WAR II GERMANY

The following Air Force report of January 3, 1952 (on the subject of UFO sightings investigated by the Air Force in the late 1940s and early 1950s) was sent from Brigadier General W.M. Garland to General John A. Samford, Air Force Director of Intelligence. It is focused on UFOs and the theory that their origins may have been in World War Two Germany:

"It is logical to relate the reported sightings to the known development of aircraft, jet propulsion, rockets and range extension capabilities in Germany and the USSR. In this connection, it is to be noted that certain developments by the Germans, particularly the Horten wing, jet propulsion, and refueling, combined with their extensive employment of V-1 and V-2 weapons during World War II, lend credence to the possibility that the flying objects may be of German and Russian origin."

The document continues: "The developments mentioned above were completed and operational between 1941 and 1944 and subsequently fell into the hands of the Soviets at the end of the war. There is evidence that the Germans were working on these projects as far back as 1931 to 1938. Therefore it may be assumed that the Germans had at least a 7 to 10 year lead over the United States."

JANUARY 4, 1965

"WE HAVE DRAWN A BLANK"

CAMBRIDGESHIRE, ENGLAND

In the early part of 1996, the British Ministry of Defense (MoD) declassified under the terms of the Government's "Thirty Year Ruling" (legislation designed to ensure that all documents, regardless of classification, were withheld from public scrutiny for a minimum of 30 years) a file that detailed a variety of UFO reports that the MoD received during 1965.

Contained within the file was an 11-page report concerning an unidentified object that was seen to come down in the vicinity of March, Cambridgeshire, England on January 5, 1965. A man named Max Beran, one of those who witnessed the descent of the object, quickly wrote to the Meteorological Office Unit (MOU) at Huntington Road, Cambridge.

Beran stated: "Whilst in the sunlight it remained visible, giving the appearance of a curved object. Perhaps a parachute, but I would have thought too fast for that. Before falling too low to be visible in the low sun it appeared to be falling to a point perhaps a mile or two Southeast of the town center from where I was watching. What could the falling object have been?"

The Senior Meteorological Officer at Cambridge immediately contacted his headquarters at Braknell, Berkshire, regarding Beran's letter. Recognizing that this was a matter for the Ministry of Defense, Braknell prepared a one-page memorandum for the MoD outlining the facts. The MoD quickly swung into action.

According to a one-page handwritten note contained within the file, the police at March had been directed by the MoD to look into the matter. "[The police] sent a car out to look for the object in the vicinity of the 'Sixteen Root Drain' but without success," stated the note.

The MoD also put numerous questions to a host of other official departments as it sought to locate and identify the UFO, including the Royal Navy, the Ministry of Aviation, and various civil aviation bodies. Whatever the object was, the MoD claimed, it was not a piece of military hardware.

"Things which may on occasion fall from aircraft include external fuel tanks, drag-chutes, cockpit canopies, access panels on doors, and sometimes accumulations of ice," the MoD informed Max Beran. "We have looked carefully into all these possibilities so far as our own aircraft are concerned, but have drawn a blank."

JANUARY 5: 1966

AN AUTHOR ENCOUNTERS SOMETHING ALIEN

IBSTONE HOUSE, ENGLAND

According to a batch of files that the British National Archive declassified a number of years ago, the well-known English writer Dame Rebecca West was inadvertently plunged into a very strange puzzle. Incredibly, she asserted, some sort of unusual aerial object, had landed in the grounds of her home – Ibstone House.

As the now aged and fading documentation at the National Archive reveals, it was 2:45 p.m. on January 7, 1966 and West was out walking in the grounds of her home when…

"As I was going down the steep hill to the farm buildings I noticed a man walking on my property at some distance to the right of the path I was following," she wrote to the MoD. "Presently, he reached a point when the wood stopped and there is a hedge which runs down to the valley along a sharp ridge. There is a gap in the hedge and the man stopped just past this and turned around, facing in the reverse direction, and stood still."

Expressing concern about "what he was going to do," West watched in amazement as what she described as "an aerial construction" appeared out of nowhere. "One moment it was not there, the next it was," Rebecca West explained. "It seemed to come down quite rapidly, on the other side of the hedge from the man, but very close to it." And what, precisely, was it that Dame Rebecca West saw? Her description was curious, to say the least.

Stressing to the MoD that the object was "strangely shaped," she stated: "It consisted of something like a metal band, grey-blue in colour, flattened at one point so as to seem almost leaf-like, crossed with a sort of herringbone system of metal strips." She elaborated further: "There was also somehow attached to these an odd object like a bag with an opening that had points, made of yellowish material. As I looked the whole thing collapsed toward the ground.

"I saw it crumpling downwards, but crumpling is not quite the word. The metal band seemed to cut backwards and disappear while the curious bag looked as if someone were squeezing the air out of the lower portion of it, so that all the points stood up, and then fell back. Comparing the height of the object with the height of the man, I should put it as something [between] fifteen and twenty."

JANUARY 6, 1995

COLLISION COURSE!

PENNINES, ENGLAND

"A close encounter between a British Airways jet with 60 passengers on board and an illuminated, triangular-shaped, unidentified flying object at 13,000 feet above the Pennines is under formal investigation by the Civil Aviation Authority," stated the *Times* newspaper on February 2, 1995.

The incident had actually taken place on January 6, 1995, as Captain Roger Wills and co-pilot Mark Stuart began their descent towards Manchester Airport, England, in a Boeing 737 twin jet. Seventeen minutes before touchdown, all was normal until a mysterious object flashed past the right-hand side of the aircraft at a distance described as being "very close."

So close that the crew actually "ducked down" in their seats as the object sped past them. An immediate check with air traffic control at Ringway revealed that nothing had been picked up on radar, save for the 737 itself.

Anticipating ridicule, the crew of flight BA 5601 did not report the incident to their colleagues; however, British Airways management was ultimately advised of what had occurred. In line with set procedures, a full report, complete with sketches of the UFO, was sent to the Joint Air Miss Working Group, a part of the Civil Aviation Authority.

A CAA spokesperson said that any suggestion that the object had been a UFO was "purely speculative," adding that the investigation could last up to six months. The spokesperson told the press: "A very small proportion of near-miss situations involving untraced aircraft remain unresolved."

This was one of those "unresolved" ones.

A POLICE-OFFICER AND A UFO

WILMSLOW, ENGLAND

One of the most fascinating of all UFO reports secured from a serving police-officer concerns an English policeman named Colin Perks, who, in the early hours of the day in question, was on duty in the town of Wilmslow. According to Perk's official log report:

"Sir, I have to report that I have been in the Police Force for almost four years. I am 28 years of age, a married man and I reside with my wife and child in [witness's address]. I am in excellent health and I have no worries of any description.

"On the night of Thursday/Friday the 6th to 7th January 1966, which was a cold clear night and started [sic] with a full moon which made visibility good. I commenced duty at 10pm on the 6th and was due to finish duty at 6am on the 7th. At 1:15am on the 7th, I had my refreshments at Wilmslow Police Station where I resumed normal patrol at 2am on this date where I commenced walking around the village. I was alone on this occasion.

"About 4am on the 7th, I was checking property at the rear of a large block of shops which are situated off the main A34 road, (Alderley Road) Wilmslow. At 4:10am I was still checking property and facing the back of the shops when I heard a high-pitched whine. For a moment I couldn't place the noise as it was most unfamiliar to the normal surroundings. I turned around and saw a Greenish/Grey glow in the sky about 100 yards from me and about 35 feet up in the air.

"I stopped in my tracks and was unable to believe what I could see. However I gathered myself together after a couple of seconds and made the following observations. The object was about the length of a bus (30 feet) and estimated at being 20 feet wide. It was elliptic in shape and emanated a greenish grey glow that I can only describe as an eerie green color. It appeared to be motionless; there was no impression of rotation. The object was about 15 feet in height with a flat bottom.

"At this time it was very bright and there was an East wind. Although it was cold there was no frost. No cloud formation was anywhere near ground level. The object remained stationary for about five seconds then without any change in the whine it started moving at a very fast rate in an East-South-East direction."

Despite an extensive investigation by the British Ministry of Defense (the official report of the MoD runs to 21-pages), the affair was never satisfactorily resolved.

JANUARY 8, 2008

A GIGANTIC UFO INVADES TEXAS

STEPHENVILLE, TEXAS

Just eight days into 2008, UFO hysteria broke out in and around the Texan city of Stephenville. It all revolved around a case that caught not just the attention of the UFO research community but the U.S. mediaas well. The Associated Press reported:

"Stephenville, Texas – In this farming community where nightfall usually brings clear, starry skies, residents are abuzz over reported sightings of what many believe is a UFO.

"Several dozen people – including a pilot, county constable and business owners – insist they have seen a large silent object with bright lights flying low and fast. Some reported seeing fighter jets chasing it.

"'People wonder what in the world it is because this is the Bible Belt, and everyone is afraid it's the end of times,' said Steve Allen, a freight company owner and pilot who said the object he saw last week was a mile long and half a mile wide. 'It was positively, absolutely nothing from these parts.'"

Then there was this from CNN: "Major Karl Lewis, a spokesman for the 301st Fighter Wing at the Joint Reserve Base Naval Air Station in Fort Worth, said no F-16s or other aircraft from his base were in the area the night of January 8, when most people reported the sighting.

"Lewis said the object may have been an illusion caused by two commercial airplanes. Lights from the aircraft would seem unusually bright and may appear orange from the setting sun.

"'I'm 90 percent sure this was an airliner,' Lewis said. 'With the sun's angle, it can play tricks on you.'

"Officials at the region's two Air Force bases – Dyess in Abilene and Sheppard in Wichita Falls – also said none of their aircraft were in the area last week. The Air Force no longer investigates UFOs."

And the *Star Telegram* told its readers:

"Stephenville's latest close encounter is weirder than any light in the sky.

"Stephenville is under assault – not by Martians, but by people hunting them.

"The phones haven't stopped ringing at Steve Allen's trucking company in nearby Glen Rose. He's the guy who was out Jan. 7 watching the sunset at a friend's house near Selden when they all saw some weird flashing lights.

"Now he can't work for all the calls from London and around the world.

"Some of the callers are scarier than space aliens.

"'I'll be OK,' he joked Tuesday, 'as long as I don't get abducted.'"

The mysterious UFO events at Stephenville still perplex the UFO research community. And the media, too.

FAIRIES AND UFOS

MARLBOROUGH, WILTSHIRE, ENGLAND

Every now and then a story will surface that is so bizarre, yet also intriguing, that it is almost impossible to categorize. Such a story comes from Janice Bakewell, a woman who encountered a small UFO – as in extremely small – in Marlborough, Wiltshire, England. Janice was walking through nearby woods with her dog early one morning when she heard a loud buzzing noise that quickly filled her ears – and clearly those of her dog, too. Puzzled, she looked around, but it was all to no avail – at least, for around two minutes. Then, everything became amazingly clear.

As if out of nowhere, a small flying saucer appeared before her, hovering at a height of around four feet off the ground, in a small clearing in the trees. It was circular in shape, silver in color, and had a red band around its middle. And, it was barely four-feet across! She watched, astonished, as the diminutive craft settled to the ground – in decidedly wobbly fashion – and a small door opened. Janice still recalls holding her breath, wondering what might happen next. She soon found out.

Out of the door flew three, three-to-four-inches long small humanoid figures: clearly female and glowing brightly, they fluttered around Janice for a minute or two, dressed in silvery mini-skirts! At one point the tiny trio landed on Janice's right arm, smiled, then flew back into the craft, which shot away into the skies, never to be seen again. Such rogue cases are so often dismissed by Ufology; yet they are weirdly engaging and not at all rare.

JANUARY 10, 1988

ALIENS IN THE BUNKER
DEEP BELOW DAYTON, OHIO

History is made in many ways. For "Harry Palmer" it occurred deep below Wright-Patterson Air Force Base in Dayton, Ohio. It is a highly secure military installation that has a reputation for being the home of a number of well-preserved – and some not so well-preserved – corpses of dead aliens, presumably recovered from more than a few UFO crashes. Many UFO skeptics ignore or write-off such claims. Harry Palmer knows better.

It was a winter's night in 1988 when Palmer was ordered to report to one particular building on the base that he had never previously been in, one which was connected to a certain weapons-storage area. On doing so, he was met by three very pale men dressed in dark suits who directed him to a door which, when opened, revealed a large elevator on the other side. Silently, the black-clad trio motioned him into the elevator. He quickly realizing he was descending – and to a fairly deep degree. He was then ushered into a corridor that had a large vault-like door at its end.

One of the three men opened it, and in a strange high-pitched voice, ordered him into the vault. The same man pointed at a large container – perhaps nine feet in length and five feet in width – and ordered Palmer to take a look inside. He did as he was told and was shocked – to the point of feeling nauseous and clammy – by the sight of a badly damaged body of what he, Palmer, could only guess was an extraterrestrial: The head was large, the eyes were huge and black, and the severed torso was skinny.

In seconds, Palmer was forcibly taken from the room, taken to yet another room, and then ordered to sign a document that effectively said that if he ever spoke of what he saw he would be prosecuted to the extent of the law for violating U.S. national security. After signing the document, a deeply worried Palmer was taken back up the elevator and unceremoniously left there to make his way back to his normal place of work.

Clearly, this affair makes no sense at all – unless someone was playing weird mind-games with Palmer, although for what bizarre reason one can scarcely guess.

JANUARY 11, 1999

A STRANGE ENCOUNTER IN THE WOODS
STAFFORDSHIRE, ENGLAND

Rob Freeman is someone who had a very weird encounter in Staffordshire, England's Cannock Chase woods. It's a large area of forest noted for being a magnet for strange activity, including sightings of UFOs, Bigfoot, and a multitude of other, unusual phenomena. Freeman, while taking a long walk in the woods – to burn off the calories ingested over the Christmas period – came across a strange, small ball of metal sitting on a trio of metal legs. The ball was around the size of an average beachball, while the legs were about two-feet in length.

Somewhat perplexed, Freeman stared at the weird contraption – wondering what on Earth it was. He admitted, however, that its flying saucer-like shape almost immediately had him thinking it was some sort of vehicle – despite its small size. His suspicions were not wrong. In mere seconds after Freeman encountered the curious object, it shot into the sky, and was out of sight in seconds. Despite contacting the local police and also nearby military bases – in an effort to try and determine if the object was something of theirs - Freeman hit a brick wall. For him, at least, the matter was never resolved.

JANUARY 12, 1988

A WEIRD INTRUDER

HARLOW, ESSEX, ENGLAND

On this day, now-released British Ministry of Defense files reveal, a woman from the English town of Harlow, Essex woke up in the early hours of the morning from a deep sleep to see before her "a tall man wearing a space helmet and a silver suit." The "man" gave a brief warning that a nuclear attack on the U.K. was imminent, after which he "disappeared in a flash."

Unfortunately, we don't know what the outcome of this affair was, as the Ministry of Defense's files do not state what action – if any – was taken. Of course, that the U.K. was clearly not nuked is suggestive of the probability that the report was simply filed away by a puzzled civil-servant.

JANUARY 13, 1893

A MYSTERIOUS WOMAN IN BLACK

RHINEBECK, NEW YORK

One of the strangest, and undeniably hair-raising, aspects of the Women in Black phenomenon – which is inextricably connected to the Men in Black enigma - is their often-reported propensity to hiss at people in menacing, and almost animalistic, fashion.

Reports of these hissing WIB date back to at least the 19th century and extend to very recent years. The *Sunday Herald* newspaper of January 13, 1893 told a disturbing tale of an encounter with just such a WIB at Rhinebeck, New York. The title of the article was "A Woman in Black." As for the sub-title, it got straight to the paranormal point: "Like Other Ghosts She is Only Seen at Night – Neither is She Dumb, but Emits a Hissing Sound Which Startles the Ear and Congeals the Blood."

According to the story, "a mysterious woman in black" was provoking "much fear" in and around Rhinebeck. It's hardly surprising when one takes note of what the *Sunday Herald* had to say next: "It is the story of a strange creature who glides noiselessly along the country roads at dead of night. She has never been known to address anybody, although she has met many. Her language is the language of signs. She invariably halts long enough to stretch out her long arm from beneath a black veil and at the same time *make a hissing noise* [italics mine]."

JANUARY 14, 2014

THE BEDROOM INVADER
POINT PLEASANT, WEST VIRGINIA

Point Pleasant, West Virginia is – beyond any shadow of doubt – noted most of all for its wave of sightings of the infamous Mothman between 1966 and 1967. Decades later, however, the town was to play host to something even stranger. The witness to the weird affair, a local woman named Denise, was jolted from her sleep by a young boy looming over her bed. This was no normal boy, however: it was one of the dreaded Black-Eyed Children — pale-skinned, hoody-wearing kids who are noted for their completely black eyes.

Denise tried to scream out, but her vocal-chords were paralyzed, as was here entire body. The eerie boy stared at terrified Denise for a few moments, then retreated into the shadows of the room and vanished. It was a nerve-jangling experience that Denise has not forgotten. Nor has she forgotten a strange wave of hang-up phone calls that occurred across the next three nights, and all around 3:00 a.m. A connection? Denise believes so.

JANUARY 15, 1948

THE FLYING TOP

JEFFERSON, TEXAS

Declassified U.S. Air Force files describe the odd encounter of a man — whose name is redacted out of the available pages of the relevant dossier — who, while driving to work around 5:00 a.m. in Jefferson, Texas, encountered what looked like a child's toy top, but which was around six or seven feet in height, and which buzzed his vehicle, as he fought to remain calm and keep his vehicle on the road. It was dark grey in color and gave off a loud humming noise. In seconds, it was gone. Both the man and the military remained baffled.

JANUARY 16, 1958

AN OVAL OBJECT OVER OHIO
DAYTON, OHIO

Dan Beckley – no relation to famous ufologist Timothy Green Beckley – encountered a large, oval-shaped UFO in the skies of Dayton, Ohio, early one morning. Notably, Dayton is home to Wright-Patterson Air Force Base – which happened to have been one of the key military facilities that handled and investigated UFO sightings at the time. That may explain why Beckley's encounter was taken so seriously – and particularly because he was a retired FBI agent, too.

The investigative Air Force team was impressed by his account of seeing the large craft as it wobbled across the sky and then suddenly shot skyward and disappeared. Notably, the file on Beckley's encounter has not surfaced under the terms of the Freedom of Information Act. It is thanks to Beckley's granddaughter that we know of the facts – which begs an important question that remains unanswered: why, exactly, has the file not been released?

JANUARY 17, 1967

STRANGERS IN THE NIGHT
CHESAPEAKE, VIRGINIA

Over the years, more than a few stories have surfaced suggesting that agencies of various governments – including the U.S. and the U.K. – have extensive background files on alien-abductees. Such a thing is not as far out as the skeptics might think. After all, back in the 1950s the FBI opened files on numerous and well-known figures in the UFO Contactee field. Under Freedom of

Information legislation, the FBI's files on such Contactees as Dr. Frank Stranges, George Van Tassel, Truman Bethurum, George Adamski, and George Hunt Williamson have all been declassified. Admittedly, files on abductees are hard to find. But, they do exist.

Also via US FOIA legislation, the FBI has released a memo dated January 18, 1967 and titled "UNIDENTIFIED FLYING OBJECT ALLEGEDLY SIGHTING, JANUARY 17, 1967." It reads as follows:

"At 4:10 a.m., January 18, 1967, [deleted] advised that he desired to report that he had observed a large oblong-shaped object which alighted in the street in front of him when he was on his way home from his television repair shop, the [deleted], Chesapeake, Virginia. He believes that he was taken into this craft which he recalls as being made of a glass like substance and being transparent. It was manned by several individuals who appeared to be undersized creatures similar to members of the human race, probably not more than 4 feet tall. They were allegedly wearing regular trouser pants and T-shirts. [deleted] believes that he was transported by this craft for an undetermined distance and returned to his point of take-off approximately one hour later."

In the second and final paragraph we're told: "[Deleted] spoke in a coherent manner although he appeared to be under certain emotional strain. He claimed he had not been drinking any intoxicants but he was unable to account for the time between 8:00 p.m. and 4:00 a.m., he stated he was telephoning from his workshop but had no recollection of being elsewhere between 8:00 p.m. and 4:00 a.m."

The FBI did not take any action regarding this story, aside from forwarding the data to the Air Force. What action the USAF made, if any, remains unknown.

AN ALIEN IS SHOT AND A COVER-UP BEGINS

BROWNSVILLE, NEW JERSEY

The following document, dated September 16, 1980 and written on official U.S. Air Force stationery, was forwarded to UFO researcher Leonard Stringfield by a source to whom Stringfield gave the pseudonym of "Jeffery Morse."

"In January of 1978, I was stationed at McGuire AFB, N.J. One evening, during the time frame of 0300 hrs. and 0500 hrs., there were a number of UFO sightings in the area over the air field and Ft. Dix MP's were running code in the direction of Brownsville, N.J. A state trooper then entered Gate #5 at the rear of the base requesting assistance and permission to enter.

"I was dispatched and the trooper wanted access to the runway area which led to the very back of the air field and connected with a heavily wooded area which is part of the Dix training area. He informed me that a Ft. Dix MP was pursuing a low flying object that then hovered over his car. He described it as oval shaped, with no details, and glowing with a bluish-green color. His radio transmission was cut off.

"At that time in front of his police car, appeared a thing, about 4 feet tall, grayish, brown, fat head, long arms, and slender body. The MP panicked and fired five rounds from his .45 cal. into the thing, and one round into the object above. The object then fled straight up and joined with eleven others high in the sky. This we all saw but didn't know the details at the time.

"Anyway, the thing ran into the woods towards our fence line and they went to look for it. By this time several patrols were involved. We found the body of the thing near the runway. It had apparently climbed the fence and died while running. It was all of a sudden hush-hush and no one was allowed near the area."

JANUARY 19, 1999

A UFO AND A CHUPACABRA
EL YUNQUE RAINFOREST, PUERTO RICO

On my first visit to Puerto Rico – in the summer of 2004 and with a crew from the SyFy Channel – I had the opportunity to speak with a woman who had a hair-raising encounter in the island's El Yunque rainforest on one particular Saturday morning. As the woman picked plantains, she was amazed to see a definitive flying saucer – silver in color and about the size of a large car – silently descend in a nearby clearing.

That amazement became trepidation when a sliding-door on the outside of the craft opened. Trepidation was immediately replaced by sheer terror when, out of the surrounding trees, a fast-running, spiky-headed Chupacabra raced towards the unearthly craft, and jumped inside it! In seconds, the object took to the skies and was lost from view. Despite the outlandish nature of the story, the woman stood by it, even sharing the facts for the Sy-Fy Channel's film-crew.

JANUARY 20, 1996

"A STRANGE CREATURE THAT LOOKED HALF MAN AND HALF ANIMAL"
VARGINHA AREA, BRAZIL

From the research team of A.J. Gevaerd and Dr. Roger Leir comes the following, based upon their in-depth research into a spectacular series of alleged alien body recoveries in the Varginha area of Brazil:

"On 20 January 1996, around 8:30 a.m., the Varginha military police headquarters began to receive telephone calls from the district of Jardim Andere of Brazil, with reports that something strange was being seen in the neighborhood. Apparently some children had reported seeing a strange creature that looked half man and half animal and that was making a sound like "a sharp anguished cry." The entity moved only when someone threw a pebble at it. The local police command then informed the ESA (Escola de Sargentos das Forças Armadas—School of Sergeants of the Armed Forces) in the neighboring town of Três Corações that something suspicious was being sighted and reported from Jardim Andere. ESA sent off a military truck with two soldiers and a sergeant to the scene in Varginha. About 9 p.m., the 13ᵗʰ Company of Special Fire Brigade was ordered to send a garrison to the place under command of Major Maciel, Sergeant Palhares, Corporal Rubens, and privates Nivaldo and Santos.

"Curious civilians were gathering around but were strictly told to evacuate the area. An hour later, a creature was spotted. It was captured with a net for catching animals. It offered little resistance and was placed within a wooden box, then loaded on the ESA truck. As it was put onto the truck, according to the Fire Brigade militaries, the alien let off a faint humming sound. The military truck headed at full speed for the city of Três Corações. Just prior to the capture, shots were heard by witnesses who later saw troops carrying bags with something moving inside."

ALIENS ON THE MOUNTAIN
PORTON DOWN, WALES

In 1996, the late Tony Dodd – a UK police officer and UFO investigator – interviewed a retired member of the British military on
the matter of a UFO crash in Wales in 1974. Dodd referred to his
source as "James Prescott." According to Prescott, on the night of
January 21, "We, that is myself and four others, were ordered to
go to Llandderfel and were under strict orders not to stop for any
civilians." The team soon reached Llandderfel, whereupon they
were ordered to load two large oblong boxes into their vehicle:
"We were at this time warned not to open the boxes, but to proceed to [the Chemical and Biological Defense Establishment at]
Porton Down [Wiltshire, England] and deliver the boxes."

A number of hours later, they reached Porton Down and the
mysterious cargo was quickly taken inside the facility. The staff at
Porton allegedly opened the boxes while Prescott and the others
looked on. Inside the boxes, to Prescott's amazement, were "two
creatures which had been placed inside decontamination suits."
The Porton staff then began the careful task of opening the suits.
Said Prescott:

"When the suits were fully opened, it was obvious the creatures were not of this world and, when examined, were found to
be dead. What I saw in the boxes that day made me change my
whole concept of life. The bodies were about five to six feet tall,
humanoid in shape, but so thin they looked almost skeletal with
a covering skin. Although I did not see a craft at the scene of the
recovery, I was informed that a large craft had crashed and was
recovered by other military units. Sometime later we joined up

with other elements of our unit. They informed us that they had also transported bodies of 'alien beings' to Porton Down, but said that their cargo was still alive. This was the only time I was ever involved in anything of this nature. This event took place many years ago and I am now retired from the Armed Forces."

A DANGEROUS DEMON
DOVER, MASSACHUSETTS

Some monsters, like Bigfoot, the Chupacabra, the Yeti, and Ogop-ogo, are seen time and again and across decades – sometimes even centuries. There are, however, a few bizarre beasts that put in very brief appearances for startled eyewitnesses, and soon vanish, never to be seen again. Perhaps there is no better example of the latter than what has become known as the Dover Demon – an entity that some UFO researchers believe may have been an extraterrestrial.

It was around 10:30 p.m. on the night of April 21, 1977 when all hell broke loose. William Bartlett, then seventeen, was driving along Farm Street, in Dover, Massachusetts, when he spotted something both amazing and terrifying sitting on a wall. It was nothing less than a small, almost goblin-like, beast of about three and a half feet in height that had huge, glowing eyes and "tendrils" for fingers. Very curiously, it lacked ears, a nose, and a mouth. As for its head, it was described as being "melon"-like and extremely pale. In some respects, it was not at all unlike the so-called Gray-aliens of Ufology.

Although a few further encounters followed, the matter was never resolved. In January 2003, however the Dover Demon was back. The witness, a teenage girl named Erica, saw the beast flash across the road as she walked home from a friend's house on a Sunday afternoon. Given that just about everyone in Dover knows the story of its resident monster – or alien – Erica was sure that what she encountered was that terrible demon, apparently having returned to its old stomping-grounds.

JANUARY 23, 1963

UFOS: A BRIEF MESSAGE
LONDON, ENGLAND

Released under the UK Government's Freedom of Information Act is a very short, but very intriguing memo concerning a woman who telephoned the old Air Ministry, London on the night in question. The memo says: "Caller, Miss [deleted] claimed to see a flying saucer at Bluebell Hill, Kent at approximately 9:15 p.m. Miss [deleted] phoned the police, who referred her to us. She claimed the flying saucer affected the lights of her car, which only returned to normal when the flying saucer flew away. Report has been sent to Air Intelligence for further investigation."

Perhaps predictably, the Air Force Intelligence report today cannot be found.

JANUARY 24, 2015

ALIENS VISIT ASHEVILLE?
ASHEVILLE, NORTH CAROLINA

On this particular date, a group of friends, heading out to a local bar around 8:00 a.m., found themselves shadowed practically the entire way by what they unanimously described as a small circle of light, around the size of a soccer ball. The light consistently stayed around three-feet from the driver's-side window, clearly exhibiting some form of intelligence – rudimentary or something much more. The group concluded there was intelligence at work, due to the fact that the ball of light carefully followed the countours of the road. Although not terrified, they were certainly a bit jangled by the experience, which they put down to an encounter with "mini-me aliens!"

A SECRET IS REVEALED
GALLIPOLIS, OHIO

On this specific day, Suzanne Clarke, then of Gallipolis, Ohio was told an amazing story by her father. According to the tale, Clarke's father decided to come clean on something that he knew of the UFO phenomenon; something amazing and, if true, something having a bearing on national security – a major bearing, in fact.

Clarke's father maintained that in 1965, three years earlier, and while employed at NORAD – the North American Air Defense Command at Cheyenne Mountain, Colorado – he saw, under circumstances that he declined to explain, a series of black-and-white, aerial photographs of three small, large-headed bodies strewn around a desert floor, and which also showed a large amount of silvery, bright debris. The location, Clarke's father said, was New Mexico, and the photos were taken in 1947. Of course, this strongly suggests the now-famous Roswell affair of 1947 – although, admittedly, Clarke's father made no reference to Roswell.

Clarke was warned by her father not to reveal what he had told her until after his death – which occurred in 1981. Such was the concern, and even fear, in his voice, however, Clarke chose to remain silent until the late-1990s. So far, there has been no knock on the door from the Men in Black.

A SECRET FILE ON CROP CIRCLES IS OPENED
NATIONAL ARCHIVE, KEW, ENGLAND

In early 1941, Sir David Petrie was appointed Director General of the U.K.'s domestic Security Service, MI5, and was given substantial resources to restructure the organization, whose origins date back to 1909. As a result, MI5 became one of the most efficient agencies of the War. After the defeat of the Nazis in 1945, it was learned that *all* of the Nazi agents targeted against Britain had been successfully identified, and in some cases recruited as double-agents, by MI5 — something that contributed to the success of the Allied Forces landing in Normandy on *D-Day* on 6 June 1944. A number of files pertaining to the wartime activities of MI5 have been declassified and are now available for public inspection at the National Archive, Kew, England. One deals with MI5 investigations of what are intriguingly described as "markings on the ground." With hindsight, today, those markings may have been nothing less than Crop Circles.

Most notable of all: from interviews conducted with Allied personnel who had taken part in the hostilities in Poland, MI5 had determined that one of the ways that Nazi spies were communicating with German Luftwaffe pilots was by "beating out signs," twenty meters in diameter, "on harrowed fields or mowing such signs on meadows or cornfields." Crop circles, as they are famously known today.

It is quite clear from examining the contents of these

now-declassified files that the foremost thought on the part of MI5 was that the wartime Crop Circles across Europe – as well as the similar formations found on the British mainland – were the work of Nazi spies, and that the designs were intended to convey a specific, coded message to German bomber-pilots.

It's also deeply important, however, to note that with regard to the truly unknown formations that MI5 studied (those from Poland, Holland, France and Belgium), the theory they were created by the Nazis was simply that: a theory, an assumption, an assessment of the fragmentary data available. Of course, in 1944, no one perceived these formations as something possibly linked to any distinctly unusual – possibly even paranormal – phenomena. But, maybe, that's *exactly* the direction MI5 *should* have been looking in.

JANUARY 27, 1966

THE PHANTOM PHOTOGRAPHER

BEAUMONT, TEXAS

Irene is a now-retired school teacher who had a very strange experience while living in Beaumont, Texas. In the early hours of the morning she inexplicably woke up and felt compelled to go to the bedroom window. On doing so, she was shocked to see a car-sized UFO – of a bright blue color – that hung in the air for a few seconds, before vanishing into the dark sky above.She raced back to the bed, terrified by what she had just seen. On the following evening, however, something even stranger occurred.

There was a knock at the door. It was a very pale-faced woman in black who claimed to work for a company that offered aerial photographs of peoples' homes – taken by an expert cameraman, then framed, that would look very nice on the living-room wall.

There was, however, something that made Irene think things were not quite right; not at all. Her instinct was right on the money. When the woman offered to show Irene one of the cameras that the company used, she agreed to see it. The woman proceeded down the drive and got in the back seat of the black car she had arrived in. In a few seconds, she was out. Irene could see the camera, but was very surprised by what happened next: the woman took a photo of the front of Irene's house, jumped back into the car, and in seconds was out of sight.

Irene quickly became convinced that the odd encounter was somehow linked to the events of the previous night. She was likely not wrong. John Keel called these odd characters "Phantom Photographers." In his book, *The Mothman Prophecies*, Keel said:

"On a rainy night in April a man from Ohio had been driving along Route 2 near the Chief Cornstalk Hunting Grounds when a large black form rose from the woods and flew over his car. It was at least ten feet wide," he claimed. "I stepped on the gas and it kept right up with me. We were doing over seventy. It scared the hell out of me. Then I saw it move ahead of me and turn toward the river.

Months later, late in October, he returned home from work and found a prowler in his apartment. "When I opened the door I saw this man standing in my living room," he reported. "I think he was dressed all in black. I couldn't see his face, but he was about five feet nine. I started to fumble for the light switch when he took my picture. There was a big flash of light, so bright I couldn't see a thing. While I was rubbing my eyes, the burglar darted past me and went out the open door. I guess I arrived just in time because nothing was missing."

Cases nearly identical to that of Irene's abounded in Keel's files.

JANUARY 28, 1977

BRIEF BUT INTRIGUING

FARNBOROUGH, ENGLAND

A short memo contained in the now-released UFO files of the British Royal Air Force provides data on a strange event that warranted and received investigation, even though the conclusions have not yet surfaced, only the aforementioned memo. It states:

"Mrs. [Deleted] of Farnborough [England] telephoned RAF Rudloe Manor to report a 'flying saucer' sighting at Devizes, Wilts., on January 28. Mrs. [Deleted] claimed to have seen a silver 'flying saucer' that changed into a large black bird! What should we do with this? Parker suggests handing over to the P&SS [Provost and Security Services] and let them deal with it."

JANUARY 29, 1983

FROM A LAKE MONSTER TO A UFO

LAKE POND OREILLE, IDAHO

Danny Cash had a very strange experience at Lake Pend Oreille, Idaho. It is a huge expanse of water, in excess of forty miles in length, and 1,100 feet in depth. And, it might accurately be said that the lake is the home of a creature not unlike Loch Ness, Scotland's legendary long-necked beast, Nessie.

Sightings of the prehistoric-looking thing date back to the 1940s and continue, albeit sporadically, into recent years. A particularly spectacular encounter with Paddler occurred on Memorial Day 1985. That was when a woman named Julie Green was on the lake with several friends when they caught sight of something huge and fantastic. It was a large, gray-colored thing that raced across the lake, seemingly partially above and below the surface of the water. That the presumed beast was only around 600 feet away meant Green and her friends were able to determine that whatever it was, it certainly wasn't a wave.

Cash saw much the same thing in 1983, but with one notable exception: only seconds after the monster dove deep below the surface, a large ball of white light shot out of the water and vanished into the skies at a phenomenal speed. It's a case as baffling as it is fascinating.

THE MAN IN BLACK
BRIDGEPORT, CONNECTICUT

There can be no doubt at all that had it not been for a 1950s UFO investigator named Albert Bender, there would not have been the phenomenon of the Men in Black. Or at least, the phenomenon would not have achieved the iconic status it has today. Bender was a curious character. He lived in the attic of a large, old house in Bridgeport, Connecticut and was fascinated by the worlds of the paranormal, the supernatural, and the occult – both in reality and in the domain of fiction, too. In terms of the latter, we're talking about horror films, sci-fi movies, and stories by the likes of Bram Stoker, Edgar Allan Poe, and H.P. Lovecraft.

One movie, in particular, that may have influenced Albert Bender's subconscious, when it came to the development of the MIB motif, is the *very* appropriately titled 1949 movie, *The Man in Black*. A UK production, it was the creation of Hammer Films, who went on to produce some of the most beloved horror movies of the 1950s and 1960s.

The Man in Black was based upon a BBC radio series, *Appointment with Fear*, which ran from 1943 to 1955. In both the movie and the radio show, the Man in Black is the narrator of the tale and is played by actor Valentine Dyall. There are a couple of things that lead me to believe that Albert Bender may very well have seen *The Man in Black*.

Of course, this would require *The Man in Black* to have been shown in cinemas in Connecticut, where Bender lived at the time. Admittedly, I have not been able to prove that. But, there are some interesting parallels between Bender's MIB-themed stories and the movie. The first thing, unsurprisingly, is the title: *The Man in Black*. The second issue revolves around the poster that was created to promote the movie. It shows a silhouette of a sinister-looking character wearing a wide-brimmed, black hat and a long, black cloak.

It should be noted that this imagery is *identical* to a piece of artwork that Bender himself created and which hung on the wall of his attic-based abode in the early 1950s. The setting of Bender's painting is an old cemetery, filled with gravestones, a solitary crypt, trees, and a large moon. As for the MIB that appears in the painting, his hat is exactly the same as that in the poster, as is the cloak. And, it's important to note that we don't often hear of the MIB wearing cloaks. Yet, Bender's artistic rendition of a MIB *was* cloaked – just like the one in *The Man in Black*.

Coincidence? Or something more?

A WEIRD PHONE CALL
BATON ROUGE, LOUISIANA

A brief story told to me by Sarah, of Baton Rouge, Louisiana. After seeing a UFO on the fringes of town late on Saturday night – one of the so-called Flying Triangles – Sarah received an approximately 3:00 a.m. phone call from a man with a robotic voice who warned her not to talk about her close encounter. It was a sighting that was very brief, and which she did not share with anyone, including friends and family. Ominously, the strange voice at the other end of the telephone warned her of "repercussions" if she did speak out. Such was the level of fear instilled in Sarah, she stayed quiet until 2014.

FEBRUARY

FEBRUARY 1, 2015

THE BOY IN BLACK

CALIFORNIA, UNITED STATES

Time and again we hear stories of the Men in Black and the Women in Black. In 2015, however, Marc encountered in California woods a Child in Black. Not a Black-Eyed Child, I should stress, but a pale-faced boy attired in black pants, black t-shirt, and a black hoody. Notably, the CIB turned up while Marc was hunting, and just a few hours after he encountered a globe-like UFO over his tent, at a height of around eighty or ninety feet. According to Marc, the boy in black appeared out of nowhere, laughed in an odd, hair-raising fashion, and then suddenly vanished into nothingness.

FEBRUARY 2, 1975

SPYING ON ALIENS ON THE MOON

THE MOON

A secret group exists that isinterested in the mysteries of the Moon, including the possibility it is home to a race of extraterrestrials that live deep below its surface: it sounds incredible. It is, however, amazing fact.

The late Ingo Swann was considered to be one of the U.S. Government's leading Remote-Viewers, those near-unique individuals whose psychic powers and extra-sensory perception (ESP) were harnessed, from the 1970s onwards, to spy on the former Soviet Union. Swann proved to be a highly skilled remote-viewer, one whose talents were employed on a number of espionage-themed operations focusing on overseas targets that might prove hostile to the United States. As a result, Swann came into contact with a variety of shadowy figures within the realm of government secrecy, and the world of intelligence-gathering, including a truly Machiavellian character known, very mysteriously, only by the name of Mr. Axelrod — seemingly a leading figure in this hidden group.

Axelrod asked Swann, pointedly, what he knew about our Moon. Now, finally, the purpose of the strange meeting was becoming much clearer. Someone within officialdom was secretly looking to have the Moon remote-viewed — which is precisely what Swann went ahead and did.

Swann, using his remote-viewing skills, was able to perceive on the surface of the Moon a wealth of domed structures, advanced machinery, additional tall towers, large cross-like structures, curious tubular constructions across the landscape, and even evidence of what looked like extensive mining operations. Someone, or something, had secretly constructed nothing less than a Moon-base.

Intriguingly, Swann was also able to focus his mind on what appeared to be a group of people — that appeared very human — housed in some sort of enclosure on the Moon, that were busily burrowing into the side of a cliff. The only oddity: they were all utterly naked. Rather ominously, and very quickly, at that point Axelrod terminated the experiment, amid dark and disturbing allusions to the possibility that the Moon-based entities were possibly acutely aware they were being spied upon via the means of astral-travel. It was even implied that Swann's very actions might now place him in grave danger, if the beings decided to turn the tables and pay him a visit of a deadly, cosmic kind — which, very fortunately for Swann, they did not.

A UFO AND A MYSTERIOUS WOMAN

MELVILLE, NEW YORK

A particularly eerie encounter occurred on this day at Melville, New York, and involved a rancher whose farm was located in a rural, isolated part of town. Only days before he received a most unwelcome visit, the man saw a definitive flying saucer hovering over one of his fields, and which – somewhat amazingly – had what was described as a "ladder" hanging from its underside. At least until the ladder was hastily retracted and the saucer shot away, high into the sky, and vanished from view. That was hardly the end of the matter, however.

Just a few days later, the man heard a knock at the door. Given that his home was in the middle of pretty much nowhere, he opened the door both slowly and cautiously. Standing before him was a "Gypsy lady" who was dressed in a gray dress that reached her ankles and who wore sandals. Just like so many of the Men in Black, her skin was noted for its deep, olive complexion, and her eyes were described as "Oriental." The rancher added that she stood around five-feet and four inches tall, and had long hair that was "so black" it "looked dyed."

The woman said to the slightly alarmed man: "I have traveled a long way. May I have a glass of water? I must take a pill."

Baffled, the man decided not to risk incurring her wrath and quickly fetched her a glass of water and watched as she swallowed a round, green-colored pill. She thanked him, turned, and walked away – which the man found very strange, given that he lived on a backroad, and walking to the nearest town would be an arduous task, to say the least.

FEBRUARY 4, 1968

"ODD PSYCHOLOGICAL EFFECTS"
HOUSE COMMITTEE ON SCIENCE AND ASTRONAUTICS

Contained in a dossier of reports provided to the House Committee on Science and Astronautics on July 29, 1968 by UFO investigator James McDonald, is this particular case-file:

"At 7:20 p.m., many persons went outdoors to investigate either (a) the unusual barking of neighborhood dogs, or (b) a disturbing and unusual sound. Soon many persons up and down several streets were observing an object round in planform, estimated at perhaps 50-60 feet in diameter, moving slowly towards the east northeast at an altitude put by most witnesses as perhaps 300 feet. Glowing ports or panels lay around its upper perimeter and 'jet-like' orange-red flames or something resembling flames emanated from a number of sources on the undersurface. Odd physiological effects were remarked by various witnesses, and the animal-reactions werenotable features of this case."

FEBRUARY 5, 1986

AN UNEXPLAINED ENCOUNTER IN THE SKIES
EAST COAST OF IRELAND

A brief UK Ministry of Defense document reveals the salient data on a UFO encounter involving a highly respectable source, an airline pilot who sighted a UFO in the airspace of Ireland. The report states:

"5 Feb 86 5427N 0530W – Bright light passed upwards in front of A/C. A/C was crossing east coast of Ireland on descent. Light travelled towards A/C from a 2.30 position range approx.

11/2 miles and passed 1000 feet above travelling right to left 1 mile ahead. Burst of green light observed at peak of its ballistic flight. A/C ht [height] 1450 ft. CAA closure – possibly flare fired at about time of OCC by Aldergrove. Pilot considered this unlikely but no other explanation has emerged."

FEBRUARY 6, 1966

THE UMMO AFFAIR
MADRID, SPAIN

Jose Pena was said to have observed the flight of a large, white-colored flying saucer over Madrid, Spain. The UFO reportedly displayed a strange, prominent symbol on its underside. A similar craft, displaying the very same symbol, was allegedly seen in May 1967, in a suburb of Madrid, and quickly photographed. Such is the controversial nature of so many UFO-themed photos, it scarcely needs mentioning that the imagery remains highly inflammatory (despite having been shown to be a hoax) and is both championed and denounced.

Particularly intriguing is the fact that the controversy did not fade away. Actually, quite the opposite: it flourished for years. And thus was born the cult of UMMO – named after the planet from which the UFOs and their alien occupants supposedly originated.

One of those that dug deep into the matter of the UMMO controversy was the late Jim Keith, the author of such books as *Saucers of the Illuminati*, *Black Helicopters Over America*, and – with Kenn Thomas – *The Octopus*. In his *Casebook on the Men in Black* book, Keith stated: "The UMMO case was created through a large number of contacts – UFO sightings, personal contacts, messages through the mail and telephone – alleged to be from space brothers

from the planet UMMO," which, Keith added, was said to be "...
located 14.6 light years from our solar system."

Notably, there were those who postulated that the story got
even weirder and wilder, to the extent that the original UMMO
hoax was, later, ingeniously hijacked and expanded upon by certain official intelligence services (chiefly, the KGB). The scenario
involved Intelligence-based personnel exploiting the original
hoax as a cover for the dissemination of psychological warfare
within the public UFO research community, as well as a means to
secretly infiltrate and manipulate that same community to gather
information.

Jacques Vallee noted of UMMO that "...some of the data that
was supposedly channeled from the UMMO organization in the
sky was very advanced cosmology." Vallee added that portions of
the material "...came straight out of the notes" of none other than
Andrei Sakharov, including certain, "...unpublished notes." Vallee
commented further that there was a degree of thought suggesting
"...somebody had to have access to those notes, to inspire those
messages, perhaps the KGB."

FEBRUARY 7, 1978

"WHATEVER THE EXPLOSION WAS, IT HAD OCCURRED IN THE AIR"

POTRERILLOS, CHILE

On this day, a UFO reportedly crashed in Potrerillos, Chile.
According to Bob Pratt, the primary investigator, "I learned about
it in March 1979 when I was in Santiago, Chile, from José Manuel
Garcia, a reporter for *Las Ultimas Notícias*, a Santiago newspaper.
According to Garcia, between two and three o'clock one morning

in 1978 (he couldn't remember the exact date), a tremendous explosion woke up virtually all three thousand people then living in Potrerillos. All the houses shook and everyone thought a blast furnace had blown up. However, a quick inspection showed that everything was intact.

"The next day, several underground shafts were found to have caved in, while on the surface a section of a road going up the side of a ravine had collapsed. Engineers determined that whatever the explosion was, it had occurred in the air and the force of the blast had been exerted downwards. Garcia felt the blast himself. He was working in Potrerillos at the time as a public relations representative for CODELCO, the government-owned mining company."

Pratt continued: "Two days after the explosion, he said, six NASA technicians showed up with radiation-detection devices and other equipment. One of them arrived in a two-man Chilean Air Force helicopter and the others arrived a little later in a panel truck with NASA emblems on it. Garcia said there was no doubt that the men were Americans, or 'gringos' as he called them."

The story got even more intriguing, as Pratt's notes show: "All six wore coveralls with NASA emblems on them. They all spoke Spanish but only one man, apparently the leader, asked questions. People throughout Potrerillos were questioned about the characteristics of the noise and where the sound had come from."

With the questions completed, the NASA team vanished as mysteriously as they have first arrived – and amid local rumors that a craft from another world had slammed into the ground, somewhere locally.

A MALFUNCTIONING UFO

PENKRIDGE, STAFFORDSHIRE, ENGLAND

In 1991, the late UFO author and collector of crash-retrieval accounts, Leonard Stringfield, revealed that he had been provided with details of an alleged 1964 UFO crash in England.

Stringfield's source, S. M. Brannigan, said that at the time in question he was stationed aboard a "specially rigged LST, a flagship" (AKA "spyship") that was attached to a naval amphibious force at an unspecified point in either the Caribbean or the Atlantic. Brannigan's specialty was the translation of intercepted Soviet military transmissions, and he recalled one particular instance when an amazing coded message was received at the ship's "crypt-machine room."

The message was given to Brannigan and he set to work translating its contents. Almost immediately, he realized that this was no ordinary interception. It told of a UFO over-flying Europe that, for reasons unknown, had malfunctioned and plummeted to earth. Whether by accident or design, as the UFO descended, it broke into two parts, the chief section of which crashed in a large area of forestland in central England known as the Cannock Chase, near the town of Penkridge, Staffordshire; while the "remains" hurtled on until they slammed into the ground somewhere in West Germany.

As Brannigan continued his work, he learned that U.S. Air Force Intelligence was implicated in the recovery – and not just of the UFO. Three dead personnel had also been found. As the enormity of the event became apparent, other U.S. forces became involved, as did various elements of NATO.

A FLYING SAUCER AND ENGINE TROUBLE

AYLESBURY, ENGLAND

In February 1962, an employee of the UK Royal Air Force Police – one Sergeant C.J. Perry – was ordered to investigate a then-recent, extraordinary UFO report. The documentation prepared by Perry is now in the public domain. It tells an intriguing story:

"At Aylesbury on 16th February 1962, at 1530 hrs., I visited the Civil Police and requested information on an alleged 'Flying Saucer' incident. I was afforded every facility by the Civil Police authorities and although no official report had been made, details of the incident were recorded in the Station Occurrence book.

"The details are as follows: Mr. Ronald Wildman of Luton, a car collection driver, was traveling along the Aston Clinton road at about 0330 hrs. on 9th February 1962 when he came upon an object like a hovercraft flying approximately 30 feet above the road surface. As he approached he was traveling at 40 mph but an unknown force slowed him down to 20 mph over a distance of 400 yards. Then the object suddenly flew off.

"He described the object as being about 40 feet wide, oval in shape with a number of small portholes around the bottom edge. It emitted a fluorescent glow but was otherwise not illuminated. Mr. Wildman reported the incident to a police patrolman who notified the Duty Sergeant, Sergeant Schofield. A patrol car was dispatched to the area but no further trace of the 'Flying Saucer' was seen. It was the opinion of the local police that the report by Mr. Wildman was perfectly genuine and the experience was not a figment of imagination. They saw that he was obviously shaken.

"I spoke to Sergeant Schofield and one of the Constables to

whom the incident was reported. Both were convinced that Mr. Wildman was genuinely upset by his experience."

FEBRUARY 10, 1964

A UFO OF THE DANGEROUS VARIETY
BIG THICKET, TEXAS

One of the most controversial UFO crash cases I investigated occurred in February 1964. The location was a large area of Texas forestland that is known as the Big Thicket. According to the story told to me by Will, on one particular night in 1964, Will and more than a few of his comrades were ordered to prepare for immediate deployment; it was clear that something important was going down. The location was the Big Thicket. It was around 9:00 p.m. when things really kicked off. With his fellow troops, Will was driven by truck to the Big Thicket – specifically an area barely a quarter of a mile from the start of Ghost Light Road. On their arrival, the entire unit was met by what Will described to me as looking like "classic CIA." Two senior military officers were also present.

Will and his fellow personnel were ordered to remain vigilant and to be ready for any eventualities, something that puzzled one and all. After all, what could be so dangerous about the heart of the Big Thicket? It wasn't long before the group found out. Will and his team were told to patrol the road and the outskirts of the Big Thicket, specifically to ensure that no members of the public tried to gain access to the area. And if they did, to detain them. Will told me that by this time he realized something very unusual was going down. The level of high-strangeness increased when, within the next twenty minutes or thereabouts, a team of personnel arrived on the scene – all dressed in white "hazmat"-style outfits.

Reportedly, what was found was a small, circular-shaped UFO designated as a "biological hazard," and, according to the primary witness, one of several such objects found between the late 1950s to mid 1960s and presented significant health issues to those that handled the alien evidence.

FEBRUARY 11, 1974

AN ALIEN INVADER

FRIMLEY, ENGLAND

The date was early 1974, and the setting, the Marconi Space and Defense facility at Frimley, England. At the time, the witness was employed as a draughtswoman in the Central Services branch – having previously served an apprenticeship in a division of the British Royal Navy – something which ensured that she had access to much of the establishment.

On arriving at work one particular morning, she was surprised to see an inordinate number of Ministry of Defense personnel swarming around one specific building which had been cordoned off. Although she was aware that something of deep significance had occurred, it was not until later that she was able to tackle a trusted colleague, a manager at the base.

"Something very serious has happened, hasn't it?" she inquired. "Yes," was the quiet response, "we've had a break-in. I can't say anymore." Over the course of several weeks, however, further pieces of the puzzle fell into place. It transpired that the break-in was far more than simply an unauthorized entry. What occurred was nothing short of the penetration of a highly sensitive facility by a living, breathing, extraterrestrial creature!

The incident had occurred late at night, and the solitary

witness was a security guard who had been patrolling the building as part of his routine duty. While walking along a corridor, the guard was startled by a dazzling blue light that emanated from one particular room. But this was no ordinary room: it was a storage facility for top secret documentation generated by Marconi as part of its work on behalf of the British Government and the Ministry of Defense, much of which was related to classified, radar-based programs.

Realizing that no one – at all – should have been in the area at that time of night, the guard burst into the room, only to be confronted by a shocking sight. There, literally sifting through pages and pages of top-secret files was a gray-skinned humanoid – but decidedly non-human – creature which quickly dematerialized before the shocked guard's eyes. Although severely traumatized by the event, he was able to provide a brief description of the being to his superiors and noted that the blue light emanated from a helmet that encompassed the head of the entity.

FEBRUARY 12, 2010

A UFO AND A CREATURE

SEATTLE, WASHINGTON

Some of the most baffling of all UFO episodes are those in which not just a UFO, but a strange creature, too, is seen. Such was the case when Kim saw a large blue ball of light hovering over her property on the fringes of the Seattle woods. It was, she recalls, bobbing up and down – "like someone bouncing a rubber ball." If that was not amazing enough, as Kim continued to watch the odd spectacle, what was described as "the largest wolf I have ever seen" walked slowly across the yard, sat under the ball of light, and stared directly at her. The unnerving situation came to a sudden end when the ball of light dematerialized, as did the wolf.

FEBRUARY 13, 1981

"SIZEABLE" AND "OVAL"

LYON, FRANCE

"13 Feb 81 Lyon – Unidentified foreign object seen on aircraft radar. A sizeable oval shaped target appeared on radar center line at limit of range tracking at very high speed. No visual sighting made."

That is the only piece of data that the UK's Civil Aviation Authority has placed into the public domain on a case that practically screams for an in-depth investigation. Maybe, it was investigated. If it was, we have yet to be told the full story.

FEBRUARY 14, 2002

AN ALIEN "MISSION"

DEATH VALLEY, CALIFORNIA

Franco's close encounter with a UFO occurred in the heart of Death Valley, California, around 9:30 p.m. Oddly, though, and for reasons which he still cannot explain, Franco felt compelled to drive out to one particular area, turn off his engine, and wait. He did not have to wait for long. In mere minutes, a typical 1950s–era flying saucer lit up Franco's car with a powerful blue light. Only seconds later, Franco's mind was filled with apocalyptic imagery of nuclear war and the end of civilization, after which the UFO quickly vanished. Franco is convinced that, for reasons which he does not fully understand, he is on a "mission," one which will see him play a major role when the apocalypse hits – a role which will involve him helping to rebuild our shattered world.

PROJECT SILVER BUG

WRIGHT-PATTERSON AIR FORCE BASE, OHIO

On this day, the Air Technical Intelligence Center, Wright–Patterson Air Force Base, Ohio, stated, in a document titled "Project Silver Bug, No. 9961," the following:

"Several news mediums have published articles concerning A. V. Roe, Canada, Limited, Project Y2 (Secret) which, when supplemented by the December *Air Intelligence Digest* article, "The Flying Disk", present an inaccurate picture of the proposed project. It was decided that a factual account of this project would be presented, in the form of a Joint Wright Air Development Center - Air Technical Intelligence Center, to the intelligence agencies to correct any misgivings brought about by the above mentioned articles.

"The subject of this report deals with a proposal for a new type of aircraft by one of Canada's most progressive members of the aircraft industry, AVRO Aircraft, limited, a member of the Hawker-Siddley group. This project should in no way be associated with any science fiction for "Flying Saucer" stories because of its external appearance. The configuration was a result of an engineering investigation into the solution of a particular problem.

"An examination of the AVRO proposal shows that the potential for a very high performance weapon system exists in the not-to-distant future. Although this proposal offers the USAF a potentially advanced weapon system having both vertical take-off and military performance capabilities, there are numerous technical problems which must be solved before a successful development can be realized.

"The proposal is for the design of a supersonic research aircraft having a circular planform and VTO characteristics. One version provides for the use of several conventional radial-flow type engines. Another unusual feature of this proposal is that the control of the aircraft is accomplished by selective direction of the exhaust gases which eliminates the necessity of conventional aerodynamic control surfaces...This proposal offers a possible solution to the USAF requirement for achieving dispersed base operations."

FEBRUARY 16, 1982

SHAPE-SHIFTING BLACK HELICOPTERS
DULCE, NEW MEXICO

The town of Dulce, New Mexico has become infamous in UFO circles, chiefly because it is said to be the home of an underground base – which is manned by hostile, dangerous aliens who engage in nightmarish genetic experiments on human abductees. So the story continues, the US Government knows all too well what goes on under Dulce, but lacks the sufficient power or ability to destroy the alien hordes. That there has been an undeniable mass of so-called cattle-mutilations in the area is an issue which cannot be denied – indeed, the FBI has declassified a sizeable number of reports of such mutilations from the area.

This brings us to the story of Bruno. On the day in question, he saw a squadron of black helicopters hovering over Archuleta Mesa – below which, the story goes, is the extraterrestrial installation. As Bruno watched, the helicopters inexplicably morphed into bright balls of light – leading him to conclude that the ETs of Dulce can camouflage their craft to resemble our aircraft, thus ensuring that, for the most part, they are never seen for what they really are.

AN ALIEN VIRUS IN OUR FUTURE?
LINCOLN, NEBRASKA

Early on the morning in question, Ralph was driving to work, in Lincoln, Nebraska, when, quite out of the blue, he heard a voice in head warning him of a looming worldwide disaster of a viral nature – a disaster that would see the overwhelming majority of the human race wiped out. Billions would be dead in a matter of weeks. The voice identified itself as Caumuan, an emissary from a faraway world. Terrified that he was going mad, Ralph pulled over to the side of the road, in a near-panic-attack state. Two days later, the message was repeated – this time as Ralph woke up for work. What was going on? Had he, at the age of 28, suddenly developed schizophrenia?

It's unlikely, as there was no repeat experience, ever. And, of course, our civilization was not exterminated as a result of a deadly virus. To this day, however, Ralph has his suspicions that, one day, the terrible disaster he was told about, will indeed occur.

A TERRIFYING INVADER
MESOPOTAMIA (MODERN DAY KUWAIT, SYRIA, TURKEY AND IRAN)
AND BABYLONIA (IRAQ)

One of the very earliest examples of a shapeshifting monster that may actually be an alien is Lilith. Her name is highly appropriate, too: in English it means "night hag." Not exactly the kind of thing any of us should aspire to cross paths with.

Lilith's dark origins can be found in the ancient mythology and folklore of Mesopotamia, and particularly so within the culture of the Babylonians. Despite the fact that she was described as a beautiful woman, with long and flowing hair, there was nothing positive about Lilith. She would regularly manifest in the homes of sleeping men, slip into their beds, and have sex with them. The purpose of which, ancient lore maintains, was to allow Lilith to steal sperm from her victims and use it to create hideous, demonic babies.

Almost certainly connected to Lilith were Lilitu and Lilu, who play major roles in the lore of the Sumerian people, thousands of years ago. This paranormal pair, too, was focused on terrifying people in the middle of the night, violating them, and then vanishing back into the darkness from which they came. Joseph McCabe, a noted expert on these two demon-like entities, and the author of *The Story of Religious Controversy*, described them as "ferocious beings" that were part-animal and part-human.

Martin Baker's encounter with just such a creature led him to conclude that, rather than being a demonic entity, his encounter with an entity that looked like Lilith was actually an alien-human hybrid engaged in gene-splicing experiments. Maybe, Baker is right on the money.

FEBRUARY 19, 1984

A UFO IN PUERTO RICO

EL YUNQUE RAIN FOREST, PUERTO RICO

Numerous witnesses reported that on February 19 1984, an unidentified aerial object crashed deep in the heart of Puerto Rico's mountainous El Yunque rain forest. The object was described by most as being circular in shape, white in color, and flying erratically before crashing into the rain forest.

In the wake of the event, according to researcher Jorge Martin, a "diversionary tactic" was put in place to the effect that the object had been nothing stranger than a meteorite. However, sources on the island interviewed by Martin reported seeing a large presence of military personnel in the area, evidence of NASA operatives on the scene, and even "pieces of metal" retrieved from the forest and loaded into wooden crates by unknown individuals and dispatched to an unspecified location.

FEBRUARY 20, 1953

SECRET FOOTAGE OF DEAD ALIENS
FORT MONMOUTH, NEW JERSEY

In 1980, in *The UFO Crash Retrieval Syndrome*, Leonard Stringfield related the testimony of a former "Air Force radar specialist, who in the spring of 1953 – specifically February 20 - was "summoned to view a film at the base theater" while stationed at Ft. Monmouth, New Jersey.

The film, Stringfield was told, showed "a desert scene dominated by a silver disc-shaped object embedded in the sand with a domed section at the top." The source of the story advised Stringfield that the UFO had been recovered in New Mexico in 1952. It was fifteen to twenty feet in diameter and was surrounded by "ten to fifteen military personnel dressed in fatigues."

Stringfield's informant told him that the movie then jumped to another scene. According to the man's recollection: "Now in view were two tables, probably taken inside a tent, on which were dead bodies. Two were on one table; one on the other. The bodies appeared little by human standards and most notable were the heads, all looking alike, and all being large compared to their body sizes. They looked Mongoloid, with small noses, mouths, and eyes that were shut."

Interestingly, Stringfield was told that the man and his colleagues were ordered by a superior officer not to discuss what they had seen with anyone and merely to "think about the movie." Two weeks later, T.E. was told: "Forget the movie you saw; it was a hoax."

FEBRUARY 21, 1999

A LITTLE MAN IN THE LONE STAR STATE
LAKE WORTH, TEXAS

Now and again a story will surface that is so bizarre it is difficult to place it into any specific category. Dave Shaw's experience in 1999 is a perfect example. While walking through the woods surrounding Texas's Lake Worth, Shaw saw what can only be described as a "little man" that raced past him at a very fast speed, and who was dressed in a yellow, one-piece outfit. "Little" is undeniably apt, as Shaw estimated that the "man" was between one-and-one-and-a-half-feet in height. The little man didn't turn back to look at Shaw; he just carried on running, vanishing into the undergrowth. Alien, sprite, goblin? There is no answer to that question.

A CHANGING HELICOPTER
PONCE, PUERTO RICO

In 2004, I traveled to Puerto Rico with a crew from the SyFy Channel to make a documentary on the Chupacabra controversy. While on the island – for a week or so – we interviewed a man named Jamie, who was originally from Florida and who had moved to Puerto Rico as a child, with his family, in 1978. Jamie encountered a silent helicopter near the town of Ponce. The helicopter – which was white in color – changed into a bright ball of light and suddenly vanished – as in dematerialized.

A SPIKY UFO
RUGELY, ENGLAND

Mavis Allen had a very strange encounter on a particular morning in 1975, in an area of woodland in central England. As Mavis walked her dog through woods near the town of Rugeley, she was amazed to see a circular, black-colored object rolling along the ground in front of her. It was around six feet in circumference and had four protrusions (that Allen referred to as "spikes") that stuck out from equal points around the middle. Allen stopped in amazement as the object rose slowly and silently, to a height of around fifteen feet and which then shot away at a fast pace.

FEBRUARY 24, 1942

LOS ANGELES INVADED

LOS ANGELES, CALIFORNIA

When the terrible events at Pearl Harbor occurred on December 7, 1941, it led to the United States to enter the Second World War, which had been raging in Europe since September 1939. People were worried and on edge that another attack might occur. Maybe it did; but these attackers were not Japanese. They were much stranger. It all began on the night of February 24, 1942. US military files tell us:

"During the night of 24/25 February 1942, unidentified objects caused a succession of alerts in southern California. On the 24th, a warning issued by naval intelligence indicated that an attack could be expected within the next ten hours. That evening a large number of flares and blinking lights were reported from the vicinity of defense plants. An alert called at 1918 [7:18 p.m., Pacific time] was lifted at 2223, and the tension temporarily relaxed. But early in the morning of the 25th renewed activity began. Radars picked up an unidentified target 120 miles west of Los Angeles. Antiaircraft batteries were alerted at 0215 and were put on Green Alert—ready to fire—a few minutes later. The AAF kept its pursuit planes on the ground, preferring to await indications of the scale and direction of any attack before committing its limited fighter force. Radars tracked the approaching target to within a few miles of the coast, and at 0221, the regional controller ordered a black-out. Thereafter the information center was flooded with reports of 'enemy planes,' even though the mysterious object tracked in from sea seems to have vanished."

Throughout the night, more and more "enemy planes" were

seen. None, however, dropped any bombs. There was no attempt to destroy the city. And everyone was baffled. They weren't aircraft of the US military. They clearly weren't Japanese, since no hostility was shown. They were, by definition, UFOs.

A MONSTER ON PUERTO RICO

MOCA, PUERTO RICO

Since 1995, Puerto Rico has been the domain of a deadly and allegedly bloodsucking creature that has infamously become known as the Chupacabra – a beast many believe to be an extraterrestrial. Long before the now-legendary beast was on anyone's radar, however, there was another vampire-like monster roaming around on the island. It was known as the Moca Vampire – its name taken from the municipality of Moca, which can be found in the northwest of the island, and which is home to around 40,000 people. Unlike the Chupacabra – sightings of which continue to this very day – the "Vampiro de Moca," as it was referred to on Puerto Rico – was a monster of a definitively "here one minute and gone the next" kind.

The controversy was all on February 25, 1975. That was when the population of Moca was plunged into a collective state of fear. And it was hardly surprising. Numerous ranchers reported how their farm animals were being violently slaughtered under cover of darkness and systematically drained of massive amounts of blood. The first area targeted was the Barrio Rocha region, where several goats, at least four pigs, numerous chickens, and more than a dozen cows, were all found dead, with puncture marks on their bodies, and deep claw-like wounds on their skin, and all missing one vital ingredient: blood.

By the end of the first week in March 1975, the death count was close to three dozen. It was in this same week that an important development was made: the blood-sucking culprit was finally seen, up close and personal, so to speak. The witness was a woman named Maria Acevedo, who caught sight of a monstrously-sized, screaming and screeching winged beast that landed atop her home, and which clambered about her zinc roof, making an almighty racket in the process.

It was clearly no normal bird: around four to five feet in height, it was described as being similar in appearance to a pterodactyl, a presumed-extinct, flying reptile of the Jurassic era. Whatever the true nature of the monster, it quickly took to the skies and vanished into the starry darkness.

FEBRUARY 26, 2001

A TERRIFYING VISITOR

NEWFOUNDLAND, CANADA

The people of Newfoundland, Canada have their own tradition of a particular shapeshifter. It is known to the locals as the Old Hag. For most people who have the misfortune to meet the monster, they describe it as a witch-like entity with long black hair and piercing, evil eyes, and dressed in a flowing black gown. She straddles her victims and either forces them into sex, or just sits on them, screaming wildly into their hysterical, wide-eyed faces. Phil Parks encountered just such a creature in Newfoundland. Like several of the people cited in this book who had similar encounters, Parks believes that the Old Hag is a "screen memory" of something extraterrestrial, rather than supernatural.

Equally disturbing is the evil imp that squats atop a sleeping, beautiful woman in Henry Fuseli's 1781 painting, *The Nightmare*. Combining horror with erotica, the artwork graphically captures the nature of these evil encounters. In Thailand, these creatures of the night are known as Phi Am. For the people of China, it's the Pinyin that they fear. Mongolia has the Kharin Buu. While, in Tibet, the Dip-non should be avoided at all costs. And Pakistan has centuries-old stories of the Shaitan. All of these things perform the same, stress-filled and sex-based acts; yet, they take on physical appearances that suit the era and the area.

FEBRUARY 27, 2016

STRANGE ENCOUNTERS
SOMEWHERE IN THE UNITED STATES

"I've met the MIB twice, 2005, about 2009, and a WIB once in the mid-1990s," Mitchell Waak told me on this date. The WIB claimed she was a 'government attorney,' had a strict intimidating manner. She had a black suit with dress, black shoes, no black hat, black briefcase. She was in a Mall Bookstore (Waldenbooks) shopping for UFO books, (strange). She told me she was looking for B. Steiger's *Project Blue Book*, the last copy of which I bought day before. She followed me out of the store and talked to me briefly. I told her that 'any ufologist (me) could be easily discredited by claiming they had watched too many *Star Wars* or *Star Trek* type movies.' She didn't smile, and then we both separated."

Waak continued: "I've met about 5 different alien races since the late 1950s starting with one group, The Elephant Skinned or Wrinkly Skinned Alien in about 1957-59 when I was 4-5 years old. This is the same group as per the 1973 Hickson/Parker. Today I am retired as a hospital pharmacist with Pharm.D. degree after

32 years of practice. I had attended UC Berkeley as a science student back in the 1970s but did not graduate there. I have NOT been involved myself that much due to these MIB approaches and subtle telepathic and verbal threats. I am a private UFO/alien researcher."

ANOTHER HELICOPTER THAT CHANGES SHAPE
WOOLSERY, DEVON, ENGLAND

Simon, of Woolsery, Devon, England – which happens to be the home-village of UK monster-hunter Jon Downes – had an extremely weird encounter in 1998. As he cycled home from school he saw in the sky – and flying at a low level – a small, black helicopter, which displayed not even a single identifying marking. Not only that, and unlike any normal helicopter, it was totally silent. Which is, of course, all but impossible. What happened next was even stranger. As Simon stared at the noiseless helicopter it suddenly morphed into an equally small flying saucer of a bright green color and soared vertically and vanished. Do UFO entities have the ability to camouflage their craft, taking on the guise of our very own technology? It's an interesting theory to ponder on.

M A R C H

MARCH 1, 1967

MYSTERIOUS MEN, UFOS, AND THE US AIR FORCE
THE PENTAGON, WASHINGTON, D.C.

On this specific day, Lieutenant General Hewitt T. Wheless, US Air Force, penned the following memo. It was widely circulated within the military:

"Information, not verifiable, has reached HQ USAF that persons claiming to represent the Air Force or other Defense establishments have contacted citizens who have sighted unidentified flying objects. In one reported case, an individual in civilian clothes, who represented himself as a member of NORAD, demanded and received photos belonging to a private citizen."

The document continues: "In another, a person in an Air Force uniform approached local police and other citizens who had sighted a UFO, assembled them in a school room and told them that they did not see what they thought they saw and that they should not talk to anyone about the sighting. All military and civilian personnel and particularly information officers and UFO investigating officers who hear of such reports should immediately notify their local OSI offices."

Clearly, the Air Force was on the trail of the infamous Men in Black. So far as we know, they never found them.

MARCH 2, 1977

"SOMETHING BETWEEN AN EGG AND A TEAR DROP"
SOMEWHERE IN THE JUNGLE OF PERU

According to Marine Corps Lance-Corporal John Weygandt, in March 1977 he was dispatched to the country of Peru "to provide perimeter security for a radar installation that... tracked drug traffic aircraft in Peru and Bolivia."

While on duty shortly afterwards, Weygandt was ordered, along with several colleagues, to attend and secure the nearby crash site of what he was told was an aircraft. On arrival at the site, however, Weygandt was certain that the object was no aircraft. There was, he said, "a huge gash in the land where something had crashed." That "something" had subsequently become embedded in the side of a nearby cliff.

Weygandt described the object as being almost completely buried in the rock; however, he was able to determine that it was "shaped like something between an egg and a tear drop." Dripping from the visible parts of the object was a "greenish-purple syrup-like liquid" that seemed to be "alive and changing."

Weygandt recalled seeing "three holes" on the object that he speculated could have been "hatches." He saw no bodies or crewmembers of the object; however, he admitted to feeling some form of "presence" from the vehicle, and stated that no less than "thirty of those guys wearing hazard suits" were in attendance at the scene of the crashed object, which Weygandt believes was shot down by a Hawk missile.

MARCH 3, 1948

"UNUSUAL PHENOMENA IN THE ATMOSPHERE"
U.S. AIR FORCE, WASHINGTON, D.C.

A U.S. Air Force document prepared on this day provides noteworthy information on the early years of official concern about UFOs:

"1. The proposal of Air Materiel Command for stationing fighter aircraft at all bases on a continuous alert status is not considered feasible for the following reasons:

"a. The outlay of aircraft and personnel would be too great consistent with the results to be obtained.

"b. Proper interception is not possible, except by accident, without complete radar coverage which the Air Force is not capable of providing.

"c. It is doubtful if fighter aircraft would be able to follow up reports emanating, for the most part, from civilian sources.

"2. It is recommended that Air Materiel Command's responsibility for "collecting" information on unusual phenomena in the atmosphere be confined to the establishment of direct channels for the receipt of such information.

"3. It is further recommended that in lieu of the proposal of Air Materiel Command, all other major demands be directed to cooperate with Air Materiel Command and to channel information directly to that command."

MARCH 4, 1950

A UFO-THEMED POEM

BERGSTROM AIR FORCE BASE, TEXAS

The March 1950 history of the 27th Fighter Group, based out of Bergstrom Air Force Base, Texas contains an odd poem titled "The Flying Saucer" and which written by Technical Sergeant Barnes.

Why? No one really knows. But, here is how it reads:

Hearing tales of little men
and speeding ships on high.
Around me all most every day,
I cast a weary eye.
Today I saw men gathered
around the hangar door.
They said they saw a Saucer.
A tiny ship they swore.
They pointed to the cloudless sky.
"Past Vapor Trails", they sigh,
I saw a far off something,
Shining in the sky.
We watched it hard, it seemed to move
As vapors drifted by
I felt the strangest feelings
Of course I know not why.
A weather balloon sent up to give
The weather for the day.
Some said a star that shines so bright,
We see it in the day.
Elusions, stars or man made things
Ships from other planets.
We watched, we talked and wondered.
But none of us could name it.
Because I could not give them
The answer is not given,
What is the thing that shines so bright
So far up in the heavens.

DEATH IN BRAZIL

ARACARIGUAMA, BRAZIL

Many UFO encounters leave the witnesses in profound states of wonder and amazement. Others provoke terror and paranoia. Just occasionally, however, the UFO phenomenon becomes downright deadly. Take, for example, the encounter of a Brazilian man named Joao Prestes Filho, a farmer from the village of Aracariguama. On the night in question, and quite out of the blue, Filho found himself bathed in a powerful glowing light, which emanated from something unknown in the skies directly above.

Whatever it was, it ensured a horrific death for Filho. The heat coming from the object was so hot that Filho fell to his knees. Worse was to come: His skin suddenly began to heat up. Then, it began to bubble. In mere minutes, he was exhibiting the physical effects of someone suffering from severe burns.

Filho's family, utterly terrified, raced him to a nearby hospital. It was all to no avail. During the journey, Folho grew progressively, and quickly, worse. His skin began to fall off his bones. One of the medics at the hospital – Aracy Gomide – confirmed poor Filho literally melted before the horrified eyes of the medical staff. Proof that not all close encounters are positive ones.

DRONE OR UFO?

SOCORRO, NEW MEXICO

In April 1964, the New Mexico town of Socorro became the site of a now-legendary UFO encounter between police officer,

Lonnie Zamora, an egg-shaped craft and a pair of diminutive ETs dressed in white coveralls. Nearly a quarter of a century later, however, aliens returned to Socorro.

On this occasion, there was no oval-shaped spacecraft and no aliens in white. Instead, according to "Mac" Sparks, there was a small, circular-shaped UFO – only about two feet in diameter - that flew over his head as he changed a tire at the side of the road early in the morning. Sparks said that the UFO was grey in color, gave off a buzzing noise, and flew in a slightly erratic fashion.

Today, we would likely conclude that Sparks saw nothing stranger than a drone. Back then? Maybe not.

MARCH 7, 2015

SHADOWED BY A UFO

SALT LAKE CITY, UTAH

While it is debatable whether or not so-called "orbs" are extra-terrestrial in origin, there is no doubt – when it comes to literal definitions – that these small balls of light, seen in and around crop circles, and in the heart of woods, are unidentified and thus making them undeniable UFOs.

Salt Lake City was the site of one such orb on this particularly day. The witness, a bus-driver, saw the approximately one-to-two foot diameter UFO "shadow" the bus for around twenty seconds while traveling along a highway around noon. As the bus was being driven for repairs, no one else, unfortunately, was on-board to see the mysterious orb. The driver, however, was adamant about what he encountered; that it was round, was dazzlingly silver in color, and was bobbing along in a bouncing motion – before suddenly shooting high into the sky – not to be seen again.

UFOS AND DEMONOLOGY

FOSTER RANCH, NEW MEXICO

On this date, a secret group within the US Government known as the Collins Elite published an extensive report on its theory that the UFO issue is demonic in nature. One notable section of the report dealt with the Roswell affair of July 1947. In what is certainly a unique fashion, they came to believe that nothing – extraterrestrial or otherwise – crashed at Roswell. Rather, the group concluded that the event was "staged" – a "Trojan Horse"-type event provoked by demons trying to deceive us into accepting the idea that vulnerable ETs had crashed at Roswell, and who were responsible for the wave of Flying Saucer encounters that gripped the nation in the summer of 1947.

For the Collins Elite, the "alien debris" and "memory metal" said to have been recovered at the crash site on the Foster Ranch, New Mexico, were nothing less than the result of diabolical "demonic alchemy." In other words, the group formed an opinion that these strange entities "weaved" the materials, then had it manifest on the Foster Ranch, thus creating the image of a crash of something exotic from the skies.

But, what of the bodies said to have been found at the site? The Collins Elite had an answer to that issue too. Their members claimed to have read reports suggesting that no literal bodies were ever found at Roswell – at all. Rather, they maintained that certain "biological materials" were recovered. Is it possible that some equally strange form of diabolical alchemy was at work to create not just the so-called memory-metal that a number of players in the Roswell saga described seeing, but also to generate a type of extraterrestrial Jackalope, a creature that looks real and that exhibits prime evidence of DNA, flesh, bone, and skin, but that is, in reality, nothing more than a brilliant piece of fakery? Possible or not, this is most certainly what the Collins Elite came to accept as gospel.

MARCH 9, 1958

OFFICIAL REPORTS ON AN AMAZING CASE
FORT CLAYTON, CANAL ZONE, PANAMA

The mystery began on the night of March 9, 1958. The location: a now-closed U.S. Army installation on the Panama Canal Zone called Fort Clayton. It was around 8:00 p.m. when a UFO was tracked by anti-aircraft personnel in the Canal Zone area. Further blips soon appeared on the screen. Clearly something unusual was afoot.

It turns out that Fort Clayton was not the only base monitoring unusual aerial activity. Radar staff at Fort Amador, Flamenco Island were also tracking something airborne and unknown. In fact, they were tracking two UFOs — both of which maintained a circular pattern above a nearby installation, Fort Kobbe. Their heights, however, fluctuated between 2,000 and 10,000 feet. It was at this time that staff at Taboga Island's Track Radar Unit confirmed they were keeping a careful watch on certain unknowns, too.

Shortly before midnight, personnel at Fort Amador chose to take a new and novel approach to try and identify the UFOs: They bathed them with powerful, ground-based searchlights. The response was incredible: in no more than a handful of seconds the UFOs headed skywards from 2,000 to 10,000 feet.

Official records on this particularly eye-opening development state: "...this was such a rapid movement that the Track Radar, which was locked on target, broke the Track Lock and was unable to keep up with ascent of the objects. As Track Radar can only be locked on a solid object, which was done in the case of the two unidentified flying objects, it was assumed that the objects were solid."

This strange and bizarre activity continued into the early hours of March 10 – something which saw UFOs hovering and accelerating to speeds around 1,000 miles per hour, and unknown objects tracked on radar. Later that same day, UFOs were monitored clearly reacting to the presence of aircraft dispatched to intercept them. The files also talk of a UFO report from the captain of a Pan American Airlines DC-6 aircraft that was described as being bigger than the plane and which was headed in a southerly direction.

MARCH 10, 1960

"SUITS OF FINE FINISH"
HUALLANCA, PERU

The details are brief, yet fascinating. At Huallanca, Peru, a number of humanoid ETs were encountered: "They were tall, with proportionate bodies and sloping shoulders. They were dressed in suits of fine finish, well fitted to the body, and of rare color, that at first seemed to shine like the fur of a seal."

MARCH 11, 1944

A SECOND WORLD WAR UFO CRASH
LONDON, ENGLAND

According to the late Gordon Creighton - a former diplomat, intelligence officer, and the editor of the magazine, *Flying Saucer Review* - a UFO crashed on UK soil during the height of the Second World War and was subsequently retrieved and studied by British authorities. The date was said to have been March 28, 1944.

Creighton further stated that details of the crash were provided in 1955 to the late journalist and television personality, Dorothy Kilgallen. It is a fact that in May 1955, Kilgallen made the following statement in an *International News Service* cable that was subsequently published in the *Los Angeles Examiner* newspaper:

"I can report today on a story which is positively spooky, not to mention chilling. British scientists and airmen, after examining the wreckage of one mysterious flying ship, are convinced these strange aerial objects are not optical illusions or Soviet inventions, but are flying saucers which originate on another planet.

"The source of my information is a British official of cabinet rank who prefers to remain unidentified. 'We believe, on the basis of our inquiry thus far, that the saucers were staffed by small men—probably under four feet tall. It's frightening, but there's no denying the flying saucers come from another planet.'

"This official quoted scientists as saying a flying ship of this type could not have possibly been constructed on Earth. The British Government, I learned, is withholding an official report on the 'flying saucer' examination at this time, possibly because it does not wish to frighten the public."

AN OMINOUS MESSAGE
DALLAS, TEXAS

On this date, Robert Davis told me of his strange encounter with a Woman in Black. In Davis' own words: "I met one once. I was walking across a parking lot when a WIB, driving a black car, came past me screaming something like 'You have nine years until what you were made for! You have nine more years!' This was back in June 1986, and until June 1995 I was constantly haunted by fear of whatever she was threatening. When the day came, there were impressions of smells as if the things might have been in the house, but otherwise, nothing happened, as is typical of alien prophecies."

A COMPACT UFO
MULHOUSE, FRANCE

Coincidentally or not, an almost identical UFO to that seen by "Mac" Sparks on March 6, 1988, was seen in the French town of Mulhouse. On this occasion, the witness was a nurse. As she walked to a bus-stop around 8:00 a.m. – her usual routine while going to work – the nurse saw an approximately three-foot-wide UFO flutter in a strange, almost malfunctioning-like, fashion over a playground built for the local kids, and at a height of around fifteen feet. The only sound was a slight swishing in the air. In seconds the UFO was gone, leaving the nurse completely floored by her encounter.

FLYING SAUCERS AND URANIUM MINES
ELIZABETHVILLE DISTRICT, CONGO

In August 1952, the CIA was informed of an amazing and highly credible UFO report from five months earlier. The relevant documentation reads as follows:

"Recently, two fiery disks were sighted over the uranium mines located in the southern part of the Belgian Congo in the Elizabethville district, east of the Luapula River which connects the Meru and Bangweolo lakes. The disks glided in elegant curves and changed their position many times, so that from below they sometimes appeared as plates, ovals, and simply lines. Suddenly, both disks hovered in one spot and then took off in a unique zigzag flight to the northeast. A penetrating hissing and buzzing sound was audible to the on-lookers below. The whole performance lasted from 10 to 12 minutes.

"Commander Pierre of the small Elizabethville airfield immediately set out in pursuit with a fighter plane. On his first approach he came within about 120 meters of one of the disks. According to his estimates, the 'saucer" had a diameter of from 12 to 15 meters and was discus-shaped. The inner core remained absolutely still, and a knob coming out from the center and several small openings could plainly be seen. The outer rim was completely veiled in fire and must have had an enormous speed of rotation. The color of the metal was similar to that of aluminum.

"The disks traveled in a precise and light manner, both vertically and horizontally. Changes in elevation from 800 to 1,000 meters could be accomplished in a few seconds; the disks often shot down to within 20 meters of the tree tops. Pierre did not regard it possible that the disk could be manned. Since the irregular speed as well as the heat would make it impossible for a person to stay inside the stable core. Pierre bad to give up pursuit after 15 minutes since bothdisks, with a loud whistling sound which he heard despite the noise of his own plane, disappeared in a straight line toward Lake Tanganyika. He estimated their speed at about 1,500 kilometers per hour. Pierre is regarded as a dependable officer and a zealous flyer. He gave a detailed report to his superiors which, strangely enough, in many respects agreed with various results of research."

MARCH 15, 1987

ALIEN BODIES AND THE MILITARY
WESTERN KENTUCKY, UNITED STATES

Briefly described by researcher Leonard Stringfield, this case concerns the discovery on ranch land in Western Kentucky in March 1987 of the skeletal remains of "two humanoid entities" and a "burned-out circle, about 4 feet in diameter, in an open grassy field." The property was reportedly owned by a retired medical doctor, a friend of Cincinnati radio host Bill Boshears, who arranged for Stringfield to speak directly with the source.

According to the doctor, the bodies had large skulls, cat-like jaws, a "barrel-like" rib cage, and long arms equipped with three fingers. The doctor quickly contacted local law enforcement personnel and was blessed the following day with a visit from the Air Force.

A colonel informed the doctor that he was there to clean up the area and remove the skeletal remains for official examination. The doctor himself was taken to an unnamed military base for interrogation, where he was shown "photos of other alien corpses" and had the "fear of god" put in him by the military. Although the doctor reportedly expressed interest in Stringfield's research and agreed to stay in touch, Stringfield did not hear from him again.

MARCH 16, 1967
"ONE SECURITY POLICEMAN WAS SO AFFECTED"
CENTRAL MONTANA, UNITED STATES

The Computer UFO Network (CUFON) states: "In central Montana, Thursday morning March 16 1967, Captain Eric Carlson and First Lieutenant. Walt Figel, the Echo-Flight Missile Combat Crew, were below ground in the E-Flight Launch Control Center (LCC) or capsule. The Echo Flight LCC was located between Winfred and Hilger, about fifteen miles north of Lewistown. Missile maintenance crews and security teams were camped out at two of the Launch Facilities (LFs), having performed some work during the previous day and stayed there overnight. During the early morning hours, more than one report came in from the security patrols and maintenance crews that they had seen UFOs. A UFO was reported directly above one of the E-Flight (LF) or silos. It turned out that at least one security policeman was so affected by this encounter that he never again returned to missile security duty."

MARCH 17, 1950
"IT WAS SEEN BY SEVERAL"
FARMINGTON, NEW MEXICO

UFO authority James McDonald stated in 1968: "…that unidentified aerial objects moved in numbers over Farmington on 3/17/50 seems clear. One witness with whom I spoke, Clayton J. Boddy, estimated that he had observed a total of 20 to 30 disc-shaped objects, including one red one substantially larger than the others, moving at high velocity across the Farmington sky on the late morning of 3/17/50. John Eaton, a Farmington realtor, described being called out of a barbershop when the excitement began and seeing a high, fast object suddenly joined by many objects that darted after it. Eaton sent me a copy of an account he had jotted down shortly after the incident. A former Navy pilot, Eaton put their height at perhaps 15,000 feet. 'The object that has me puzzled was the one we saw that was definitely red. It was seen by several and stated by all to be red and traveling northeast at a terrific speed."

MARCH 18, 1990

UFOS INVADE BELGIUM
EAST OF LIEGE, BELGIUM

Beginning in 1989 and continuing through 1990, Belgium was the focus of intense UFO activity. There was not a single flying saucer in sight, however. Rather, people were reporting encounters with what became known as black-colored "Flying Triangles." Superficially, they resembled the U.S. Stealth bomber and fighter. There were, however, significant differences: the FTs flew silently, could hover, and were able to fly at speeds as slow as 20 miles per hour and in excess of 1,000 miles per hour. While, in some quarters, there was a nagging suspicion that the Flying Triangles were aircraft still on the secret list, most observers dismissed such a theory. After all, why not test-fly them above the deserts of Area 51, where they would not be seen?

It wasn't just the general public, UFO investigators, and the

Belgian military that were concerned. The U.S. Defense Intelligence Agency was too. A 1990 DIA report, titled "Belgium and the UFO Issue," reveals the facts concerning a wealth of Flying Triangle encounters, including the following, which occurred on March 18, 1990. According to the DIA:

"Source A cited Mr. Leon Brenig, a 43-year-old professor at the Free University of Brussels in the field of statistics and physics… Mr. Brenig was driving on the Ardennes auto-route in the Beaufays region east of Liege, Sunday, 18 March 1990 at 2030 hours when he observed an airborne object approaching in his direction from the North. It was in the form of a triangle…and had a yellow light surrounding it with a reddish center varying in intensity. Altitude appeared to be 500–1000 meters, moving at a slow speed with no sound. It did not move or behave like an aircraft."

MARCH 19, 1964

AN EARLY CROP CIRCLE
CUMBERLAND, ENGLAND

On March 23, 1964, T.E.T. Burbury, the Rector at Clifton Rectory, Penrith, Cumberland, wrote to the National Physical Laboratory at Teddington describing an encounter which had occurred some days previously:

"Dear Sirs: Does an apparent column of blue light about 8-feet in diameter and about 15-feet high which disappears and leaves a mark of very slightly disturbed earth, the same diameter, mean anything to you? This occurred about 9.30 p.m. last Saturday night about 2 miles from here. It was seen by a person who is very short sighted who would have been unable to see anything, except the light, even if it had been present.

"I examined the ground which is about 100 Yards from the nearest building and there are no pylons near. There was no sign of burning, either by sight or smell, the grass growing between the exposed ground appeared quite normal. There were no signs of bird tracks or droppings: the ground simply appeared to have been lightly raked over in an almost perfect circle. "For your information only, I told the farmer to have a sample of the earth collected and analyzed for bacteria content, but don't know whether he has done so. Yours faithfully: T.E.T. Burbury."

Note the words of the rector: "…the ground simply appeared to have been lightly raked over in an almost perfect circle." Does this not sound somewhat familiar?

Burbury's reference to "the farmer" strongly suggests that the circle was found on farmland. And: What of the column of blue light? Realizing that this was out of their jurisdiction, staff at the National Physical Laboratory forwarded a copy of the rector's letter to the Meteorological Office at London Road, Bracknell. In turn, Mr. H.M. Race of the Meteorological Office advised Burbury that: "This does not appear to be a meteorological matter and we are therefore passing your letter to a London office who may be able to deal with it." The "London office" to which Race was referring was an element of the old Air Ministry called S4. Its staff examined the available data but came away baffled.

MARCH 20, 1979

AN EERIE INCIDENT

PASADENA, CALIFORNIA

Pasadena, California was the site of a strange encounter with a definitive Man in Black. The witness, Charlie H., had seen a UFO two nights earlier as he drove near to what is known locally as Devil Gate Dam – a place with a great deal of paranormal activity attached to it. The UFO, says Charlie, was not particularly large, and was circular and bright pink in color. Charlie, who was driving home from a shift that ended at 2:00 a.m., said that the UFO came close to his car – around eighty or ninety feet away – then shot away into the sky.

Two days later, and as he happened to look out of his living-room window, Charlie saw a man dressed in a black fedora, black suit, black trench-coat, white shirt, and black tie, get out of an old, black Cadillac and take a photo of his home. The MIB then got back into the vehicle and drove away. John Keel termed this particular brand of MIB as "phantom photographers."

MARCH 21, 2003

A TEXAN UFO
EDINBURG, TEXAS

Reports of sightings of what are popularly known as "Flying Triangles" within the realms where the ufologically-minded hang out are extremely common. Angelo saw just such a craft on this particular night outside of Edinburg, Texas. A story that surfaced on local radio at the time, it told of Angelo's encounter with a huge, black, triangular UFO that flew very slowly and in complete silence for a few moments, after which it rose vertically and slowly into the sky.

MARCH 22, 1979

UFOS AND INTIMIDATION IN THE DEAD OF NIGHT

PASADENA, CALIFORNIA

On this day, our witness from March 20, Charlie H., experienced yet another aspect of Men in Black lore: namely, a host of phone calls in the middle of the night. According to Charlie, the phone rang five times between around 1:00 a.m. and 3:00 a.m. On three occasions, he could here strange static that, rather oddly was mixed in with piano music that Charlie said reminded him of a "horror-movie soundtrack." On the other two occasions, Charlie heard a fast-chattering voice, speaking in an unknown language.

If the intent of the calls was to intimidate and scare Charlie, the tactic worked.

MARCH 23, 1966

"OCCASIONALLY THEY TILTED, GLINTING IN THE LATE-AFTERNOON"

FISHER'S PEAK, TRINIDAD

In a 1968 statement, James McDonald revealed, "Mrs. Frank R. Hoch paid no attention when her son first tried to call her out to see something in the sky. Knowing it was kite season, dinner preparations took precedence, and she told the 10-year-old boy to go ride his bike. The second time he was more insistent and she went outside to look. Two objects, domed on the top but nearly flat on the bottom, shaped like a cup upside down, having no rim or 'sombrero brim,' she said, were moving slowly westward from Fisher's Peak, which lies just south of Trinidad.

"Her son, Dean, told her he had seen three such objects when he tried to get her to come out earlier. (Mr. Louis DiPaolo, a Trinidad postman whom I interviewed, had also seen three objects.) Interestingly, when Mrs. Hoch saw the objects, one was between her and the ridge, the other just above the low ridgeline. The ridge is about a half-mile from the Hoch residence. A photo of the ridge, with roughly-scaled objects sketched on it, suggests an angular diameter of perhaps a degree (object size of order 100 feet), in disagreement with her earlier angular estimates.

"It was clear that Mrs. Hoch was, as are most, unfamiliar with angular-size estimating. The objects, Mrs. Hoch said, moved up and down in bobbing manner as they progressed slowly westward along the ridgeline. Occasionally they tilted, glinting in the late-afternoon sun as if metallic. No sound was mentioned by any witness except one young boy whose attention was drawn to the object by a 'ricocheting sound,' as he put it."

MARCH 24, 2016

"NO-ONE'S GONNA BELIEVE THIS"
ANDERSON, SOUTH CAROLINA

On this day, Dennis Carroll told me: "Well, about a year ago I was a guest on Lon Strickler's Radio show Arcane Radio and I kind of jokingly issued an invitation to the Men in Black. I told them to come and see me. Well, I kind of forgot about that statement and a couple a months went by and one evening I stopped at a nearby convenience store. As I came of the store I noticed what looked like an almost brand new looking black Cadillac a good way out in the parking lot it looked like a '63 or '64 caddy about the time I noticed it a greenish kind of light came on in the interior and I swear I saw two men in black suits intently looking my way. They also we wearing aviator sunglasses. At night at that. Well, I couldn't really believe what I was seeing. So I reached for my cell phone to take a photo as I thought that no one is gonna believe this, lol. I discovered, however, that I left my cellphone in my truck. At the same moment the green light went out in the car, the caddy started slowly easing out of where it was parked. I rushed to get in my truck with the intention of following these guys to get a picture. By the time I got quickly into the truch, the rolling car was completely, almost supernaturally like, gone. And that place has a huge parking lot. There is no way this vehicle could have gotten gone that quickly. I think I may have just gotten an answer to my invitation, lol, thinking back I feel like that they definitely wanted me to see them. They were sending me a message of sorts. I have written several books and researched and investigated the paranormal for over 40 years and that, other than the very dramatic UFO sighting I had several years ago, is one of the strangest things I've had happen. But ever since that sighting a lot of weird things have taken place."

MARCH 25, 1948

ROSWELL'S LITTLE BROTHER
AZTEC, NEW MEXICO

Next to the so-called Roswell Incident of July 1947, certainly the most talked-about "UFO crash" of all is that which is alleged to have occurred in the vicinity of Aztec, New Mexico, in 1948. According to information related to the author Frank Scully in the late 1940s (and subsequently published in his best-selling 1950 book, *Behind the Flying Saucers*), as a result of a number of separate incidents in 1947 and 1948, the wreckage of four alien spacecraft, and no fewer than 34 alien bodies, had been recovered by American authorities, and were being studied under cover of the utmost secrecy at defense establishments in the United States.

As Scully reported, the majority of his data came from two individuals: Silas Mason Newton (described in a 1941 FBI report as a "wholly unethical businessman") and one "Dr. Gee," the name given to protect eight scientists, all of whom had supposedly divulged various details of the crashes to Newton and Scully. According to Scully's sources one such UFO was found in Hart Canyon, near the town of Aztec, in March 1948.

Although the Aztec affair has attracted the attention of numerous UFO researchers over the years, it's a fascinating piece of documentary evidence relative to the Aztec case that surfaced in the late 1990s I wish to bring to your attention. It came thanks to the late, investigative author and former CIA employee, Karl Pflock, and it is one that may ultimately shed more important light on the psychological warfare angle of the crashed UFO mystery.

As Pflock stated: "In 1998, under curious circumstances, I was made privy to a fascinating document about one of the most controversial cases of the Golden Age of Flying Saucers, the so-called Aztec crash of 1948. I had little more than passing interest in the case until 1998, when a source, who insists on complete anonymity, showed me a handwritten testament, set down by the key player in this amazing, often amusing, truth-is-stranger-than-fiction episode. The contents of this 'journal' seem to lift the veil of mystery and uncertainty from important aspects of the case, while at the same time drawing it more closely around others."

The story as told to Pflock was that the military was keeping a secret and close watch on Silas Newton when his tales of the Aztec UFO crash were at their height. More remarkably, military personnel were dispatched to visit Newton and told him something amazing: they knew his Aztec story was utterly bogus, but, incredibly, they wanted him to keep telling it. To confuse the controversy surrounding real crashed UFOs? Maybe!

MARCH 26, 1997

UFOS AND MASS SUICIDE
SAN DIEGO, CALIFORNIA

Marshall Herff Applewhite, Jr., gained infamy in 1997 when he convinced thirty-eight of his followers in the so-called Heaven's Gate cult to take their own lives – chiefly because doing so would see them return in reanimated, immortal form. But before we get to death, reanimation and immortality, let's see what it was that led to that terrible tragedy.

On March 26, 1997, Applewhite started brainwashing his duped clan into believing that if they killed themselves they would all reanimate – in some angelic dimension far different to, and far away from, our own earthly realm. Since the comet Hale-Bopp was just around the corner, so to speak, Applewhite even weaved that into his story. There was, he said, a huge UFO flying right behind the comet, and when death came for the group it would transfer them to that same UFO and new and undead lives elsewhere.

His loyal followers eagerly swallowed every word. To their eternal cost, they eagerly swallowed something else, too: highly potent amounts of Phenobarbital and vodka. In no time at all, almost forty people were dead, all as a result of the words of Applewhite. Aliens did not call upon the members of the Heaven's Gate group. No UFO was ever detected behind Hale-Bopp. And the dead did not rise from the floor of the Heaven's Gate abode, which was situated at Rancho Santa Fe, California, and where one and all took their lives. Their bodies stayed exactly where they were until the authorities took them to the morgue for autopsy.

THE UFO-CHUPACABRA CONNECTION
EL YUNQUE RAIN FOREST, PUERTO RICO

As a Puerto Rican woman named Rosario told me, in a 2004 interview, it was on this date that she was working in a grove near the foot of the island's El Yunque rain-forest, where she picked plantains. Her attention was suddenly drawn to a deep, resonating hum, one that was coming from directly above her.

Looking up, Rosario was startled to see a black, triangular-shaped object – about 25 to 35 feet in length - that was hovering overhead at a height estimated to be around 90 to 120 feet, and which had a glossy, shiny surface. Surprise and amazement turned to shock when a pencil-thin beam of light shot out of the base of the craft, fanned out, and enveloped Rosario in a pink glow.

For what almost seemed like an eternity, Rosario was rooted to the spot, while her mind was flooded with images of widespread nuclear destruction and environmental collapse in the Earth's near-future. The final image was of a large, bald head with huge, black eyes that closely resembled the alien face on the cover of Whitley Strieber's 1987 best-selling book, *Communion* – which Rosario was inexplicably drawn to read in the immediate aftermath.

Suddenly, the light retracted and the flying triangle rose into the sky, heading slowly towards the heart of the rain forest. Interestingly, in the wake of the encounter, Rosario developed an overwhelming interest in environmental issues, and quite literally overnight – after a lifetime of eating meat – became a staunch advocate of vegetarianism.

That was not all: three days later, and only a couple of hundred feet from where Rosario was working on that fateful day, two girls spotted a chupacabra of the bipedal, spiked and decidedly menacing kind. The beast spotted them, too. Evidently, however, it was a monster on a mission, since, after peering at them for a few moments it fell down on all-fours and bounded away into the heavy undergrowth. It was an event that – due to both the time frame and the proximity – led Rosario to conclude the chupacabra was somehow linked to the UFO phenomenon.

MARCH 28, 1965

A SQUADRON OF FLYING TRIANGLES
RICHMOND, NORTH YORKSHIRE, ENGLAND

As many students of Ufology will be aware, the last couple of decades or so have seen a rise in reports of one particular type of UFO. It has become known as the Flying Triangle. The FTs are triangular in shape and very often black in color, hence the name, of course. They often emit a low humming noise, and have a trio of lights on their underside. They usually have rounded corners too, rather than sharply angled edges.

While digging through a whole host of formerly classified files on UFOs at the National Archives at Kew, England in 1996, I came across a one-page report dated March 28, 1965 that, I confess, I almost overlooked. On closer inspection, however, I realized that it was potentially one of the most important UFO-related documents that I had ever come across. According to the MoD paperwork, on the night in question a witness saw at approximately 9:30 p.m. over moor-land near Richmond, North Yorkshire, England: "Nine or ten objects – in close triangular formation each about 100ft long – orange illumination below – each triangular in shape with rounded corners, making low humming noises."

Interestingly, as noted in the first paragraph of this entry, the "rounded corners" and "low humming noise" are precisely what many witnesses to Flying Triangle-style UFO encounters are reporting today – in a world-wide capacity, no less.

Recognizing the significance of this, I made a photocopy of the document and set about locating the witness, who is named in the files, I should stress. This did not prove to be a difficult task. I introduced myself and explained that I had located at the National Archives a copy of the original report that dealt with his sighting all those years ago. It is fair to say that the man was shocked, to say the least, to find that details of his long-gone encounter had been kept on file by the MoD for more than thirty years.

As he explained, on March 28, 1965 at approximately 9:30 p.m., he had been driving through the North Yorkshire moors. On approaching the village of Skeeby, he encountered something remarkable: "I saw this light. It was about one hundred feet from end-to-end, about one hundred feet above the moors and shaped like a huge triangle and white, milky-white in color.

"It kept coming towards me and then stopped about two hundred yards from me over the moors. It hovered for a while – nothing came out of it, but there was a light below it that just pulsated like a light bulb. There could have been quite a few lights on it but from a distance the light just looked like a glow. Then without a warning, it just took off at a speed that isn't recognized. Good gracious, I thought, it must be a UFO!"

MARCH 29, 1979

UFOS OVER CHINA

MEXICO CITY, MEXICO

Even though UFOs were reportedly sighted across China as long ago as the Sino-Japanese War in the 1930s and 1940s, there was an official reluctance in the post-war years to recognize the phenomenon because of a widely held belief that they were American spy planes, according to [Wendelle] Stevens. "The Russians convinced the Chinese government that UFOs were a United States trick," he says. "They persuaded the Chinese to give them all the information they had. During those years the only cases anyone heard about were the spectacular ones."

That changed on March 29, 1979 when two dish-shaped objects reportedly flew backwards and forwards over Beijing at a height of about 150 meters. There were thousands of witnesses, and the first official reports of flying saucers in China's state media meant the newspapers were full of the incident the following day.

Stevens, co-author of *UFOs Over Modern China*, which documents 400 sightings, said: "When those newspaper stories appeared, people who had had experiences thought the lid was off so they began writing letters to newspapers describing what they had seen – thousands and thousands of letters."

A group of scientists at Wuhan University, led by former diplomat Professor Sun Shili, was given permission to start researching the phenomenon. A network of UFO enthusiasts' clubs was formed under the umbrella of the Chinese UFO Research Organization. Stevens recalls his first meeting with Sun, in Mexico City in the early 1980s.

"My opening words were, 'Do the Chinese have crashed

UFOs in their possession?' He answered: 'Of course.' Although Sun did not elaborate on the whereabouts of these aircraft, he said China was taking a different approach to the US with its research. Sun said the Chinese were researching crashed UFOs to produce airliners that could rise and descend vertically, and unlocking the secret of unlimited supplies of energy. The US was using the technology from crashed UFOs to build bigger and better weapons.

"The Chinese are quite far along in that field [aeronautics]. They have experimental vehicles that rise and descend vertically. They haven't got them in production but when they do – and it might take 10 years – the economic balance of the world could shift. They are going into space using the knowledge they have got from the examination of crashed vehicles," Stevens says.

MARCH 30, 1905
"MYSTERIOUS AERIAL LIGHTS"
BARMOUTH, WALES

Ray Boeche, of Lincoln, Nebraska, is an Anglican priest and a former state-director for the Mutual UFO Network: MUFON. A firm believer in the existence of the UFO phenomenon, Boeche does not believe it has extraterrestrial origins. Rather, his conclusion is that the phenomenon is demonic – and that includes the darkly-suited figures known as the Men in Black and the Women in Black. Boeche says:

"The Welsh airship flap of 1909 resulted in many MIB-like encounters, the mysterious visitors usually reported to have been speaking in some strange, unknown language. An event from four years earlier, in 1905, may be even more interesting. During the spring of that year, Wales was inundated with sightings of mysterious aerial lights. On March 30, 1905, the *Barmouth Advertiser* carried this item: 'In the neighborhood dwells an exceptionally intelligent young woman of the peasant stock, whose bedroom has been visited three nights in succession by a man dressed in black. This figure has delivered a message to the girl which she is too frightened to relate.' It is interesting to note that this event comes in the midst of the great Welsh Christian revival of 1904-05."

"HE WAS LOOKING AT THIS MASSIVE, TRIANGULAR-SHAPED CRAFT"

SHAWBURY, SHROPSHIRE, ENGLAND

One of the most significant UFO reports of the 1990s attracted the deep attention of the UK Ministry of Defense. The case was investigated by Nick Pope, who, now retired from the MoD, writes and lectures regularly on the UFO mystery. Pope shares the details of the March 31, 1993 incident, which was reported by the primary witness, the Meteorological Officer on duty at Royal Air Force Shawbury, Shropshire, England. It was an encounter that occurred in the early hours of the morning:

"There was literally just a skeleton staff operating, so the Meteorologicalj Officer was, essentially, on his own…he could see this light coming towards him and it got closer and closer and lower and lower. Next thing, he was looking at this massive, triangular-shaped craft flying at what was a height of no more than two hundred feet, just to the side of the base and only about two hundred feet from the perimeter fence.

"Military officers are very good at gauging sizes of aircraft and they're very precise. His quote to me was that the UFO's size was midway between that of a C-130 Hercules and a Boeing 747 Jumbo Jet. Now, he had eight years' worth of experience with the Royal Air Force, and a Met. Officer is generally much better qualified than most for looking at things in the night sky. And there were other factors too: he heard this most unpleasant low-frequency hum; he saw the craft fire a beam of light down to the ground. He felt that it was something like a laser beam or a searchlight. The light was tracking very rapidly back and forth and sweeping one of the fields adjacent to the base.

"He also said — and he admitted this was speculation — that it was as if the UFO was looking for something. Now, the speed of the UFO was extremely slow — no more than twenty or thirty miles per hour, which in itself is quite extraordinary. He said that the beam of light retracted into the craft, which then seemed to gain a little bit of height. But then, in an absolute instant, the UFO moved from a speed of about twenty or thirty miles per hour to a speed of several hundreds of miles per hour — if not thousands."

The UFO was gone. Despite intensive inquires, the case remained unexplained.

APRIL

SEX WITH REPTILIANS
SEDONA, ARIZONA

"Audrey," is a thirty-eight-year-old woman who claims seven very close encounters with male Reptilians – lizard-like humanoids that are a staple part of Ufology - between 2001 and 2007. A resident of Sedona, Arizona – a place renowned for a wide range of paranormal phenomena – Audrey was first abducted by what she later recalled, in somewhat of a drugged, hypnotized state, was a group of military personnel in black fatigues, late one night on the edge of town.

As she drove home, and after visiting a friend in Flagstaff, Audrey caught sight of a black van following her, one that loomed out of the shadows and ran her off the road. The next thing she remembered was being manhandled into that same van. After that, it was lights out. She later woke up to find herself strapped down to a table in a brightly lit, circular room. In front of her were three men in those same fatigues. For a while, at least.

As Audrey craned to sit up as she watched in terror as all three men suddenly shimmered – as if caught in something akin to a heat haze. In no more than around six or seven seconds they were replaced by a trio of approximately eight-foot-tall, green-colored monsters that looked like Godzilla's younger and smaller brothers.

Audrey states that the aliens moved towards the table, unstrapped her, and one by one, had sex with her. She was somewhat embarrassed to admit that the encounter was exciting, if fraught. She was, however, unable to shake off the taboo of what she described as having sex with animals. If that's what they really were. According to Audrey, all of the other experiences occurred in her own home – again, late at night – and sex was the only thing that went down, so to speak.

"FACES LIKE FROGS"
AUSTIN, TEXAS

After attending a gig in Austin, Texas, Sally, Jen, and Mary drove back to their home-city of Waco – also situated in the Lone Star State. On the way back, however, something strange happened around 2:00 a.m.: the three teenage friends had a period of what in UFO/alien abduction research circles is known as "missing time."

Austin to Waco is not a particularly long journey; however, all three girls were shocked to find there was a period of around three hours that could not be accounted for when they got home. All three soon began having nightmarish dreams of being taken on-board a UFO by dwarfish creatures that had "faces like frogs." All three stated that they were subjected to intrusive medical procedures and all were told they would forget the experience – which, as it transpires, they clearly did not.

None of them sought out counsellors or UFO researchers, preferring to confide in their families alone – that is until 2009, when Jen chose to share their story with a Texas-based UFO group.

AN ASTRONAUT SEES DEAD ETS
MCCLELLAND AIR FORCE BASE, SACRAMENTO, CALIFORNIA

Within the pages of his *UFO Crash/Retrievals: Is the Cover-Up Lid Lifting?* Leonard Stringfield revealed: "In 1985, Chris Coffey, of

Cincinnati, who was a close friend of astronaut Ellison Onizuka, revealed to me that she had asked him when they met after one of his visits to Wright-Patterson AFB, about his interest in UFOs. He admitted he kept an open mind on the subject and added that his curiosity was aroused when he and a select group of air force pilots, at McClelland AFB in 1973, were shown a black-and-white movie film featuring 'alien bodies on a slab.'"

Stringfield added: "In his state of shock, he said he remembered saying aloud, 'Oh, my God!' Chris, knowing my work in C/R [Crash/Retrievals], had arranged for me to meet Onizuka to discuss UFOs after his scheduled flight on the space shuttle *Challenger*. As it turned out, fate intervened when the shuttle exploded."

In 2011, after writing about this affair in my book, *The NASA Conspiracies*, I was informed that the date cited above is the correct one.

APRIL 4, 1957

CAPTURED ON RADAR

BALSCALLOCH, SCOTLAND

On the morning of April 4, 1957 – according to now-declassified British Royal Air Force documents housed at the National Archive, Kew, England – radar operators at Balscalloch, Scotland reported to RAF West Freugh, Wigtownshire that they had detected a number of "unidentified objects on the screens of their radars." And it quickly became apparent this was no Cold War penetration of British airspace by Soviet spy-planes or bombers.

As the mystified radar-operators watched their screens, they were amazed to see a large, stationary object hovering at 50,000 feet that then proceeded to ascend vertically to no less than 70,000 feet. According to the files: "A second radar was switched on and detected the object at the same range and height."

The *X-Files*-style report continued: "The unidentified object was tracked on the plotting table. After remaining at one spot for about 10 minutes the pen moved slowly in a NE direction, and gradually increased speed. A speed check was taken which showed a ground speed of 70 mph, the height was then 54,000 feet."

And further reports began to pour into military bases across Scotland, as the following extract reveals: "At this time another radar station 20 miles away, equipped with the same type of radars, was asked to search for the object. [An] echo was picked up at the range and bearing given and the radar was locked on."

In fact, it appears that there were multiple UFOs in the area, as the RAF made clear in its report to the Air Ministry at Whitehall: "After the object had traveled about 20 miles it made a very sharp turn and proceeded to move SE at the same increasing speed. Here the reports of the two radar stations differ in details. The two at Balscalloch tracked an object at about 50,000 feet at a speed of about 240 mph while the other followed an object or objects at 14,000 feet. As the objects traveled towards the second radar site the operators detected four objects moving in line astern about 4,000 yards from each other. This observation was confirmed later by the other radars."

Most significant of all at this stage was the assessment by the radar experts of the incredible proportions of the UFOs: "It was noted by the radar operators that the sizes of the echoes were considerably larger than would be expected from normal aircraft. In fact they considered that the size was nearer that of a ship's echo."

APRIL 5, 1948

CREDIBLE WITNESSES AND THE AIR FORCE

HOLLMAN AIR FORCE BASE, ALAMOGORDO, NEW MEXICO

In 1948, the US Air Force noted no shortage of high-quality encounters involving military personnel. One such case is written-up in the following fashion: "On 5 April 1948, three trained balloon observers from the Geophysics Laboratory Section, Watson Laboratories, N.J. reported seeing a round, indistinct object in the vicinity of Hollman Air Force Base, New Mexico. It was very high and fast, and appeared to execute violent maneuvers at high speed. The object was under observation for approximately 30 seconds and disappeared suddenly."

APRIL 6, 1956

ALMOST MULDER AND SCULLY

WASHINGTON, D.C.

A UFO encounter of a very close kind, one involving the FBI? Sounds like *The X-Files*, right? Yes, except for one thing: this story is not the stuff of sci-fi. Declassified FBI records show that this affair was all too real. It involved a woman who is referenced in the files as a "Miss Richards," who worked at FBI Headquarters in Washington, D.C.

As the files reveal, on April 6, 1956, Miss Richards and her fiancé left Washington, D.C. by car with the intention of travelling to Morven, North Carolina, for a family celebration. At around 5:00 a.m. on the following morning, something truly eye-opening occurred, as the now–declassified documentation demonstrates clearly:

"...while driving on Route 1 north of Henderson, North Carolina, the pair was startled by what appeared to be a round low-flying object coming directly toward the car. The object appeared to pass over the car and Miss Richards turned to see it appear to speed up and then veer off out of sight. She and [her fiancé] both felt they had seen something unusual which was difficult to explain and certainly did not appear to be an optical illusion."

Then there is this, from the same document stash:

"The object appeared to be flying very low as it came toward them, moving at great speed and gave off no particular sound. The object, to the best of her belief, was at least as wide as the highway and appeared to be no more than two to four feet in thickness."

The report expands on what happened next: "She recalled the object approached their car on the driver's side straight ahead at a height which she thought to be less than 25 feet. She was unable to estimate the speed of the object. She described it as being oval shaped, being very bright and having a light blue color. It made no sound that she could hear. She advised her fiancé would be able to state exactly where they had observed the object in North Carolina, inasmuch as he was familiar with that area."

Both Miss Richards and her fiancé were interviewed by personnel from the FBI's Domestic Intelligence, and all of the data was shared with "interested military agencies."

A real *X-File*? Undoubtedly.

APRIL 7, 1962

TWELVE DEAD ALIENS

TIMMINDORFER, EAST-WEST GERMAN BORDER

According to retired United States Army Command Sergeant-Major Robert Dean, between 1961 and 1964 NATO's Supreme Headquarters, Allied Powers in Europe (SHAPE) conducted a classified investigation into the UFO subject that resulted in the publication of an eight-inch-thick document entitled *The Assessment*. Dean further stated that SHAPE's studies concluded that a number of extraterrestrial civilizations and species were visiting the earth and were undertaking an in-depth surveillance program. Dean also added that, according to *The Assessment*, in 1962 (April 11) British military forces were implicated in the recovery of a UFO that had crashed on the East-West German border—specifically at Timmendorfer, near the Baltic Sea.

The first to arrive on the scene, said Dean, was a corps of British military engineers who succeeded in gaining entry to the crashed object. Contained inside were twelve dead alien creatures – all small in stature with large bald-heads, black eyes and gray skin. Dean stated additionally that a series of extensive autopsies of the aliens had been undertaken by the British military, who discovered the intriguing fact that all of the bodies were identical: clones, or as Dean suggested, "laboratory products."

Dean added: "I saw all the photos taken of the beings and I couldn't believe it."

In 1998, data that may have a bearing on this case surfaced from a now-retired Inspector of Equipment with the British Ministry of Defense. The source was working with the Royal Electrical and Mechanical Engineers (REME) at the time that the incident recalled by Robert Dean allegedly occurred. "I tried to look into it," stated the source. "When Bob Dean's story was first publicized, I asked my superior, who was a major in the REME, to make a few inquiries. As I was working for the REME at the time, too, I thought I had a good chance of finding someone who perhaps knew something about it."

The result of the man's inquiry was perhaps predictable: "The major said he was told: 'Leave it well alone.' Now, this was in England; I wouldn't say where as I don't want things pinning down, but that's what he was told."

APRIL 8, 1947

"MOVING RATHER RAPIDLY"
RICHMOND, VIRGINIA

According to the US military, "During April 1947, two employees of the Weather Bureau Station at Richmond, Virginia, reported seeing a strange metallic disk on three occasions…One observation was at 15,000 feet when a disk was followed for 15 seconds. The disk appeared metallic, shaped like an ellipse with a flat bottom and a round top…The disk appeared to be moving rather rapidly, although it was impossible to estimate its speed."

APRIL 9, 1987

THE GRINNING MAN
SAN FRANCISCO, CALIFORNIA

In 1987, the Maxwell family spent a week vacationing in and around San Francisco, staying with friends in Menlo Park. On their way back home, they traveled along California's famous Highway

101, which provides a panoramic view of the Pacific Ocean for mile upon mile. They chose to drive through the night, when the highway would be at its least busy, thinking that it would be to their benefit. How completely and utterly wrong they were. As fate would destine to have it, after a couple of hours of driving, the family of four spotted a strange light in the sky. It was described as a bright green ball of light, about the size of a beach-ball, one which paced their car and that stayed with them for a couple of miles, at a height of around sixty feet. There was nothing frightening about the encounter. Rather, they were all amazed and excited. It wasn't long, however, before things got very disturbing.

The day after the Maxwell family got home was a Sunday, meaning they had an extra day before returning to work and school. It was while one of the teenaged children sat on the porch playing music on an old Walkman that she caught sight of a man on the other side of the road. He was dressed completely in black, aside from a white shirt. He even wore black gloves, on what was a bright, summery day. The girl was particularly disturbed by the fact that the man sported a weird grin and was staring right at her. So unsettled was she that she went back into the home and told her father of what had just happened. He quickly went to the door but – no surprise – the MIB was gone.

APRIL 10, 1961

AN EARLY SHADOW PERSON
BOSTON, MASSACHUSETTS

Today, the phenomenon of so-called Shadow People is very well known. Their name is most apt: these usually one-dimensional entities are dark, human-like in appearance, and dangerous. Theories for who, or what, they may be range from aliens to demons, and shapeshifters to time-travelers. Whatever their point of origin – or maybe even multiple origins – an early encounter with one of these wretched things happened in Boston, Massachusetts by a young woman named Sally Salisbury.

In the early hours of a winter's morning, Salisbury was woken from a deep sleep by the terrifying sight of one of the Shadow People looming over her and oozing negativity and hatred, senses that Salisbury immediately picked up on. Paralysis set in – also immediately – andlasted for around two minutes, after which the entity vanished.

Interestingly, and very likely directly connected, on the following night Salisbury had a graphic dream – if that is all it was – of being taken on-board a UFO and subjected to traumatic and intrusive procedures of a medical and gynecological nature.

APRIL 11, 1967

WHEN FACT AND FICTION MIRROR EACH OTHER

The Invaders was a short-lived, but excellent, TV series that starred Roy Thinnes and which ran for just two seasons, from late 1967 to early 1968. One of the episodes was titled "Panic." It was first broadcast on April 11, 1967. The guest-star is Robert Walker, Jr., who plays an alien who uses the alias of Nick Baxter. There is, however, something very wrong with Baxter. He is infected with a deadly virus which has a bizarre effect on anyone he touches. The virus literally freezes them to death. It isn't long before David Vincent – Thinnes' character - is on the trail of the infected alien, who is causing havoc and death in rural West Virginia.

Few people with a knowledge of the Mothman saga will need

telling that the vast majority of the 1966-1968 events described in John Keel's *The Mothman Prophecies*, and in Gray Barker's *The Silver Bridge*, occurred in rural parts of West Virginia.

"Panic" also introduces us to a character named Madeline Flagg (played by Roy Thinnes' wife from 1967 to 1984, Lynn Loring). Flagg has a pet German Shepherd that meets a grisly end when the alien freezes it to death. In the pages of *The Silver Bridge*, Gray Barker describes the mysterious disappearance of Bandit, also a German Shepherd, who vanished on the night of November 14, 1966, from his home near Salem, West Virginia. Keel also tells the story of Bandit in *The Mothman Prophecies*.

Of course, all of these odd and intriguing crossovers and connections between the worlds of fiction and fact – and all focused on West Virginia in the 1960s – may simply be due to coincidence. Or, perhaps, the writers of *The Invaders* kept a careful watch on the high-strangeness that was afoot in West Virginia in 1966-1967, and chose to make use of it on the show. Albeit in somewhat altered form, of course. The same could be said for the production team on *The Mothman Prophecies*.

On the other hand, is it possible that the very act of developing a fictional story and characters can provoke the spontaneous manifestation of real-life counterparts and situations?

APRIL 12, 1954

"ABNORMALLY PROPORTIONED" ALIENS
WALKER AIR FORCE BASE, ROSWELL, NEW MEXICO

From the research team of Fred Schaefer, Gerald Miskar and Linda Robinson comes the account of "KA," who joined the Air Force in early 1954. After having completed his basic training at Sampson

Air Force Base, Geneva, New York, KA was transferred to Walker Air Force Base, New Mexico, where he "began special training in the Sikorsky H-19 helicopter...in relation to desert search and rescue operations."

According to KA, on the night of 12 April 1954, he and his crew were scrambled to take part in a rescue mission, following a "crash in the desert." KA informed Schaefer, Miskar and Robinson that after having been flown for approximately 25 miles from Walker into the heart of the desert, his team came upon a "saucer-like" object that had crashed "edgewise into the sand" and that was approximately 40-50 feet in diameter.

"Scattered outside the craft" were four small bodies that were "abnormally proportioned," and approximately four to four-and-a-half feet in height that KA was ordered to photograph.

"Scuttlebutt" suggested that the craft and bodies were taken to Walker, asserted KA. Shortly afterwards, under the false accusation that he had subsequently gone AWOL and discussed classified data pertaining to the crash without official authority to do so, KA was dismissed from the Air Force.

APRIL 13, 1964

THERE'S SOMETHING IN THE RIVER
WALTHAMSTOW, ENGLAND

At around 8:40 p.m. on the night in question, bus-driver Bob Fall was driving alongside the River Lea in the town of Walthamstow, England when his attention was drawn to a fast-moving aerial object that barely missed his bus as it plunged into the depths of the river. He said:

"I just glanced into the sky and saw something coming

towards me very, very fast. It flew straight across the road and, had I been a few yards further forward, it would have hit the top deck of the bus. At first I thought the back windows of the bus had come in and, as I turned around, I saw all the passengers looking out towards the river. There was a big splash in the water. I stopped as soon as I could to report it. The thing was at least nine feet long, cigar-shaped and silver," he insisted. "If it had been a bird or birds I [would] have seen the wings. Besides, it was going too fast."

As a result of the media publicity afforded this event, a British UFO investigator, Ronald Caswell of Harlow, Essex, looked into the case and uncovered a wealth of data that had been almost completely overlooked by his contemporaries. His notes state:

"I have a piece of one of the telephone wires broken by the object. A newspaper shows great coils of it on the towpath. The police spokesman's suggestion that a duck, or even four ducks, could have broken those wires is ridiculous. Neither could a swan. The length of the wire across the river would have moved away at the pressure of a plummeting bird, and the bird would certainly have been badly injured, if not killed."

Notably, Caswell also said that he learned "…when it was late enough for the general public to have cleared off, heavy lifting equipment was brought in and a find was made in the early hours of the morning."

What that "find" was, has never been disclosed.

A LEGEND PASSES
BRIDGEPORT, CONNECTICUT

I knew that, in all likelihood, it would happen soon. After all, he was getting perilously close to a century in age. But, I have to say, it was still sad to see the news when it surfaced. You are most likely wondering whom I'm talking about. None other than the passing of Albert Bender, the guy who began the Men in Black mystery back in the early 1950s, and whose 1962 book on the subject, *Flying Saucers and the Three Men*, remains a must-read for MIB enthusiasts. Despite having been threatened, taunted and tormented by a trio of blazing-eyed Men in Black in his Bridgeport, Connecticut home all those years ago, Bender lived to the ripe old age of ninety-four – proof that being confronted by the MIB does not necessarily mean death is looming just around the corner!

Although April 14 was the date on which the story of Bender's death surfaced on the Internet, it turned out that he had passed away just a couple of weeks earlier, specifically on March 29. Both Loren Coleman and I wrote obituaries on Bender, which got sizeable coverage and commentary online. In part, mine read like this:

"Given that there have been claims Bender died in the early 2000s, a few people have already asked me if the Wiki page is accurate. Yes, it is. Bender had a full life and outlived just about everyone else who got involved in Ufology in the late 1940s and early 1950s. Over the years I have written quite extensively on the life and experiences of Albert Bender (my book, *Women in Black: The Creepy Companions of the Mysterious M.I.B.*, delves into his experiences even more.) And both *Flying Saucers and the Three Men* and *They Knew Too Much about Flying Saucers* were books I read as a kid. As many people know, the mystery of the MIB is one of my particular interests. It's likely that interest would not have developed as it has without the words and experiences of Albert Bender. RIP, Mr. B."

APRIL 15, 1976

"HOW COULD IT RISE UP LIKE THAT?"
CORNWALL, ENGLAND

In 1976 the dense trees surrounding Mawnan Old Church, Cornwall, England became a veritable magnet for a diabolical beast that was christened the Owlman. The majority of those that crossed paths with the creature asserted that it was human-like in both size and design, and possessed a pair of large wings, fiery red eyes, claws, and exuded an atmosphere of menace. No wonder people make parallels with Mothman – the fiery-eyed monster linked to Men in Black and UFO encounters in Point Pleasant, West Virginia in the 1960s.

It all began during the weekend of Easter 1976, when two young girls, June and Vicky Melling, had an encounter of a truly nightmarish kind in Mawnan Woods. The girls were on holiday with their parents when they saw a gigantic, feathery "bird man" hovering over the 13th Century church.

It was a story that their father, Don Melling, angrily shared with a man named Tony "Doc" Shiels. I say "angrily" because Shiels was a noted, local magician who Melling came to believe had somehow instigated the whole affair. Or as Shiels, himself, worded it: "...some trick that had badly frightened his daughters." Shiels denied any involvement in the matter whatsoever. But that was only the start of things.

Another one to see the Owlman was Jane Greenwood, also a

young girl. She wrote a letter to the local newspaper, the *Falmouth Packet*, during the summer of 1976 that detailed her own startling encounter: "I am on holiday in Cornwall with my sister and our mother. I, too, have seen a big bird-thing. It was Sunday morning, and the place was in the trees near Mawnan Church, above the rocky beach. It was in the trees standing like a full-grown man, but the legs bent backwards like a bird's. It saw us, and quickly jumped up and rose straight up through the trees. How could it rise up like that?" How, indeed?

APRIL 16, 2016

TREVOR JAMES CONSTABLE

NEW ZEALAND

That was the day on which the death of yet another ufological old-timer – Trevor James Constable – was revealed. As Loren Coleman noted, Constable died just two days after Albert Bender, at the age of ninety. It so transpires that Constable had a deep interest in the Bender/MIB affair and concluded, back in 1962, that Bender's MIB were definitively occult-based in nature and origin. How do I know this? Because back in sixty-two Gray Barker published a follow-up title to Albert Bender's *Flying Saucers and the Three Men*. Its title: *Bender Mystery Confirmed*. It was essentially a 100-page collection of letters from readers of Bender's book and who wanted to offer their thoughts and theories. One of those people was Trevor James Constable.

The author of *They Live in the Sky*, and someone who believed that at least some UFOs are living, jellyfish-like creatures, Constable wrote the following letter to Gray Barker, which the latter duly published in *Bender Mystery Confirmed*:

"Dear Gray, It is difficult indeed for me, as an occultist with some firsthand experience of this field of UFOs, to sort out Bender's journeys back and forth across the threshold line between the physical and the astral. A biometric examination of Al Bender would probably indicate similar things to what it revealed about certain other researchers – total inability to distinguish between events on two planes of reality."

Constable continued to Barker: "Bender's honesty I do not for a moment doubt. His discrimination I would deem non-existent. It seems almost incredible that the man could relate the full story of the construction of his chamber of horrors in the attic in the way Bender has. This is what convinces me of his honesty. Nothing could be more logical, in an occult way, than that the invisible entities he invited by the preparation of this locale, should indeed manifest to him, and thereafter proceed to obsess him for a protracted period, using hypnotic techniques that brought the man completely under their control."

APRIL 17, 1897

AN ALIEN IN THE CEMETERY

AURORA, TEXAS

Perhaps no other crashed UFO account aside from the Roswell, New Mexico story of 1947 and the Aztec, New Mexico affair of 1948 has generated more controversy than the allegation that an alien spacecraft crashed in a small Texas town called Aurora in the latter part of the 19th Century.

One of those who believes the Aurora case has merit is the noted author and investigative reporter Jim Marrs, says:

"April 17, 1897, dawned clear and cool in North Texas when

out of the south came a large silver cigar-shaped object dropping lower and lower as it approached the small hamlet of Aurora, Texas, less than 20 miles northwest of Fort Worth. There it struck a windmill and exploded, scattering debris - and at least one small body - in all directions. Or did it?

"Despite straight-faced coverage in the local newspapers at the time, the Aurora crash continues to be a source of controversy [and] every few years the story is brought up again by various newspapers and periodicals. Each time, some debunker argues that the Aurora spaceship crash story was a hoax, a fake story planted in the newspapers to draw attention to the little town that was dying after being bypassed by the railroad."

APRIL 18, 1964

UFO VS METEOR

ONEIDA, NEW YORK

The bulk of research and revelations pertaining to this case can be credited to the late Frank Edwards, radio host, and to Kevin Randle, the writer and researcher who also co-authored (with Don Schmitt) several books on the Roswell controversy. Richard M. Dolan, author of *UFOs and the National Security State,* here provides an outstanding summary of the case:

"On April 18, 1962, an unidentified, red, glowing object was moving west very rapidly over Oneida, New York. Was it a meteor? If so, it was quite unusual. In the first place, it was tracked on radar which, while possible, is exceedingly rare. Second, as it passed across the country, Air Defense Command alerted all bases along its path and at least two Air Force bases - Luke AFB near Phoenix, and Nellis AFB in Nevada - sent jet interceptors after it. Why pursue a meteor? Finally, the entire sighting from New York to Nevada lasted minutes. This gives an average speed of 4,500 mph, well below the slowest speed ever recorded for a meteor."

"When the object passed over Nephi, Utah, people on the ground heard jets following it. The object then landed at Eureka, Utah. Several witnesses saw it as a 'glowing orange oval' which emitted a low whirring sound.' When it landed, it disrupted the electrical service from a nearby power station. It then rose, maneuvered, and headed toward Nevada. It was seen at Reno, then turned south and was spotted somewhat east of Las Vegas, where it went off the radar screens. Many witnesses saw it as a 'tremendous flaming sword.' By now it had been seen by thousands of people. It exploded near Mesquite, Nevada, at which time it was being pursued by armed jet interceptors from Nellis AFB."

The *Las Vegas Sun* reported the incident in its April 19th edition under the headline, "Brilliant Red Explosion Flares in Las Vegas Sky." The article broached the UFO topic, and mentioned the Air Force alert in several states. The Clark County sheriff's office was swamped with calls. They investigated the incident but found nothing of consequence. On May 8, 1962, the Air Force sent Blue Book Chief Robert Friend and J. Allen Hynek to investigate. Their results were quite unsatisfactory. The two did not go to Nevada, but confined themselves to central Utah. Despite their knowledge that jets had pursued the object, they concluded it was a bolide, an especially fiery meteor.

A CLOSE ENCOUNTER OF THE BREAKFAST KIND

EAGLE RIVER, WISCONSIN

On April 19 (not April 18, as has been incorrectly stated on so many previous occasions) a UFO encounter occurred in Eagle River, Wisconsin that many researchers of the flying saucer phenomenon have seen fit to relegate to the domains of hoaxing and/ or fantasy. It just might have been something else. It was the late morning and the tasty brunch of a man named Joe Simonton was about to be rudely interrupted by visitors from another world. Talk about bad timing.

A chicken farmer, Simonton was about to eat when he was shaken to his core by the thundering sound of what he thought was a jet-plane flying low overhead. It was not. He raced outside and was confronted by nothing less than a flying saucer, around thirty feet in diameter, hovering above his yard.

Simonton could only stand and stare, in awe, as a doorway opened and a man approached him. He and his comrades inside the UFO were all short — around five feet at the most — and wore outfits similar to military jumpsuits. The completely mute man approached Simonton with what clearly resembled a terrestrial jug, and managed to make Simonton understand that he wanted water.

Simonton quickly obliged. As a "thank-you" the aliens gave Simonton a hot plate of what appeared to be small pancakes, fresh off of ET's grill. Yes, really. It was a good trade-off for the farmer. The leader of the group gave a strange salute and returned to the craft, which shot away, into the heavens. Simonton ate his somewhat unappetizing pancakes — or, at least, he ate one of them. By all accounts, one was enough.

PROJECT MOON DUST
WASHINGTON, D.C.

In the 1950s, the U.S. military created a program called Project Moon Dust. Its secret mandate was to recover and secure crashed and landed foreign technology of a highly advanced nature. We are talking about the likes of Soviet space-satellites. Notably, there are longstanding rumors that Moon Dust personnel have taken part in the recovery of crashed UFOs. An April 1961 official Air Force document on Moon Dust provides notable data:

"Based on estimates of the time and place of foreign earth satellite vehicle (ESV) atmospheric re-entries, Headquarters USAF (AFCIN) initiates MOON DUST Alerts. They are issued as far in advance as practicable (normally 10 days) and are automatically cancelled three (3) days after the re-entry prediction date stated in the alert message. It is necessary that the alerts be issued on a world-wide basis until such time as techniques are developed that will make possible the prediction of the precise time and place of impact.

"During the periods when MOON DUST Alert is in effect, it is important that interested personnel receive, as rapidly as possible, accurate sighting data on the final (estimated) orbits from as many different sources as possible. The following guidance may assist in reporting observations of space vehicle re-entry. The re-entry of a space vehicle can be seen over great distances, and even the qualified observer cannot estimate the distance from point of observation to the sighted object with any great degree of certainty. At these distances, the re-entry would appear to resemble a meteor travelling in a near horizontal or descending path and, as the distance decreased, would appear as a brilliant object or cluster of objects visible during daylight conditions. In addition, an audible rumbling sound like thunder, arid possibly sharp explosion-like sounds might be correlated with the sighting.

"Because of the intelligence connotations of MOON DUST regarding retrieval and examination by ATIC of a descended Soviet space vehicle, the overall project is classified Confidential, and MOON DUST Alerts are normally on a Confidential basis because of the intelligence association with decay estimates. The basic decay estimates (identification of the- object and estimated date and hour of decay) are in themselves normally unclassified. Thus, decay estimates, as such, can be released to observers or observatories cooperating with U.S. collectors purely on the basis of international cooperation in the scientific aspects of space knowledge."

APRIL 21, 1991

"WHAT HAPPENED IS A MYSTERY"

KENT, ENGLAND

On the night of April 21, 1991, the term "close encounter" took on an altogether more significant meaning for the crew and passengers of a London, England-bound airliner. At 9:00 p.m., Captain Achille Zaghetti – who was piloting a McDonnell MD-80 aircraft – was amazed to see a missile-like unidentified flying object pass his aircraft as it flew over the English county of Kent, at a height of more than 22,000 feet.

As the UFO was no more than 1,000 feet above the airliner, and the incident was therefore classified as a "near miss," an official inquiry was launched by the Civil Aviation Authority.

Approximately two weeks later, the CAA issued a statement to the media that read as follows: "The pilot said the object was light brown, round, 3 meters long, and did not describe any means of propulsion."

The statement continued: "The aircraft was under the control of the London air traffic control center who had no other aircraft in the vicinity but consistent with the pilot report, a faint radar trace was observed 10 nautical miles behind the Alitalia aircraft."

In conclusion, it was stated: "The air traffic controller submitted an occurrence report and investigatory action began immediately. Extensive enquiries have failed to provide any indication of what the sighting may have been."

One of the most interesting things about this particular incident is the attitude taken by the British Ministry of Defense at the time: "What happened is a mystery. It was yet another UFO," said a spokesperson for the MoD on the same day that the CAA issued its findings on the case.

APRIL 22, 1949

AN EARLY FLYING TRIANGLE

VICKSBURG, MISSISSIPPI

In 2013, I had an interesting debate with a fellow researcher of the UFO phenomenon, on the topic of that one particular type of UFO that has become known as the Flying Triangle. When the conversation got going, it didn't take long before I was assured that (in words broadly like the following): "They're just military aircraft, and still classified. But one day they will be unveiled for us all to see – just like what happened with the Stealth fighter and the Stealth bomber."

Frankly, I get tired of people assuming – often without doing *any* deep research – that the FTs are domestic in origin. The reason why they reach that conclusion is actually very simple. There seems to be an assumption on the part of many in Ufology that the Triangles are phenomena that have only been seen since the 1980s onwards. Or, at the very earliest, the late 70s. Now, if that was the case, then yes, of course, an argument could be made that these craft are (a) ours; (b) still-classified; and (c) far in advance of the aforementioned Stealth aircraft.

Unfortunately for those who prefer to see the Flying Triangles as vehicles of the military and nothing else, there is a major problem: reports of craft identical to those seen today date back more than sixty years. The issue here is that the "Flying Triangles are ours and ours alone" meme is one that has been fully embraced by lazy souls who simply will not look at the bigger, historical picture. If they did, their views might change – and change significantly, too.

On the date at issue, a UFO was seen at Vicksburg, Mississippi that was flying at a significant speed and that was distinctly triangular in shape. Indeed, in the official U.S. Air Force file on the affair – which is housed at the National Archives in Maryland – the object is actually described in the official report (by Special Agent Bernard A. Price) as a "flying triangle."

APRIL 23, 1965

MAKING CONTACT

SCORRITON, COUNTY OF DEVON, ENGLAND

The story revolves around a man named Ernest Arthur Bryant, a resident of an old village in the English county of Devon called

Scoriton. Or, as some prefer to spell it, Scorriton. As for Devon, it's an ancient and mysterious land, and which is made famous by the fact that Sir Arthur Conan Doyle set his classic Sherlock Holmes novel *The Hound of the Baskervilles* in Devon's Dartmoor National Park.

On this day, Bryant (who served with the British Commandos in World War Two) saw something amazing hovering over a field close to his home: a flying saucer. Bryant stared, shocked and amazed for a few moments, and then made his cautious way to the field. As he did so, and seemingly in response to his actions, the circular-shaped craft gently touched to the ground.

As Bryant arrived, a group of three, human-like beings attired in shiny, silver suits motioned him not to come any closer. He did as he was told. Bryant looked on, stunned, and noticed that the beings had overly long foreheads, seemed to have problems breathing in the Earth's atmosphere, and, somewhat oddly, had no thumbs. One of the beings then moved towards Bryant and reeled off typical, absurd, Space Brother-themed spiel. The entity claimed his name was "Yamski" and that he and his comrades hailed from Venus, no less.

The alien then made a comment along the lines of, "If only Des were here." Or, suggested Bryant, it may have been "Les," rather than "Des." This, along with the "Yamski" name is all very interesting, since only one day before the encounter, the world's most famous Contactee, George Adamski, died. Plus, Adamski's co-author on his *Flying Saucers Have Landed* book was Desmond Leslie.

Also in typical Contactee/Space Brother style, Bryant was given a "tour" of the UFO – which was, allegedly, split into three sections. The aliens then made a cryptic statement suggesting they would contact Bryant again. As Bryant watched from a safe distance, the UFO then rose into the sky and vanished from sight. It was then end of a strange encounter that still baffles ufologists.

INVADERS FROM MARS
SOCORRO, NEW MEXICO

That was the date of a near-legendary UFO encounter which occurred at Socorro, New Mexico. The witness was a police-officer named Lonnie Zamora, who stumbled upon a landed UFO and its dwarfish crew on the afternoon of the 24th. Moments later, the object took to the skies in fiery fashion. The story is a classic within Ufology. Far less well-known, is an equally intriguing case that occurred on the very same day.

Around ten hours before the Socorro affair, a young farmer named Gary Wilcox got the shock of his life when he saw a strange craft land in woods near his Tioga City, New York home. Like the craft Zamora saw, this one was also white, egg-shaped, and crewed by a pair of small aliens. It appeared that the aliens were collecting soil-samples — as evidenced by the trays of dirt the extraterrestrial duo were holding.

Incredibly, one of the aliens proceeded to speak to Wilcox. In English, no less. The ETs - who claimed to come from Mars — engaged Wilcox in conversation on issues which ranged from farming to man-made pollution, and from outer-space activity to the Cold War. Finally, the aliens were done and, before leaving, warned Wilcox not reveal what had just occurred — nor the nature of the conversation. Wilcox chose to ignore their words and, as a result, briefly became famous in the world of Ufology.

"DO NOT ACCEPT PEOPLE INTO YOUR HOUSE"

GLOUCESTER, ENGLAND

On this day, the British Police Force was chasing down an eerie Woman in Black – the female equivalents of the notorious Men in Black. The U.K's *Daily Mail* was carefully following the strange affair. On April 25, the newspaper's Damien Gayle noted that: "Parents have been told to be vigilant after a bogus social worker called at a house and examined a baby. The woman, who claimed to be from Gloucestershire social services, tricked her way into the home in Quedgeley with fake ID and listened to the child's heartbeat with a stethoscope. She told the mother there were concerns for the welfare of her four-month-old son."

Detective Inspector Andy Dangerfield, of Gloucestershire Police, assured the press that the woman had at no time come into physical contact with the baby, but added: "We don't know what the motivation for this was but clearly it is very concerning. Our inquiries are ongoing. We have visited houses in the area to warn local people and would urge everyone to be vigilant. Remember, do not accept people into your house unless you are 100% sure you know who they are. You can always tell them to stay outside until you have made your own inquiries and if you are suspicious in any way, then call police. We have liaised with our partners at Gloucestershire social care services and they have alerted their staff to this incident."

A NAZI FLYING SAUCER

MIAMI, FLORIDA

An intriguing FBI document concerns a man who appeared at
the Miami Office of the FBI on April 26, 1967, and furnished the
following information relating to a circular-shaped aircraft that
he allegedly photographed during November 1944: "Sometime
during 1943, he graduated from the German Air Academy and was
assigned as a member of the Luftwaffe on the Russian Front Near
the end of 1944, he was released from this duty and was assigned
as a test pilot to a top secret project in the Black Forest of Austria."

During this period, recorded the FBI, the man was witness
to a strange, flying vehicle. It was, he told the interviewing agents,
"…saucer-shaped, about twenty-one feet in diameter, radio-con-
trolled, and mounted several jet engines around the exterior
portion of the craft. He further described the exterior portion
as revolving around the dome in the center which remained stationary. It was his responsibility to photograph the object while in
flight. He asserted he was able to retain a negative of a photograph
he made at 7,000 meters (20,000 feet)."

The FBI further detailed: "According to him, the above aircraft was designed and engineered by a German engineer whose
present whereabouts is unknown to him. He also assumed the
secrets pertaining to this aircraft were captured by Allied Forces.
He said this type of aircraft was responsible for the downing of at
least one American B-26 airplane.

"He has become increasingly concerned because of the
unconfirmed reports concerning a similar object and denials the
United States has such an aircraft. He feels such a weapon would

be beneficial in Vietnam and would prevent the further loss of American lives which was his paramount purpose in contacting the Federal Bureau of Investigation."

APRIL 27, 1950

"A GLOWING RED OBJECT"
CHICAGO, ILLINOIS

While presenting for the House Committee on Science and Astronautics on July 29, 1968, James McDonald, PhD stated: "Another early airline sighting that seemed worth personally crosschecking involved the crew and passengers of a TWA DC-3 on the evening of 4/27/50 I have interviewed both the pilot, Capt. Robert Adickes, and the copilot, Capt. Robert F. Manning, and confirmed all of the principal features first reported in detail in a magazine account by [Major Donald] Keyhoe The DC-3 was at about 2000 feet, headed for Chicago, when, at about 8:25 p.m., Manning spotted a glowing red object aft of the starboard wing, well to their rear. Manning sent to me a copy of notes that he had made later that night at his Chicago hotel."

APRIL 28, 1977

"A LARGE, DAMAGED OBJECT"
SOUTH-WEST AUSTRALIAN BORDER

The well-known Australian researcher Bill Chalker writes: "In about 1977 a UFO first seen as a purple-green 'fireball,' was observed to 'crash' near the South Australia–West Australia border, some distance north of the Eyre Highway."

According to Chalker's source for the account, who claimed

to have been a "direct participant," a quick-response team headed to the crash site and found a "large, damaged object, completely unlike any conventional aircraft," that had "something of a triangular appearance."

The witness informed Chalker that "two beings" were located within the craft, one apparently injured and one deceased. Both appeared to be around 5 feet in height, "pot-bellied," with long arms and black eyes. Chalker's source also confided to him that the retrieval team was a "joint US-Australian operation," and that he was personally aware of "4 apparent UFO crash events."

In 2014, a further source came forward, claiming personal involvement in the case and tying the date down to April 26, 1977. That same source claimed that the bodies of the dead ETs are, today, held deep below the ground in a secure "vault" at Pine Gap – which is the Australian equivalent of the United States' National Security Agency.

APRIL 29, 1957

"THE OBJECT WAS CIRCULAR WITH A WHITE SLIGHTLY CURVING TAIL"

ODIHAM RAF BASE, HAMPSHIRE, ENGLAND

At around 10:20 a.m., on the morning of April 29, 1957, two UK Royal Air Force *Hunter* aircraft took to the skies from an RAF base called Odiham, which is located in the English county of Hampshire. The plan was for the aircraft to take part in a mid-air military training exercise. Things didn't quite turn out as planned, however. When the planes reached a height of roughly 45,000-feet, one of the pilots found himself confronted by what can only be described as an undeniable, unidentified flying object.

And you don't have to take my word for it. The following is a word for word account of what took place, and which is extracted from a now-declassified British Air Ministry file on the case which can be found at the National Archives, at Kew, Surrey, England:

"…when over Hayling Island Mission 28 No. 2 saw a large white object at 10 o'clock slightly above. The object was circular with a white slightly curving tail hanging below. The time was approximately 1110. Formation leader was informed and both pairs turned east onto a northerly heading to look for the object. At first the object was thought to be a parachute but later it was realized that the object must have been larger and at a greater distance because of the slow passing speed."

And matters were far from over. They had, in fact, barely begun. At 8:38 p.m. that night, the pilot of a Royal Air Force *Javelin* aircraft – also based at RAF Odiham – was vectored onto a UFO reportedly tracked on radar some twelve miles from his position. The pilot made no visual contact,, and he eventually returned to base. This particular affair received brief coverage in a number of newspapers – after one of the base staff tipped off a local reporter on what had gone down – and, as a result, an Air Ministry spokesman made a *very* brief statement to the press. It went as follows: "All we can say is that we are investigating the matter. Until inquiries are completed we have nothing further to add."

APRIL 30, 1957

UNKNOWN OBJECTS AND THE MILITARY

SHANKLIN, ENGLAND

According to UK Ministry of Defense records, a member of the public, a Mr. L. Humfreys, telephoned Royal Air Force Ventnor to report that he could see two metallic-appearing objects to the south-east of Shanklin, England, at a height of what was estimated to be approximately 30,000 feet. Mr. Humfreys – whose sighting was backed-up by three additional witnesses – said: "The object appeared as a steady, metallic, very bright pinpoint of light, with a suggestion of a smaller round object immediately behind."

At 8:10 p.m., staff at the nearby radar station at Beachy Head reported to RAF Ventnor that they were tracking two unidentified responses flying at a height of 25,000 feet. Almost one hour later, Beachy Head contacted Ventnor again, this time to report that RAF St. Margaret's was also plotting two fast-moving targets, but were unable to ascertain their heights. One of the objects was reported to be traveling in a Southwesterly direction, at a speed of between 750 and 800 knots.

Since all attempts to identify the objects failed – and no evidence surfaced suggesting they were linked to any kind of exercise referred to by George Ward – a detailed report was prepared by Pilot Officer R.F. Coles of RAF Ventnor, and all the relevant data (which included the radar-based material) was forwarded to the Air Ministry at Whitehall, London for scrutiny. The six-page report has now been declassified and can be examined by one and all at the National Archives.

MAY

MAY 1, 1994

A "BOOMERANG" ATTRACTS OFFICIAL, SECRET ATTENTION

NORTHOLT RAF BASE, BOVINGDON, ENGLAND

Under the terms of the UK Freedom of Information Act, the following, brief extract from a much longer, and still withheld, file offers the following, tantalizing insight:

"1 May 1994 – Sighting of unusual object. Member of public reported seeing a black boomerang-shaped object, which appeared to hover over RAF Northolt, above 30,000 feet, before tumbling approximately 2000–3000 feet, while rotating through 180 degrees on its axis. No other reports of anything unusual received – possibly A/C in Bovingdon stack seen from odd angle in setting sun."

MAY 2, 1962

MONITORING A UFO

NEATISHEAD RAF BASE, ENGLAND

British Air Ministry documentation of May 23, 1962 reveals that five days earlier, radar-based personnel stationed at Royal Air Force Neatishead on the east-coast of England, tracked an unidentified flying object maneuvering, and even briefly, hovering over the coastline at a height of slightly more than 11,000 feet between approximately 1:20 and 1:30 a.m. Although a fighter-plane was launched and vectored onto the target, it was to no avail: the UFO, clearly reacting to the presence of the aircraft, shot vertically into the sky – leaving the pilot and the radar personnel utterly baffled. The matter was never resolved.

AN EERIE SILENCE
WREXHAM, ENGLAND

Declassified UK military papers show that late in the afternoon a pair of schoolgirls heading to their homes in Wrexham, England, saw a large "bowl"-shaped UFO flying over the area at a low level and which briefly hovered over a field only a couple of hundred yards from where the girls were standing. Oddly, during the twenty to thirty seconds that the UFO was in view, everything went very quiet and still – as if the pair was in some strange vacuum-like state. This somewhat spaced-out feeling has been noted in many encounters. Ufologist Jenny Randles refers to it as the Oz-Factor.

AN ENCOUNTER IN LOS ANGELES
LOS ANGELES, CALIFORNIA

Although a fairly minor cog in the UFO Contactee wheel, Orfeo Angelucci wrote a number of well-received books, even though they failed to sell in large quantities. They included *The Secret of the Saucers* and *Son of the Sun*. May 17, 1952 was the day – or, rather, the night – on which everything changed for Angelucci. It started out as a strange day – even before the ETs arrive on the scene. From the moment he woke up, Angelucci felt agitated, worried, and had a strange sense that the day was going to turn out very weird. He was not wrong.

At the time, Angelucci was employed by the Lockheed Aircraft Corporation and was working night-shifts. It was shortly after midnight on the evening in question that Angelucci got in his car and drove home. He didn't know it then, but he was about to have a detour, and an experience, of a very weird kind. It was as Angelucci crossed a bridge over the Los Angeles River – a bridge that was eerily empty of any other vehicles at the time – that he caught sight of a large, blue-colored ball of light that was clearly shadowing him. The beach-ball sized circle of light took a sudden turn, appearing directly in front of Angelucci's car. Shocked to the core, Angelucci slowed his car to practically walking pace, and watched, amazed, as two small, green balls of light emerged from the larger one and floated towards him.

Via telepathy a booming voice informed Angelucci that he had been watched for a number of years. Angelucci was about to ask a question when the two balls closed in on each other, and eventually merging into one, larger, green light. In mere seconds, the ball changed into the disembodied images of a man and a woman – or, as Angelucci came to learn – the floating heads of a pair of aliens who could pass for you or me. Like so many of the Contactees, Angelucci was asked – in a noticeable and slightly bullying and patronizing fashion – to "spread the word" of the supposedly utterly benevolent ETs.

MAY 5, 1980

ABDUCTED BY ALIENS AND THE MILITARY

KIRTLAND AIR FORCE BASE, ABLBUQUERQUE, NEW MEXICO

One of the strangest alien abduction events involved a woman named Myrna Hansen, who had a notable and controversial UFO encounter late one night while driving to New Mexico after vacationing in Oklahoma. After realizing that a substantial amount of time seemed to be missing from the journey, and having vague,

UFO-related memories concerning the night's events, she underwent hypnosis to try and determine what had taken place. It transpires that she was abducted by a group of small, black-eyed aliens that took her on board a UFO, and on which she was treated in a fashion very similar to that of Betty and Barney Hill back in 1961. That's to say, as the human equivalent of a lab rat. In many respects, what happened next was even weirder.

Hansen's hypnotically retrieved memories revealed that, when the aliens were done with her, she was taken to some form of subterranean installation. This was no alien base, however. What it actually was, was something quite different. When word of Hansen's experience and recollections began to circulate amongst ufologists, sources at Kirtland Air Force Base, New Mexico, who were secretly following the story, instantly realized that what Hansen had described was – rather incredibly – a classified, off-limits bunker that was a part of the base's weapons storage area.

The implication – given that Hansen was not an employee of the Air Force, and as a result, did not have a security clearance to access the weapons storage area – was that elements of the military were monitoring the alien abduction, and then, when it was over, flew Hansen, in a darkened helicopter, to Kirtland, where she was subjected to a grilling by military personnel, demanding to know what occurred while she was on the UFO. Whatever the Air Force learned, it remains unknown outside of the world of the underground domain of what are known as MILABS – military abductions.

UFO DOWN!

BERMEJO, BOLIVIA

On May 15, 1978, the U.S. Department of State hastily circulated – from the American Embassy in La Paz, Bolivia – a document concerning an event which occurred three days earlier. It reached the U.S. Secretary of State, the CIA, the NSA, and NASA. Titled *Report of Fallen Space Object*, the document outlined the extraordinary facts:

"The Bolivian newspapers carried this morning an article concerning an unidentified object that apparently recently fell from the sky. The object was discovered near the Bolivian city of Bermejo and was described as egg-shaped, metal and about four meters in diameter. The Bolivian Air Force plans to investigate to determine what the object might be and from where it came. I have expressed our interest and willingness to help. They will advise."

"Request the department check with appropriate agencies to see if they can shed some light on what this object might be. The general region has had more than its share of reports of UFOs the past week. Request a reply ASAP."

The CIA was soon on top of things, as the following memo, also of May 15 shows: "Many people in this part of the country claim they saw an object which resembled a soccer ball falling behind the mountains on the Argentine-Bolivian border, causing an explosion that shook the earth. This took place on May 6. Around that time some people in San Luis and Mendoza provinces reported seeing a flying saucer squadron flying in formation."

Officially, nothing was found: no wreckage, no bodies, and no craft. Unless, that is, the CIA secretly knows better.

AN APOCALYPTIC WARNING
BECKENHAM, KENT, ENGLAND

In the early hours of the morning in question Leonard Murray was awakened from a dead sleep by a "spaceman" wearing a "fish-bowl"-style "space helmet" and a light blue outfit. The other-world character warned Murray that a Third World War was on the horizon and that he and his family should prepare to try and survive the looming Apocalypse. Cold War-era anxieties? Or a real encounter with an extraterrestrial concerned about our future as a species? More than half a century later, the chances are we will never find out the truth of this odd encounter.

"THE GOVERNMENT IS CONCERNED"
DECATUR, TEXAS

Gloria is an elderly woman currently living in Decatur, Texas. On July 19, 2012, she briefly saw what can only be accurately described as a flying saucer, which hovered over her home, as she sat in her backyard, reading a book, and with her two dogs for company. In fact, it was the barking of both dogs, and which stared at the sky, that alerted her to the weird craft. It didn't stay around for long, however. But that was not all.

The next afternoon, that of the 20th, there was a knock at the door. It was a pale-faced woman of about thirty, wearing a long black wig and dressed in a black jacket, white blouse, and long black skirt. And then there were the huge sunglasses. Gloria felt deeply uncomfortable as, upon opening the door, the Woman in

Black proceeded to warn her not to talk about the UFO she had encountered the previous day, due to the claim that "the government is concerned."

Clearly, however, the WIB was not from the government: according to Gloria, the woman didn't even look human. After asking what the time was, the WIB turned, walked down Gloria's driveway and vanished. Never to be seen again.

THE MYSTERIOUS "BELL"
BEAUMONT, TEXAS

According to Sallie-Ann, of Beaumont, Texas, late one night after visiting a friend in the town of Orange, Texas, she encountered a very weird object on an isolated stretch of country road. It was a bell-shaped object, about nine or ten feet in height, which hung over the road, at a height of around fifty feet, and which glowed bright yellow. As she approached the object, Sallie-Ann was unsure as to whether she should slow down her car or speed up. She chose the latter – which, perhaps, was a wise choice.

A "TENTACLED" UFO
OTTAWA, CANADA

Canadian military files refer to the sighting of a fairly small UFO described as being "octopus"-like, and which was seen on the outskirts of Ottawa late one night by a group of friends. The report is brief – which is unfortunate because, according to the witnesses, the story was pretty amazing: the UFO flew through the air by flicking what were described as "tentacles," in much the same way that oars are used to propel a rowing-boat. The reference to tentacles suggests some sort of flying monster of unknown proportions. The witnesses, however, were sure that the object was metallic. It was only briefly in view, but long enough to convince the friends of what they had seen.

MAY 11, 1950

A FLYING SAUCER AND A FESTIVAL

MCMINNVILLE, OREGON

Seeing a UFO is astounding enough on its own. Photographing it is even more so. How about photographing it twice? Incredible good luck or a case of just too good to be true? Those are the questions that surround a couple of now-infamous photos taken by a farmer named Paul Trent, of McMinnville, Oregon, on the evening of May 11, 1950. It was Trent's wife, Evelyn, who alerted her husband to the circular-shaped object soaring across the skies. He grabbed his camera, aimed, and before you could say "take me to your leader," UFO seekers all across the nation were almost foaming at the mouth.

For the last seventeen years the people of McMinnville have celebrated Paul Trent's good fortune by holding a four-day-long festival in his honor at the town's Hotel Oregon. Saucer- seekers flock to the town and ufological luminaries lecture to the flying saucer faithful. Their number includes Coast to Coast AM's George Noory and Dr. Roger Leir, described at the festival's website as an "alien implant removal specialist."

It's all good fun. Even when it's not, there's no need to worry. For just $4.00 you can purchase a "UFO Fest Alien Stress Toy."

Now we come to McMinnville's very own "elephant in the room." UFO skeptics have noted that Paul Trent's "flying saucer" closely resembles – and very suspiciously resembles - the side-view mirror of a 1950 Ford Coupe. Done with mirrors? Say it ain't so!

MAY 12, 1999

AN ENCOUNTER IN THE BEDROOM
COLLINS, NEW YORK

Phyllis is a retired school teacher who had a strange experience on this particular night in her hometown of Collins, New York. It was around 2:00 a.m. when Phyllis was violently woken up by the sight of a large, humanoid entity that resembled a huge lizard, one that stood upright and which hissed at her in a malevolent fashion. Within the field of UFO research, such entities have become known as the Reptilians. For some investigators of this strange ufological offshoot, the Reptilians are either shapeshifting entities from another dimension, the modern day descendants of an ancient terrestrial race, or extraterrestrials from a faraway world. Whatever they are, the Reptilians have become a staple part of Ufology.

As for Phyllis, her encounter was downright horrific and apocalyptic: the green monster loomed over her, at which point her mind was filled with visions of flying saucer-style craft soaring across the skies of a devastated Earth. Landscapes were burned to a crisp, cities were obliterated, the skies above were filled with millions of tons of dust, and billions were dead. It was a nightmarish scene of what Phyllis believes will one day come true: namely, the destruction of the Human Race by ETs. Although why Phyllis was given insight into the world that is still to come, she has no idea.

AN EERIE ENCOUNTER IN A LIBRARY
UNIVERSITY OF PENNSYLVANIA, PHILADELPHIA, PENNSYLVANIA

On this day, a man named Peter Rojcewicz wrote-up a fascinating account of an experience he had in November 1980. On the day in question, Rojcewicz was working on his PhD thesis in folklore. It was while doing research at the Library of the University of Pennsylvania that Rojcewicz had an encounter of a type that will instantly be recognizable, in terms of its relation to Jane's, some thirteen years earlier. Rojcewicz's very own words are suggestive of the menace that was soon to follow: "It was a strange day, weather-wise, with erratic shifts of rain and wind and sun. It would get very blustery, and then it would become very calm. It was approximately 4:30 P.M. and already on the dark side."

As Rojcewicz studied hard, and as nightfall loomed, he suddenly became aware of a darkly-clad, tall and thin man in his midst. The odd character had tanned skin, black and greasy hair, sunken eyes, and a hard to define accent, but one that had a strong European flavor to it. In addition, he wore a Texan-style string tie. Its color doesn't even need describing; one and all surely can surely deduce that by now.

The man asked Rojcewicz what he was working on, and Rojcewicz told him that he was researching the UFO phenomenon. The MIB then proceeded to ask Rojcewicz if he had ever seen a UFO. He replied he was more interested in accounts of UFOs than whether or not they were alien craft. The MIB was not happy by Rojcewicz's response. In a loud voice he said, "Flying saucers are the most important fact of the century, and you're not interested?!" The man then stood up – "as if mechanically lifted"

– put his hand on Rojcewicz' shoulder, and added, as he walked away, "Go well in your purpose."

A MONSTER AT A UFO CRASH SITE
AZTEC, NEW MEXICO

Danielle B. is a woman who, for a number of years, lived in the New Mexican town of Aztec – which, just like the far more famous New Mexican town of Roswell, has a crashed UFO legend attached to it. It's a legend that dates back to March 1948, when, reportedly, a near-intact flying saucer and its crew of diminutive dead pilots were found. But, according to Danielle, she encountered something far stranger at Aztec than deceased extraterrestrial dwarfs and a wrecked flying saucer.

It was on one particular day in May 2004 that Danielle decided to spend a few hours hanging out in Aztec's Hart Canyon – which, curiously enough, is *exactly* where the alleged UFO is said to have fallen to earth, back in the 1940s. It was also where Danielle had an encounter with something far worse than aliens. On what was a warm and sunny day, Danielle found a place to sit, where she could read a book, and have her snacks and drinks at hand. It was a perfect way to spend a day off work. Or, for a while it was, at least.

All was normal for a couple of hours. That is, until Danielle noticed a small, black helicopter approaching her in the distance. Far more correctly, she assumed that it was a helicopter. Certainly, at a distance that's what it appeared to be. But it was no normal helicopter: there was no "thud-thud" sound that one associates with the fast-moving blades of a helicopter. And, on top of that, it appeared to be carrying below it a small calf, held tightly in place by thick ropes! Most definitely not the kind of thing you see every day. When the helicopter got close to Hart Canyon, however, Danielle could see that the helicopter was actually nothing of the sort. It was a large, obscene-looking insect of around four meters in length. The presumed rotor-blades of the helicopter were actually the fast-beating wings of the monster-creature. As for those ropes, they were nothing less than powerful-looking black limbs.

MAY 15, 1971

UFOLOGICAL DEATHS
WORLDWIDE

Otto Binder – who died on October 13, 1974, at the age of sixty-three – is most remembered for his work in the field of superhero comic-books. He wrote for DC Comics' "World's Finest Comics" and "Mystery in Space," Marvel Comics' "Young Allies," and Fawcett Comics' "Bulletman," amongst many others. As someone who finds superhero stuff to be utterly ridiculous, I'm pleased that Binder did more than just focus his time on spandex, cloaks, masks, and stupid "super-powers." He was also the editor of *Space World* and had a deep interest in UFOs. In 1967, Binder's book *What We Really Know About Flying Saucers* was published.

On May 15, 1971, however, Binder penned a feature for *Saga* magazine. Its title was "Liquidation of the UFO Researchers." As you might guess – and guess correctly – the article was focused upon alleged mysterious deaths within the field of Ufology. It began in eye-catching fashion:

"Over the past 10 years, no less than 137 flying saucer researchers, writers, scientists, and witnesses, have died – many under the most mysterious circumstances. Were they silenced, permanently, because they got too close to the truth? Before the 1967 Congress of Scientific Ufologists, Gray Barker, the chairman, received two letters and one phone call telling him that Frank Edwards, the noted radio newscaster and champion of flying saucers, would die during the convention. One day after the meeting was convened there was an announcement that Frank Edwards had succumbed to an 'apparent' heart attack. How could anybody know that Edwards was going to die, unless it was planned?"

How, indeed?

STRANGENESS AMONG THE BOOKS
MOUNT MISERY, NEW YORK

Jane and Richard were driving around the roads of Mount Misery when Richard, quite out of the blue, fell ill. He managed to pull the car to the side of the road, immediately after which he fainted at the wheel. Panic-stricken, Jane didn't know what to do. As it transpired, the decision of what to do next was suddenly, and violently, taken out of her by-now-clammy hands. A near-blinding white light flooded the vehicle, having originated somewhere in the deep, almost impenetrable, woods that surrounded the car. Jane found herself completely immobilized in her seat by some unseen, paranormal force. It's clear there was a degree of missing time involved, since the next thing the couple remembered was driving along Mount Misery's Old County Road, some distance from where all of the terror exploded.

A couple of days later Jane received a disturbing telephone call. The mysterious woman instructed Jane to go to her local library, to ask the staff for a specific book on Native American history, and to then turn to page forty-two and read it. *Very* carefully. Jane reached the library around mid-morning. Even her arrival was dominated by profound oddities: aside from the librarian and Jane herself, the building was completely empty of people and was vacuum-like in its silence and stillness.

Jane described her as only a Woman in Black can be described: her hair was black, her eyes were "very black," her skin was olive, and her black-colored outfit was curiously out of time. In Jane's words, the WIB was dressed in "an old-fashioned suit like something out of the 1940s, with a long skirt, broad shoulders, and flat old-looking shoes." Most astonishing of all, before Jane could say anything, the WIB handed her – from under a desk - a copy of the very book Jane had been instructed to seek out by her mysterious caller.

Jane, unsettled, but determined to find out what was going on, took a seat, opened the book and turned to page forty-two. As she did so, the writing on the page changed from large to small, and back again, several times. Rather amazingly, the writing then did something else: it magically morphed into a message. Jane was able to remember the entire, length message – word for word – something which suggested it had been subliminally implanted in her mind. She carefully wrote it down:

"Good morning, friend. You have been selected for many reasons. One is that you are advanced in auto suggestion. Through this science we will make contact. I have messages concerning Earth and its people. The time is set. Fear not. I am a friend."

MAY 17, 1974

"WAS THERE POLITICAL PRESSURE ON THE PART OF THE AIR FORCE?"

WASHINGTON, D.C.

On this day, a US Air Force paper, titled "Should the USAF Reopen Project Blue Book?" Blue Book being one of the Air Force's various UFO programs, and which was closed down in 1969. The authors were Major William E. Brummett, Major, USAF, and Captain Ernest R. Zuick, USAF. In part, their paper stated:

"The purpose of this study is to determine whether or not Project Blue Book should be reopened. To better guarantee an unbiased study, one of the writers will present arguments supporting the closure of Project Blue Book. These arguments will embrace supportive evidence such as the "Condon Report", the review of the "Condon Report" conducted by the National Academy of Sciences, and the findings of Project Blue Book. The other writer will present arguments for reopening Project Blue Book. These arguments will contain supportive evidence such as a critical analysis of Project Blue Book and the Condon Report, new developments regarding two former UFO sightings, and two important new sightings which occurred in 1973.

"...After completing the UFO research and after scrutinizing the original Project Blue Book files, the writers have concluded that both Project Blue Book and the Condon report seem to lack credibility. Both investigations appear to be biased, shallow attempts at explaining the complex mysteries of UFOs. But why? Why should Project Blue Book, with the world's best facilities readily available, end in such dismal failure? The lack of a satisfactory answer to this question has given rise to other questions concerning Project Blue Book. Was there political pressure on the part of the Air Force or some other governmental agency to cover-up or influence the investigation and conclusions of the Project Blue Book staff? Why didn't the Air Force transcribe their UFO findings to data processing and a central memory bank for easier cross-reference? Did the constant changing of Project Blue Book's directorship upset the stability of the investigation?"

As intriguing as all the above questions are, Project Blue Book was never revived.

MAY 18, 1909

A UFO LANDS ON A WELSH MOUNTAIN

CARDIFF, WALES

That was the night on which one of the most amazing of all UFO encounters occurred. A Mr. C. Lethbridge was walking to his Roland Street, Cardiff, Wales home, via the 271-meter-high Caerphilly Mountain. As he did so, Lethbridge was astonished by the sight of a cigar-shaped vehicle – in excess of forty-feet in length – which was sitting on the grass, at the edge of a mountain road. In his very own words...

"When I turned the bend at the summit I was surprised to see a long tube-shaped affair on the grass on the roadside, with two men busily engaged with something nearby. They attracted my close attention because of their peculiar getup; they appeared to have big heavy fur coats and fur caps fitting tightly over their heads. I was rather frightened, but I continued to go on until I was within twenty yards of them, and then my idea as to their clothing was confirmed.

"The noise of my little spring cart seemed to attract them,

and when they saw me they jumped up and jabbered furiously to each other in a strange lingo — Welsh or something else; it was certainly not English. They hurriedly collected something off the ground, and then I was really frightened. The long thing on the ground rose up slowly.

"I was standing still at the time, quite amazed, and when it was hanging a few feet off the ground the men jumped into a kind of little carriage suspended from it, and gradually the whole affair and the men rose in the air in a zigzag fashion. When they had cleared the telegraph wires that pass over the mountain, two lights like electric lamps shone out, and the thing went higher into the air, and sailed away towards Cardiff."

 MAY 19, 1986

UFOS INVADE BRAZILIAN AIRSPACE
SAO PAULO TO RIO DE JANEIRO, BRAZIL

One of the most notable encounters with not just one UFO, but a squadron of them, took place in the skies of Brazil on May 19, 1986. A U.S. Defense Intelligence Agency report describes the facts:

"According to sources, at least 20 unidentified objects were observed by several aircrews and on radar the night of 19 May, 1986. The objects were first seen by the pilot of a Xingu aircraft, transporting Ozires Silva, former President of Embraer, between Sao Paulo and Rio de Janeiro. Fighters were launched from Santa Cruz AFB at approximately 2100 hours. Although all three made radar contact, only one of the three pilots managed to see what he described as red, white and green lights. Shortly afterward, radar contact was made with similar objects near Brasilia and three Mirages were launched from Anapolis AB. All made radar and visual contact at 20,000 feet. They reported that they were escorted by thirteen of these discs with red, green and white lights at a distance of one to three miles."

The report comes to an end in a decidedly intriguing fashion: "...there is too much here to be ignored. Three visual sightings and positive radar contact from three different types of radar systems, leads one to believe that something weird arrived over Brazil on the night of 19 May."

MAY 20, 1952

A CONTROVERSIAL CRASH
ISLAND OF SPITSBERGEN, NORWAY

If there are two things we can say for sure about reports of alleged crashed UFOs, it's that (A) there are a lot of them; and (B) many are highly controversial in nature. And one of those cases that falls firmly into category B is alleged to have occurred off the coast of Norway on the island of Spitsbergen in mid-1952. It's a case that a few UFO researchers accept as being genuine, but that a great many believe to be nothing less than a complete and outrageous hoax. There's another possibility too, however: that the story was a deliberate, government-created "plant" to confuse the truth about tales of UFOs crashing to earth, whatever that truth might really be.

Now-declassified CIA files of 1952 on the Spitsbergen affair begin: "Writing in the German magazine *Der Flieger*, Dr. Waldemar Beck says that a flying saucer which recently fell at Spitsbergen has been studied by eminent Norwegian and German rocket experts. He writes that Dr. Norsal, a Norwegian expert in rocket construction, went to the place where the flying saucer had fallen a few hours after it had been discovered in the mountains of Spitsbergen by Norwegian jet planes."

The CIA continued: "In the wreck of the apparatus the expert is said to have discovered a radio piloting transmitter with a nucleus of plutonium transmitting on all wavelengths with 934 hertz, a measure that has been unknown so far. The investigation has also shown that the flying saucer crashed because of a defect in its radio piloting system. The saucer, which carried no crew, has a diameter of 47 meters. The steel used in the construction is an unknown ally. It consists of an exterior disc provided at its peripheral with 46 automatic jets. This disc pivots around the central sphere which contains the measurement and remote control equipment. The measurement instructions have an inscription in Russian."

Was there some substance to this report? And if so, was this crashed flying saucer Russian or extraterrestrial in origin? Having an interest in the case, I dug further, and came across several pages of U.S. Air Force material that showed shortly after the incident was reported by the media, the intelligence arm of the U.S. Air Force made inquiries with the Norwegian military who asserted that they had no knowledge of the crash. But still the story refused to die.

A seldom-seen account of the crash was printed in a Stuttgart newspaper, the *Stuttgart Tageblatt*. A translation of the account read: "Oslo, Norway, Sept. 4, 1955 – Only now a board of inquiry of the Norwegian General Staff is preparing publication of a report on the examination of remains of a UFO crashed near Spitsbergen, presumably in early 1952. Colonel Gernod Darnbyl, during an instruction for Air Force officers, stated: 'The crashing of the

Spitsbergen disc was highly important. Although our present scientific knowledge does not permit us to solve all the riddles, I am confident that these remains from Spitsbergen will be of utmost importance in this respect.'"

Despite all of this circumstantial evidence, the case is, today, said to have been nothing but a hoax or a piece of government disinformation.

MAY 21, 1966

"IT WAS CIRCULAR IN PLANFORM AND HAD NO WINGS"
PHILADELPHIA, PENNSYLVANIA

According to James McDonald, PhD:

"Skipping over many other pilot observations to a more recent one which I have personally checked, I call attention to a close-range airborne sighting of a domed-disc, seen under midday conditions by two observers. One of them, William C. Powell, of Radnor, Pa., is a pilot with 18,000 logged flight hours. He and a passenger, Miss Muriel McClave, were flying in Powell's Luscombe in the Philadelphia area on the afternoon of 5/21/66 when an object that had been first spotted as it apparently followed an outbound flight of Navy jets from Willow Grove NAS made a sharp (non-banking) turn and headed for Powell's plane on a near-collision course. As the object passed close by, at a distance that Powell put at roughly 100 yards, they both got a good look at the object. It was circular in planform and had no wings or visible means of propulsion, both witnesses emphasized to me in interviews. The upper domed portion they described as 'porcelain-white,' while the lower discoid portion was bright red ('dayglow red,' Powell put it)."

MAY 22, 1949

A UFOLOGICAL DEATH
WASHINGTON, D.C.

Within the field of Ufology there are longstanding rumors that the May 22, 1949 death of James Forrestal – the first U.S. Secretary of Defense – was linked to the UFO phenomenon. So the story goes, while suffering from severe depression and anxiety, and ultimately spiraling into a complete nervous breakdown (as a result of his exposure to what the US Government knew about UFOs), Forrestal was on the verge of revealing his knowledge of an alien presence on Earth. The theory continues that powerful figures decided such a thing simply could not be allowed to occur. The result was that Forrestal had to go. And "go," he certainly did: out of a window. In the early hours of May 22, Forrestal plunged to his death from the 16th floor of the Bethesda Naval Hospital. The big question is: was he pushed or did he jump?

There's no hard proof in the public domain that Forrestal was briefed on the more sensational and top-secret aspects of the UFO phenomenon. Although logic dictates that he would have been briefed (at least to some degree), since he accepted the position of Secretary of Defense in 1947 – the year in which the flying saucer was "born" and when the military was indeed taking the mysterious matter very seriously. Even outside of Ufology, there are suspicions that Forrestal's death was no suicide.

MAY 23, 1953

AN "UNKNOWN" ON RADAR

CAPE OF GOOD HOPE, SOUTH AFRICA

Just two days after an alleged UFO crash at Kingman, Arizona on May 21, 1953, a curious event occurred in South Africa. It should be noted, however, that the local media did not report on the affair for more than six months. Finally, on November 27, the basic facts were revealed, when the South African military decided to come clean. The press said:

"Headquarters of the South African Air Force announced that on May 23rd, 1953, radar operators picked up an unknown object which passed over the Cape six times at a speed definitely exceeding 1,250 miles an hour. Each time it passed it was within radar range for sixteen seconds at distances varying from 35,000 to 50,000 feet, and altitudes between 5,000 and 17,000 feet.

The acclaimed UFO researcher Aime Michel, concluded on this affair: "There is no suggestion that what was seen above the Cape was some creation of playful radar, or a refracted radar or reflected image, or a sound balloon, or Venus, or anything of the kind. It was simply an 'unknown object,' which passed overhead six times in succession."

MAY 24, 1986

"THERE IS NO ATTEMPT AT A COVER-UP"

ENCOUNTER BAY, VICTORIA HARBOR, AUSTRALIA

Calls For Crashed UFO Probe was the headline that appeared in the June 1, 1986 edition of the South Australian *Sunday Mail* newspaper. The headline and accompanying article detailed an event that had occurred one week earlier, on 24 May. Similar headlines appeared in numerous other newspapers, including *The Sun*; *The Advertiser*; and *The Border Watch*, which collectively told a remarkable story.

It was around midday on May 24, 1986 that numerous witnesses saw a "family-car-sized" object crash in Encounter Bay, Victoria Harbor, just off the South Australian coastline. Literally dozens of people from Mount Gambler, Robe, Kingston, Salt Creek and even Western Australia saw the unknown object as it hurtled through the air to its final destination in 120 feet of water in Encounter Bay.

MAY 25, 2015

A CHALLENGER MYSTERY

CAPE CANAVERAL, FLORIDA

The day began for me as it always does: I checked my emails and Facebook messages, and then got to work. Just a few days later – I was due to speak at the annual *Contact in the Desert* gig at Joshua Tree, California. The subject of my lecture: the UFO Contactee phenomenon. One of the things I planned to speak on (and *did* speak on) was the matter of a certain Contactee who had an intriguing but very controversial story. Back in 1986, she was interviewed by the FBI, as part of the Bureau's investigation into the January 1986 explosion of NASA's *Challenger*.

Declassified under the terms of the Freedom of Information Act, the files record that the woman (whose name is deleted from the available documentation – although it is known to me) said the Shuttle was sabotaged. According to the heavily-redacted documentation that the FBI has been willing to release into the public domain, a source of some standing, one that was apparently very well known to Bureau agents, had come into contact with a woman – whose name the FBI has been extremely careful to completely delete from the available papers – who "claims to be in contact with certain psychic forces that provide her with higher information on selected subjects. She refers to these forces as 'Source' and when providing information from Source she often speaks in the collective 'we.' [The woman] claimed that she had come to Washington, D.C. to provide information concerning the Challenger Space Shuttle explosion on 1/28/86."

Well, I decided to reference all of this in my lecture at Joshua Tree. So, I surfed the Net for a good picture of the ill-fated *Challenger* that I could insert into my PowerPoint presentation. A couple of hours later, I had to make a call to my agent, Lisa Hagan – on the matter of none other than my then-forthcoming MIB book.

During the course of the conversation, Lisa said that something very strange had happened to her earlier that same day. I asked what it was and she told me how she received a phone call – number not available – from someone who spoke just two words: "*Challenger* exploded." Lisa is one-hour ahead of me, and when we checked it turned out that she got the call right around the time I was searching for the photo. It scarcely needs to be said that Lisa was amazed - and a bit unsettled, too - when I told her I was looking into the *Challenger* issue the very morning she got the call. I had a deep suspicion – one that has not gone away – that my every online move was being monitored; probably Lisa's, too.

MAY 26, 2002

THE RETURN OF THE SPACE-BROTHERS
HOOVER DAM, OUTSIDE LAS VEGAS, NEVADA

Despite being perceived by many within Ufology as old-hat, the long-haired, so-called Space Brothers – who were at their peak, in terms of visibility and interest, in the 1950s – still continue to surface. One such encounter comes from Ken Craig, who swears he saw a flying saucer land near the Hoover Dam, Nevada as he drove over the dam itself.

It was around 3:00 a.m. and Craig was heading to Henderson, Nevada, after completing a late-shift at work. He pulled his car to the side of the road, close enough to see two tall, silver-suited individuals – both with very long blond hair and which almost came down to their waists. Craig watched in amazement as they scooped a sizeable amount of soil into two large buckets, returned to their craft and took to the skies – but not before giving Craig a friendly wave!

MAY 27, 1949

"THEY COULD POSSIBLY HAVE BEEN EGG-SHAPED"
RED BLUFF, CALIFORNIA TO BURAS, OREGON

In the early summer of that year, the FBI was the recipient of a number of notable UFO reports from the US Navy's Office of Naval Intelligence (ONI). One particular document, of June 23, 1949, describes the encounter of a pilot who had served with the Navy during World War Two, and who was described as being:

"…married and has three children. He has a BS and BA degree from the University of Southern California, Los Angeles,

California; has also had two years of law at the University of Southern California. Source is thirty years of age, but appears to have a background of experience few men his age possess."

The report continues:

"On Friday, 27 May 1949, source was flying his own SMJ-type aircraft from Red Bluff, California, to Buras, Oregon, a distance of 305 miles. He left Red Bluff at 1332 and arrived at Burne at 1458 PST. At 1423 PST, Friday, 27 May 1949, source observed the sun reflecting on an object or objects at a considerable distance ahead, a few points to the starboard. He continued to watch the course taken by the reflecting material expecting it to materialize into conventional aircraft as the distances lessened between him and the object or objects.

"As the object reached the long bluffs which run for a number of miles along the east side of some dry lakes, he saw that instead of a single object there were several, which seemed to be flying in formation. At this point the objects appeared to have changed their course so that they were paralleling his course and were following the bluff's rim at about 1,000 to 1,500 feet below source's altitude, at a distance which he estimates to have been 5 1/2 to 7 1/2 miles. Source is certain that it could not have been as far as 10 miles since the bluffs were less than 10 miles away and he could see the objects outlined against the bluffs.

"The objects that source saw are described by him as follows: Size of each object: Considerably smaller than a fighter plane, probably less than 20 feet in length. All of the separate objects appeared the same in size.

"Shape of object: There was no break in the outline. Source is certain he would have recognized conventional aircraft. They had a solid configuration, and no great thickness. They were elongated, oval, perhaps twice as long as wide, perhaps five times as long as thick. They could possibly have been egg-shaped, and could conceivably have been perfectly oval. The objects seemed definitely solid objects as there was nothing ethereal about them. Source is confident they were traveling at least as fast as source's own plane (212 MPH)."

MAY 28, 1996

"KEEP THEIR NOSES OUT OF IT AND THEIR MOUTHS SHUT"
BOYLE, IRELAND

Joseph W. Ritrovato says that, "…in May 1996, a UFO apparently went down near Boyle, Eire (Ireland). One night during that month many witnessed an unusual object glide down towards the Curlieu Mountains north of Boyle. It appeared to be an aerial craft coming into land, but had misjudged its approach, clipping the tops of trees and landing in a lake. Several occupants were said to have been taken into custody by a retrieval team and much military activity (including American soldiers) continued in the area for a six-month period following the incident. Civilians were prevented from going near the scene and the local police were instructed to keep their noses out of it and their mouths shut."

MAY 29, 1952

"THE OBJECTS HAD A BUBBLE DOME ON THE TOP"
OVER THE GULF OF MEXICO

"At approximately 1700 hours two elliptically shaped objects, larger than a fighter aircraft, were observed from the USN aircraft carrier Oriskany CV-34," says On This Day. "One observer watched the objects through a telescope, while the radar officer viewed the objects on the radar scope. The objects had a bubble dome on the top. Each object flew at an estimated altitude of between 10,000 and 15,000 feet at a supersonic speed and left a white vapor trail. The objects' course paralleled that of the carrier. The duration of the sighting was from 15 to 20 seconds."

MAY 30, 1958

"A RED LIGHT MADE...A 90 DEGREE TURN"
URAL'SK, KAZAKSTAN, USSR

"At 9:20 p.m. a science writer in Ural'sk, Kazakstan, USSR, watched as a red light made the start of a pattern to land at the south edge of an airfield, but then stopped, stood motionless for a few moments, made a 90 degree turn, stopped again, and after several minutes got smaller. A second red light joined the first, then they separated and silently flew away."

While the story is a brief one, it was investigated by Lloyd Mallan, the author of the 1967 book, *The Official Guide to UFOs*, and whose information on the case reportedly came directly from sources within the United States Air Force.

MAY 31, 1967

"THEY FOUND A 30-BY 50-YARD SEMI-CIRCULAR AREA THAT WAS STILL IN FLAMES"
BEAUSEJOUR, MANITOBA, CANADA

Also from On This Day: "On the 31st of May in 1967 a woman living on a farm outside of Beausejour, Manitoba, Canada (about 45 miles from Winnipeg) was sitting on her front porch at 11:30

p.m. waiting for her husband to return home. She saw a brilliant red light with a smaller blue light beside it come towards her from the south. The light lit up the ground and appeared to land. She became frightened and ran inside her house. The next morning she and her husband went out to investigate where the object had landed. They found a 30 by 50 yard semi-circular area that was still in flames. The strange fact about this case is that on June 15th the area was still smoldering, despite considerable rain having fallen in the area. Radioactive soil was found at the site."

JUNE

TRYING TO UNDERSTAND THE ROSWELL WRECKAGE
ROSWELL, NEW MEXICO

In the summer of 1997, one of the most controversial UFO-themed books ever written was published. Its title: *The Day After Roswell*. Ghosted by William Birnes, the editor of the now-defunct *UFO Magazine* and the star of History Channel's also defunct *UFO Hunters*, the book tells the story of one Philip Corso. Specifically, Lieutenant Colonel Philip J. Corso. U.S. Army. Corso's story was both amazing and groundbreaking. But, was it true? While some in the field of Ufology embraced the story, many certainly did not, preferring instead to view the book as either government disinformation – designed to confuse the truth of what really happened at Roswell, New Mexico back in the summer of 1947 – or nothing more than an elaborate and ingenious hoax designed to make money.

According to Corso, he, near-singlehandedly, spearheaded a secret program designed to seed alleged alien technology and wreckage - recovered from the Foster Ranch, Lincoln County, New Mexico by the U.S. Army Air Force's 509th Bomb Wing in July 1947 - into the private sector. As a result of this clandestine operation, so Corso maintained, the United States was soon able to understand, and even back-engineer, at least *some* of the extraterrestrial materials. Fiber-optics, transistors, night-vision equipment, and computer chips, were all, allegedly, a direct outgrowth of the extensive studies of the Roswell materials.

True or not, Corso's story still provokes significant debate, years after it was published.

AN ALIEN CALLS

SKIES ABOVE NORWICH, ENGLAND

After very briefly encountering a UFO – shaped like a classic, 1950s-style flying saucer of the sort seen in the likes of *The Day The Earth Stood Still* and *Earth Vs. The Flying Saucers* – above their Nor- wich, England home, the Parr family received several very strange, early hours, phone calls from an alleged alien named Carva, who had a strange robotic voice and who warned Mr. Parr that if he, his wife, and daughter knew what was good for them they would say nothing of their brief encounter of the non-human kind. Perhaps, very wisely, they did exactly that, until they finally revealed all in 2012 – still feeling somewhat concerned about doing so.

There is an unusual afterword to this strange case. The rea- son why the Parr family chose to go public more than a quarter of a century after their encounter is because in May 2012, they received yet another warning-filled call from the alleged alien known as Carva. According to Mr. Parr, he felt that going public would prevent "anything from happening to us." By "us," he meant his family.

DON'T SAY A WORD

PERTH, AUSTRALIA

Not unlike the Parr family of England in 1986, the Marshall fam- ily of Perth, Australia had a near-identical encounter after seeing a huge, black, triangular shaped UFO flying completely silently, and at a dangerously low level, as they headed home after a night out. Although the Parrs did not tell anyone about their experience (at least, not at the time, anyway), late on the following night the phone rang. It was a man with a strange, somewhat European accent who warned them not to talk about the craft they had seen. In this case, the Parrs forgot about the experience until years later when they saw a TV documentary on the Men in Black enigma –which referenced the issue of the MIB making threatening phone calls to UFO witnesses. Today, the Parrs are fully convinced that what they experienced was full–blown intimidation from a menacing MIB.

ALIENS AT A CAMP-SITE
SOMEWHERE IN THE WILDLANDS, ARIZONA, UNITED STATES

Still on the matter of large, black, triangular-shaped UFOs, one of these curious craft – that some UFO researchers believe are alien spacecraft, while others conclude they are secret technologies of the US Government – was seen in the wilds of Arizona on the night in question. The witness Sam was suddenly enveloped by a beam of light as he crawled out of his tent to investigate the loud humming noise which had suddenly envelope the area. When Sam looked up, he knew exactly what was making the sound.

Sam watched in awe as the massive, noiseless vehicle hung in the air at a height of what Sam estimated was no more than 200 feet – at most. In a split second it raced away, lost in the dark skies above. Sam was left to stare in wonder and fear at what it was he encountered on that strange night.

THE GIANT ORANGE
HALIFAX, NOVA SCOTIA, CANADA

Late one night, in the town of Halifax, Nova Scotia, Canada, a young man named Andy was heading home after an evening out with friends when, as he rounded the corner of one particular street, he came face to face with what can only be describe as a UFO resembling, in Andy's words, "a five-foot [diameter] orange."

For only around three or four seconds, the orange ball of light bobbed in the air, after which it slowly took the skies, winking out as it reached a height of around seventy or eighty feet. Whether some strange weather anomaly – such as ball-lightening – or something of another world, we don't know. What we can say for sure, however, is that in literal terms it was an unidentified flying object.

BUTCHERS FROM THE STARS?
DULCE, NEW MEXICO

Just outside the town of Dulce, New Mexico a slaughtered and extensively mutilated cow was found on local ranchland. FBI papers on the grisly affair reveals that the animal was missing both eyes, its tongue, left ear, and had a large, circular burn mark on its stomach. Most bizarre of all, its four legs were broken. The conclusion of a veterinarian brought in by the FBI was that the cow had been dropped to the ground from a height of somewhere around twenty feet or more. In no time at all, rumors that alien entities were the culprits quickly circulated, as did the rumor that it was all the work of a rogue group in the government undertaking research in the field of biological weapons. The mystery was never solved.

AN AFFIDAVIT OF THE ALIEN KIND

KINGMAN, ARIZONA

It's not every day that someone signs an affidavit concerning his UFO encounter, but it does happen occasionally. Take, for example, the case of the late Arthur Stansel, who held a master's degree in engineering and who took part in the D-Day landings at Normandy, France in the Second World War. He also worked at the top secret Nevada Proving Ground. In Stansel's own words:

"I…do solemnly swear that during a special assignment with the U.S. Air Force, on May 21, 1953, I assisted in the investigation of a crashed unknown object in the vicinity of Kingman, Arizona.

"The object was constructed of an unfamiliar metal which resembled brushed aluminum. It had impacted twenty inches into the sand without any sign of structural damage. It was oval and about 30 feet in diameter. An entranceway hatch had been vertically lowered and opened. It was about 3-1/2 feet high and 1-1/2 feet wide. I was able to talk briefly with someone on the team who did look inside only briefly. He saw two swivel seats, an oval cabin, and a lot of instruments and displays.

"A tent pitched near the object sheltered the dead remains of the only occupant of the craft. It was about 4 feet tall, dark brown complexion and had 2 eyes, 2 nostrils, 2 ears, and a small round mouth. It was clothed in a silvery, metallic suit and wore a skullcap of the same type material. It wore no face covering or helmet.

"I certify that the above statement is true by affixing my signature to this document this day of June 7, 1973."

JUNE 8, 200

A NEAR-COLLISION OVER WALES
BRISTOL CHANNEL TO NORTH DEVON COAST, WALES

Shortly before 1:00 a.m. on June 8, 2008, a South Wales Police helicopter, carrying a crew of three, was over the Ministry of Defense St. Athan, awaiting permission to land and refuel. As they held their position in the skies, the crew's attention was drawn to a "brightly lit" object above them that was reported as being "flying saucer shaped." Suddenly, without warning, the object raced towards them at "great speed" – something that caused the pilot to take immediate, evasive action to avoid a potential collision. The object then sped away and the helicopter crew decided to follow. Their pursuit took them over the Bristol Channel until, as they neared the North Devon Coast, a lack of adequate fuel forced them to abandon the chase.

What may have been the same object was seen later that same day by George Withrington, who happened to be a retired RAF glider pilot from St. Mellons, Cardiff. He said the unknown intruder was "peculiar with lots of flashing lights" and added that: "I was looking at an airplane overhead when I spotted this thing that was in the corner of my eye. It shifted direction very quickly, in the blink of an eye. I looked at it for quite a while. I was watching it for at least 10 minutes. It flew off towards the east, towards Newport."

Media coverage was intense; which led South Wales Police to state that: "We can confirm the Air Support Unit sighted an unusual aircraft. This was reported to the relevant authorities for their investigation. The crew are very experienced and responded in a professional manner in relation to what they saw. In today's skies, there are a wide variety of aircraft which come in a range of different shapes and sizes and in all probability, this sighting has just confirmed that one of these was in the area at the relevant time."

Today, the case remains steeped in controversy, with some UFO researchers perceiving the incident as prime evidence that aliens were flying over South Wales on that fateful night. Others, meanwhile, suggest that nothing stranger than Chinese Lanterns and media exaggeration were the cause of all the cosmic fuss.

JUNE 9, 192

A UFO DOWN IN RUSSIA

STAVROPOL PROVINCE, RUSSIA

In March 1957, A.A. Mikhaylov, the Chairman of the Astronomical Council of the USSR Academy of Sciences, received a letter from a woman named Ol'ga Vasilievna Maslennikova, who informed him of a story told to her by her landlord that concerned a "strange apparition [that] flew into a village of the Stavropol province" many years previously, specifically on June 9, 1921. She continued: "Three dark-skinned men came out of it. They were breathing hard, making signs, and soon died since they could not breathe air. The village residents quickly pulled apart the thing in which they had landed."

A similar account came from Irina Danilova of Moscow, whose letter apparently corroborating the story of Ol'ga Vasilievna was published in the newspaper *Anomaliya* in 1985. She had heard a practically identical tale from her grandfather, but was able to add that the object that the mysterious men arrived in "resembled a big arrowhead," and "subsequently the local people disassembled the machine, using the metal for manufacturing household gods...."The bodies of the crew were reportedly "buried without cross or church ritual."

No date was provided for this case; however, research undertaken by Dr. Yuriy N. Mozorov, a professional folklorist and a graduate of the philological faculty of Moscow University, suggests that it probably occurred in "the late 19th century." Although Dr. Mozorov has appealed for additional, corroborative data on this case, thus far it has not been forthcoming—which may not be a surprise, considering the age of the incident. Nevertheless, he states: "...the story itself remains an intriguing and thought-provoking one. At least in these respects it seems to be worthy of its title - the Russian Roswell."

JUNE 10, 168

"THE INTENT OF THE EXTRATERRESTRIAL BEINGS IS UNKNOWN"

WASHINGTON, D.C.

This was the day on which Major John R. King, of the US Air Force, prepared a document titled "The UFO Problem: Time for a Reassessment." Major King came to some eye-opening conclusions:

Based on an exhaustive review of the literature available to the public, the writer of this paper comes to the following conclusions:

1. Many objects reported as UFOs are misidentifications of natural phenomena or man-made objects.

2. Many objects reported as UFOs are space vehicles.

    a. These vehicles originate extraterrestrially.

    b. These vehicles are controlled by some intelligence either on board the vehicles or at some extraterrestrial location remote from the vehicles he space technology or the extraterrestrial intelligence is far superior to ours.

    c. It is likely that contact has been made with Man on an individual and covert basis.

    d. It is not known why overt contact with Man has not been made.

    e. The intent of the extraterrestrial beings is not known.

3. The implications for the world in the existence of UFOs is presently signifiant, and will become even more significant if overt contact is made.

4. The Air Force has been inept in its handling of the UFO problem.

5. The Air Force has lost some of its esteem in the eyes of a large segment of the U.S. population because of the manner in which the Air Force has handled the UFO problem.

6. Defense of the anti-UFO position has been weak. Charges and allegations against the Air Force have not been satisfactorily answered.

7. The gravity of the implications for mankind in the existence of UFOs may be the root cause for the puzzling official pronouncements and approach to the problem.

A DEATH VALLEY ENCOUNTER
DEATH VALLEY, CALIFORNIA

U.S. Weather Bureau files reveal that on this particular day, a gold prospector working in Death Valley, California encountered a strange, glowing ball of light that hovered in the air in front of him for around a minute or two, as the man stood rooted to the spot – partly amazed and partly terrified.

While the man placed his curious encounter in a UFO context, for the U.S. Weather Bureau, it was a case of ball-lightening, a very rare phenomenon that sees lightening take on the form of a sphere.

Wikipedia provides a solid, concise explanation of ball-lightening: "Ball-lightening is an unexplained atmospheric electrical phenomenon. The term refers to reports of luminous, spherical objects which vary from pea-sized to several meters in diameter. Though usually associated with thunderstorms, it lasts considerably longer than the split-second flash of a lightening bolt. Many early reports say that the ball eventually explodes, sometimes with fatal consequences, leaving behind the odor of sulfur. Until the 1960s, most scientists argued that ball lightening was not a real phenomenon but an urban myth, despite numerous reports from around the world. Laboratory experiments can produce effects that are visually similar to reports of ball lightening, but how these relate to the natural phenomenon remains unclear."

A 500-FOOT-LONG UFO

DINKELSBUHL, GERMANY

A public service corporation, the Civil Aviation Authority was established by the British Parliament in 1972 as a specialist aviation regulator and provider of air traffic services. Following its separation from the National Air Traffic Services in 2001, the CAA became the U.K.'s independent aviation regulator, with all civil aviation functions (such as economic regulations; airspace policy; safety regulations; and consumer protection) integrated within a single, unified body. The CAA has declassified into the public domain a number of documents that tell of extraordinary encounters with UFOs, as the following, startling extract demonstrates:

"12 Jun 82 Dinkelsbuhl – Large translucent object 500 feet long at 41,000 feet. ATCC [Air Traffic Control Center] requested subject aircraft to investigate this object which was found to have the form of a double rectangle surmounted by a globe (egg shape) crowned by a silver cone. Object observed by all on board."

The strange saga of this absolutely huge UFO was never resolved.

A MYSTERIOUS MUTILATION

DULCE, NEW MEXICO

Cattle mutilations are one of the United States' most baffling and grisly mysteries. It's also a mystery that many UFO researchers believe has connections to the UFO enigma. Are aliens harvesting cattle? They just might be. Officer Gabe Valdez, of the New

Mexico State Police investigated a particularly weird case on June 13, 1976. Valdez's report states that he headed out early on the next morning to the ranch of Manuel Gomez, in the town of Dulce. The sight was shocking: Gomez had found a cow dead, with its left ear, tongue, udder, and rectum all removed with what appeared to have been a sharp instrument. Valdez's official report makes for amazing and disturbing reading:

"Investigations continued around the area and revealed that a suspected aircraft of some type had landed twice, leaving three pod marks positioned in a triangular shape. The diameter of each pod part was 14"…Emanating from the two landings were smaller triangular shaped tripods 28" apart and 4" in diameter. Investigation at the scene showed that these small tripods had followed the cow for approximately 600'.

"Tracks of the cow showed where she had struggled and fallen. The small tripod tracks were all around the cow. Other evidence showed that grass around the tripods, as they followed the cow, had been scorched. Also a yellow oily substance was located in two places under the small tripods. This substance was submitted to the State Police Lab. The Lab was unable to detect the content of the substance."

Notably, the report continues that when radiation readings were taken at the site – and specifically in the indents made by the tripods – the levels were twice the normal level. Valdez investigated numerous, similar cases between 1976 and 1979, all of which were forwarded to the FBI for study. The Bureau was as puzzled as the New Mexico State Police. Cattle mutilations continue to this very day.

THE AUTHOR SEES A GHOST LIGHT

BIG THICKET, TEXAS

Located in the Piney Woods area of East Texas, the Big Thicket has a most apt moniker: it is a huge, 83,000-acre area of woodland. "Dense" barely begins to describe the massive, forested environment, which is home to numerous wild animals, including alligators and wildcats.

Running through the heart of the Big Thicket is a long, thin, and incredibly sandy old road called Bragg Road. That's not what the locals call it, though. To them, it is known as Ghost Light Road. There is a very good reason for this: for at least three centuries, people have reported seeing weird, small balls of light flitting through the trees late at night. But, we're not talking about anything quite as down to earth as fireflies. These particular lights vary in size from – approximately – a tennis ball to a beach ball.

They also exhibit evidence of intelligence: witnesses describe the lights approaching them, even circling them, in what is occasionally perceived as a playful fashion. Such is the interest that the lights provoke in the people that live there, and in visitors too, a historical marker has been erected at the start of Bragg Road and which details the strange story of the lights.

I know all this, as I have seen one of the mysterious ghost lights myself, late on the night of June 12, 2005. I was standing on Bragg Road when the approximately basketball-sized light appeared – very briefly. What it was, I have no idea. But, it was there all the same.

"IT'S STANDING ABOUT 20 FEET HIGH OFF THE ROAD"

DUGWAY PROVING GROUND, UTAH

From the files of Open Minds, we have an intriguing story:

"The reporting witness and two friends were invited by a mutual friend to go bowling on June 15, 1992. She was living with her grandparents in Dugway on the military base," the witness stated. 'We started driving out towards Dugway in late afternoon. Just before dark we crossed Johnson pass, which is a small mountain pass just before a long straight road leading up to the army base.' The witness was riding with two friends. 'I was in the front passenger seat. My friend Jeremy was driving. And Ryan was in the back seat of the car.' The group noticed something ahead of them in the roadway."

As for what they encountered, "It looks like a big piece of plastic or a parachute because the edges of the object were kind of fluttering around on the edges, but it can't be because it's standing about 20 feet high off the road. It also had a white light that was either coming from behind or from inside of the object. I didn't see any direct light. It seemed to be all indirect."

Suddenly, the UFO changed shape – into that of a cone. Both the craft and the light then shot away at incredible speeds, not to be seen again.

JUNE 16, 1963

"CONTACTS OF ONE KIND OR ANOTHER WITH SPACE
PEOPLE ARE NOT NEW"

ALBUQUERQUE, NEW MEXICO

UFO Evidence states: "Apolinar (Paul) Villa, a mechanic of Albuquerque, New Mexico, had a unique privilege having prearranged meetings with Space People for the specific purpose of taking pictures of their craft. They told him they came from the galaxy of Coma Berenices, many light years distance…Apparently, contacts of one kind or another with space people are not new to Mr. Villa. He says that he has been taught telepathy by extraterrestrial intelligence since he was five years old."

Gabriel Green was a well-known ufologist in the 1950s and 1960s. He had a particular interest in the Villa affair and, in 1965, said, "Villa says that prior in photographing his first series of saucers in 1963, he had seen about five Flying Saucers in the previous five years, and he had talked with spaceman previously. He said that his first picture-taking contact was his second in-person meeting with extraterrestrial beings. The first was in 1953 while he was working for the Department of Water and Power in Los Angeles. While on the job one day in Long Beach, he had a strong urge to go down to the beach, a feeling he did not understand. There he met a man about seven feet tall.

At first Villa was afraid and wanted to run away. But the man called him by name, and told him many personal things about himself. Billa realized that he was communicating with a very superior intelligence, and then became aware that this being was a spaceman. He knew everything I had in my mind and told me many things that had happened in my life," Villa says.

DEATH IN THE LAB
PASADENA, CALIFORNIA

The time is shortly after 5:00 p.m. on the afternoon of Tuesday, June 17, 1952. The location is a large and imposing pre-war mansion on South Orange Grove Avenue in Pasadena, California. And complete and utter carnage and chaos is currently reigning supreme. Within the deep bowels of the old house, a laboratory packed with all manner of chemicals and scientific gadgetry is enveloped in flames. The Hell-like inferno is borne out of two terrifying explosions, the rumbling and reverberating echoes of which can still be heard at least a mile away, and which cause the neighbors to run screaming onto the streets, petrified that an all-destructive Third World War has just begun.

Lying on the floor of the laboratory is a man whose body has been horribly mutilated as a result of the awesome power of the explosion and the inferno. A sickening, bleak hole dominates what is left of the man's lower-jaw. The bones of his left arm are violently broken, and both of his legs are completely shattered. Half of his right arm is missing, and the remainder is a tangle of exposed muscle, sinew, and bloodied bone. The man's life is ebbing away fast — and what is left of his mind knows it, too. A wild and careering ride in an ambulance is undertaken to try and save the man from the icy clutches of that grimmest of all reapers, but it is to no avail. He expires at 5:45 p.m. at Pasadena's Huntington Memorial Hospital.

Some people insisted, in hushed tones, that the man got everything he deserved — and then some. After all, for years he had been working to summon up unholy entities from some vile netherworld and may very well have succeeded in doing so, too. Entities, that some observers of his death say, were dangerous and manipulative ETs.

This story is made all the more incredible by virtue of the fact that the man at the center of this event was no mere fantasist, mentally-deranged dreamer, or wannabe Satanist. Rather, without this man – whose life ended so violently and terribly on that long-gone day in 1952 – the world would be very different one today. Without him, neither John Glenn nor Gordon Cooper would have likely ventured into space. Without him, Neil Armstrong would probably never have uttered those immortal, famous words of July 1969, when he took his first, tentative steps on the surface of the Moon.

In short, without this man there might well have never been a U.S. space-program, no NASA, no Apollo missions, and no space shuttle. In his own way, and in his short-but-packed lifetime, the man did not just change history or influence the present day, he arguably played an integral role in creating both. His name was Jack Parsons – a man who came to believe he ushered in the 1947 wave of UFO encounters by supernaturally opening a portal, or doorway, to another realm of existence.

JUNE 18, 1963

ETS AND A HAIR-COVERED MONSTER
NEW SOUTH WALES, AUSTRALIA

There is no doubt that the world's most famous hairy man-beast is Bigfoot. It's not alone, however. China is home to a very similar creature: the Yeren. On the Himalayas, the Yetis – or the Abominable Snowmen, as they are also known – are said to lurk. Even the

UK has its own version: the Big Grey Man. Then, there is Australia's Yowie, which is also a large, hair-covered humanoid.

On the morning of the day in question, a man named Bob Hamer claimed to have seen a Yowie on Australia's Blue Mountains, which are situated west of Sydney, in Australia's New South Wales. There was something very strange about Hamer's encounter, however: according to the man himself, the beast loomed out of a dense area of trees, stared at him for a few moments — and Hamer did likewise — and was then suddenly bathed in a gold-yellow beam of light that came from the sky. As Hamer looked up he was amazed to see a large, silent, oval-shaped UFO hovering above. In seconds the Yowie was "beamed up" into the UFO, which then vanished into the distance at a high speed. As bizarre and as outlandish as this story is, Bigfoot researcher Stan Gordon has uncovered a number of UFO-Bigfoot cases in his native Pennsylvania. Is Bigfoot an alien? Maybe…

JUNE 19, 2012

A MINIATURE UFO
WILTSHIRE, ENGLAND

A brief report from the UK's Civil Aviation Authority states that the pilot of a light aircraft coming in to land at an airfield in Wiltshire, England encountered a small UFO, around the size of a Mini-car, that passed by his plane at a fast pace and which was sparkling white in color and that moved in a "rolling" fashion.

Checks made with local military bases — to try and determine if some kind of sophisticated drone was the cause of all the fuss - drew nothing bit blanks.

Interestingly, the witness — a pilot with twelve years experience at the time of the encounter —quickly developed a deep interest in the UFO phenomenon. Futhermore, he claimed an abduction-style event in 2013, and "felt drawn" to visit of series of Crop Cirle formations in the fields are the work of benevolent who are concerned about our future and our warlike ways.

JUNE 20, 1975

A HELICOPTER AND AN UNSOLVED DEATH

DULCE, NEW MEXICO

Yet another dead and mutilated cow was found on the fringes of Dulce, New Mexico, and once again the FBI was brought in to take a look at the situation. Notably, according to the rancher whose animal was killed, on the night before he found the dead animal, a large, double-rotor helicopter was seen on his property and flooded the ranch with a powerful beam of light. Such was the illumination, the rancher was able to fully determine that the helicopter completely lacked any kinds of identifying markings. It was clearly what, in UFO lore, has become known as a "black helicopter." The culprits were never caught.

As the FBI personnel had a behind-closed-doors meeting, in August 1975, with Pentagon officials on the matter of the mysterious helicopters. The military denied any involvement in the cattle mutilation controversy and maintained that it did not have any squadrons of unmarked hilicopters. The FBI failed to resolve the matter of who was flying the strange craft.

THE MYSTERY OF MAURY ISLAND
PUGET SOUND, WASHINGTON

So the story goes, on the morning in question, a man named Harold Dahl, his son, and two still-unidentified individuals witnessed six, disc-shaped aircraft — one in the middle, wobbling in a strange fashion while the remaining objects surrounded it — flying in formation over Puget Sound, Washington State, at a height of around 2,000 feet. Dahl described the objects as being "shaped like doughnuts," and with "five portholes on their sides."

Suddenly, the central disk began to wobble even more and dropped to a height of no more than 700 feet. The remaining discs then broke formation, with one of them descending to the same height as the apparently malfunctioning disc and then proceeded to "touch it."

Without warning, the malfunctioning disc then began to "spew forth" what appeared to be two different substances: a white-colored material that Dahl described as a thin, white "newspaper-like" metal that floated down to the bay; and a black substance, that also hit the water, and that was reportedly hot enough to "cause steam to rise." Indeed, sections of the black substance allegedly hit both Dahl's son and his pet dog that were also on the boat, and reportedly killed the animal outright.

According to the story, Dahl reported the events in question to his superior: Fred Crisman, a man with a long and complicated life story, and suspected ties to the murky world of American Intelligence. Since Dahl had supposedly retained samples of the recovered debris, he convinced Crisman to go to the Maury Island shore and take a look for himself. Crisman later claimed that he saw on the shore an "enormous amount" of both the black and the white material, and recovered some of it for his own safekeeping.

Crisman duly reported his experience to the publisher Ray Palmer (of *Amazing Stories* fame), who hired none other than Kenneth Arnold to investigate the Maury Island affair. Arnold, whose own, historic encounter came three days after Dahl's encounter at Maury Island, delved deeply into the story, and was later joined by two Air Force investigators, Captain William Lee Davidson and First Lieutenant Frank Mercer Brown, who were working under General Nathan Twining to collect information on the then-current wave of UFO encounters being widely reported across the United States.

Crisman turned over samples of the mysterious debris collected at Puget Sound to the Air Force investigators, who intended to fly it to their final destination at Wright Field, Ohio. Fate would have another outcome, however. Shortly after Brown and Davidson departed from Washington State, their plane crashed, killing both men. A team was dispatched to clean up the site. Reportedly, however, the strange debris could not be located. No wonder that the Maury Island controversy continues to provoke furious debate, decades later.

JUNE 22, 2016

"I'M NOT GOING TO LET THEM INTIMIDATE ME"

DALLAS, TEXAS

Kimberly Rackley, a psychic and friend, messaged me at Facebook, clearly in a state of fear and stress. She wrote: "Had an experience last night / morning. A little drained this morning. Freaked me out. I was awoken by what seemed like thousands of voices that were excited and upset. I sometimes hear the astral plane at night but this was crazy. I need to make it stop so I lift into astral and all these entities are everywhere in agitated state.

"I ask what's wrong and they all circle me and then this being very tall and slender all in black suit but with a long coat and gray eyes comes straight for me. The entities circling me close in tighter. They are trying to protect me. But he pushes them away with flick of his hand and I'm suddenly back in my body. There in my room was the man. He had same non-aura energy, like MIB. He pointed at me and the place in my wrist where the previous MIBs always try to place a chip in me started burning. Then I passed out. I feel electric inside, like I'm going to jump out of my skin and I'm nauseated. Kind of frightened. I look like death."

She added: "No I didn't. I'm freaked out now. I don't freak easily with supernatural stuff except with MIB. This one makes the ones that come in my sleep look like puppy dogs.

"I'm kind of nervous about channeling or going into theta today. Too close to astral.

"We need to find out why! I'll see if I can psychically discover anything. I'm not going to let them intimidate me."

JUNE 23, 1915

LIGHTS OF THE "FLOATING" KIND

MT. RAINER, WASHINGTON

Official investigations within the UK of unusual aerial phenomena started long before Kenneth Arnold's June 24, 1947 sighting of a squadron of flying saucers at Mt. Rainier, Washington State. One of the most notable "pre-Arnold" reports can be found within the archives of the UK Admiralty and dates from, rather incredibly,

1915 (and into 1916). Prepared by a Lieutenant Colonel W.P. Drury, the Garrison Intelligence Officer at Plymouth Garrison, Devon, England, the four-page paper is titled "Report on the Dartmoor Floating (or Balloon) Light."

It concerns a series of strange events that occurred on the wilds of Dartmoor (the setting for Sir Arthur Conan Doyle's classic novel, *The Hound of the Baskervilles*). Lt. Col. Drury advised his superiors at the Admiralty that on June 28, 1915 he and a colleague, one Lt. C. Brownlow of Naval Intelligence, had interviewed a Miss Cecilia Peel Yates at Dolbeare Cottage, Ashburton, about an unusual experience she had on June 23, 1915:

"She informed us that a few mornings previously, just before dawn, having been awakened by the barking of dogs, she saw from her bedroom window a bright light in the sky, bearing N., and apparently suspended a short distance above the earth. It was too large and bright for a planet, and, as she watched, it swung to the N.E., and disappeared. Haytor is due North of Ashburton and 4 miles distant as the crow files."

Initially, a study of the document makes clear, Lt. Col. Drury and Lt. Brownlow were more than skeptical of Miss Peel Yates's UFO-like encounter: "Although we had entirely failed to shake the lady's evidence by cross-examination, we deemed her story so wildly improbable that we excluded it from our official report. But shortly afterwards reports of a similar phenomenon were received from the neighborhood of Hexworthy Mine, which is 5 miles to the N.W., across Dartmoor.

"On July 12th, Lieutenant Brownlow and I proceeded to Sherril, near Hexworthy, and interviewed Mrs. Cave-Penny and her daughter, from whom the report emanated. Their house, an isolated farm on the moor, commands a clear view of the mine, which is two-and-a-half miles distant. They stated that on several occasions they had watched a bright white light rise from a point a few hundred yards to the Eastward of the mine, swing across the valley to about the same from Totnes, and a paddock some distance West of it, and disappear."

Despite the fact that the initial report of June 23 prompted a flood of reports that continued for a year, the matter of the curious light of Dartmoor remained a mystery.

JUNE 24, 1947

SUPPORT FOR A FAMOUS ENCOUNTER
CASCADE MOUNTAINS, OREGON

That was the date upon which one of the most famous of all UFO encounters occurred. Namely, that of an American pilot named Kenneth Arnold, who, on the afternoon in question, encountered a squadron of UFOs near Mt. Rainier. However, Arnold's story is so well-known that I have chosen to select another case from this historic day – a case which offers distinct support to Arnold's claims.

The story revolves around the testimony of a man named Fred Johnson. He was a prospector who may have seen the very same objects encountered by Arnold. Both military intelligence and the FBI took an interest in what Johnson had to say. It should be noted that the FBI has chosen to black-out Johnson's name on its paperwork; however, the military chose not to delete his name. Declassified files state:

"Fred Johnson reported without consulting any records that on June 24, 1947, while prospecting at a point in the Cascade Mountains approximately five thousand feet from sea level, during the afternoon he noticed a reflection, looked up, and saw a disc proceeding in a southeasterly direction. Immediately upon sighting this object he placed his telescope to his eye and observed the disc for approximately forty-five to sixty seconds."

We're then told that Johnson "…remarked that it is possible for him to pick up an object at a distance of ten miles with his telescope. At the time the disc was sighted by Mr. Johnson, it was banking in the sun, and he observed five or six similar objects but only concentrated on one. He related that they did not fly in any particular formation and that he would estimate their height to be about one thousand feet from where he was standing. He said the object was about thirty feet in diameter and appeared to have a tail. It made no noise.

"According to Johnson he remained in the vicinity of the Cascades for several days and then returned to Portland and noted an article in the local paper which stated in effect that a man in Boise, Idaho, had sighted a similar object but that authorities had disclaimed any knowledge of such an object. He said he communicated with the Army for the sole purpose of attempting to add credence to the story furnished by the man in Boise."

JUNE 25, 1999

UNCONVENTIONAL AIRCRAFT
NATIONAL ARCHIVES, KEW, ENGLAND

While the British Government has declassified into the public domain literally thousands of pages of documents on UFOs, many of the dossiers are fairly tame in terms of content. There is one file, however – a file that I found while digging through old records held at the National Archives, Kew, England in 1999 – that hardly ever gets a mention. Why, exactly, I have no idea, since it's one of the most important UK–UFO files to have ever surfaced officially.

The file is titled *Unconventional Aircraft* and is of interest and significance for a number of reasons. First, much of the material contained within it was classified at *Secret* level (with a considerable number of papers stamped *Top Secret*). Second, the file makes it very clear that the Air Ministry was not the only department involved in the UFO subject during the late 1940s. And third, there is evidence to show that, at the time, the UK Government was monitoring the UFO subject on what was, quite literally, a global scale.

With respect to unidentified flying objects, what, precisely, does the relevant paperwork tell us? In the period 1948-1949, sources within the British Government were extremely interested in determining the extent to which the Nazis had succeeded in constructing flying saucer-like aircraft during the Second World War; and furthermore, those same sources were expressing concern regarding the extent to which the Soviets might have capitalized on this technology.

This can be amply shown by virtue of the fact that as far back as September 1949, the Air Ministry's Scientific and Technical Intelligence Branch (STIB) was regularly receiving clippings culled from all manner of publications on both Nazi saucers and various other UFO reports. To illustrate this, on 14 September, 1949, the STIB received from the Press Information Room of the Air Ministry's Intelligence Division, a selection of newspaper reports concerning UFO activity over Vienna, Austria. *Now it's Flaming Saucers*, proclaimed one such clipping from the *Daily Herald* on 12 September 1949.

Similarly, only months later, the STIB received from the Press

Information Room, a large batch of magazine articles photocopied from German newspapers and science periodicals on both highly-advanced flying saucer designs postulated by the Nazis during the Second World War, as well as post-War designs on the drawing-boards of the Soviets and the Americans.

JUNE 26, 1982

THE FLYING "DOUGHNUT"
BRINDISI, ITALY

The following documentation is scant, but offers an interesting insight into a case that quickly caught the attention of the UK's Civil Aviation Authority several days earlier in 1982:

"21 Jun 82 Brindisi – Unidentified object sighted by pilots. Object passed down left hand side at same height as aircraft (FL230) & 2 miles away. Black shiny doughnut shape about the size of a car. Object was tumbling and judged to be stationary."

JUNE 27, 1979

MILITARY HELICOPTERS AND A CRASHED SAUCER
SOUTHEASTERN OREGON

Admittedly lacking in detail, an incident was reported to researcher Bruce Molon of Indiana that occurred on June 27, 1979 in a "wild area of forested mountains in southeastern Oregon."

A former marine allegedly involved in the event informed Molon that a circular shaped object with a "low dome" had crashed deep within the forested area in question, damaging trees and depositing an amount of unusual debris in the vicinity that was described as being similar to "fresh cast iron" and of extremely light weight. Crates were loaded onto helicopters to transport the material from the site, which was then "cleaned up" by the military.

JUNE 28, 1947

A SQUADRON OF UFOS OVER THE UNITED STATES
LAKE MEADE, NEVADA

US Air Force documents of 1948 reference an intriguing encounter with not just one UFO, but multiple unknowns. According to the USAF: "While flying at 10,000 feet on a course of 300 degrees, 30 miles northwest of Lake Meade, Nevada, an Air Force lieutenant reported seeing five or six while circular objects in close formation and traveling at an estimated speed of 285 miles per hour."

The Air Force's response was notable and is spelled out as follows: "Since the Air Force is responsible for control of the air in the defense of the U.S., it is imperative that all other agencies cooperate in confirming or denying the possibility that these objects have a domestic origin. Otherwise, if it is firmly indicated that there is no domestic explanation, the objects are a threat and warrant more active efforts of identification and interception... It must be accepted that some type of flying objects have been observed, although their identification and origin are not discernible. In the interest of national defense it would be unwise to overlook the possibility that some of these objects may be of foreign origin."

Clearly, behind the scenes, matters of a UFO nature were being taken very seriously.

ALIENS AND AN AIRLINER
GOOSE BAY, NEWFOUNDLAND, CANADA

A fascinating encounter involving multiple UFOs occurred on this particular night. The source was both credible and impeccable: Captain James Howard, who was piloting a Boeing Stratocruiser aircraft from New York to London. The flight was heading towards Goose Bay when, shortly after 1:00 a.m., ground-control advised Captain Howard that he would have to make a change in direction, towards Cape Cod. All was normal until the aircraft reached a point near Seven Islands, Quebec and a number of unusual aerial craft loomed into view. Captain Howard takes up the story:

"They were moving at about the same speed as we were (approximately 230 knots) on a parallel course, maybe 3 or 4 miles to the north west of us (we were heading NE). They were below the cloud at this time, at a guess at 8,000 ft. Soon after crossing the coast into Labrador, the cloud layer was left behind and the objects were now clearly in view, seeming to have climbed more nearly to our altitude. At this time the sun was low to the northwest, sky clear, visibility unlimited.

"There was one large object and six smaller globular things. The small ones were strung out in a line, sometimes 3 ahead and 3 behind the large one, sometimes 2 ahead and 4 behind and so on, but always at the same level. The larger object was continually, slowly, changing shape, in the way that a swarm of bees might alter its appearance. They appeared to be opaque and hard-edged, gray in color, no lights or flames visible."

JUNE 30, 1908

UFO CRASH IN RUSSIA?

TUNGUSKA, RUSSIA

That's a date that has gone down in history, chiefly due to the fact that it is shrouded in mystery, controversy, and conspiracy. It was just as dawn was breaking that an unknown, and unearthly, entity entered the Earth's skies. Whatever it was, it exploded spectacularly and violently over Tunguska, Russia, at a height of around four to six miles. The precise location was an area of heavily forested hills near Siberia's Lake Baikal. By all accounts the object was huge: somewhere in the vicinity of 200 to 600 feet in length.

Such was its pummelling force the unknown intruder flattened entire swathes of the landscape for miles and miles. Trees were laid down like matchsticks, the sky lit up in ominous fashion, and the terrifying sound of a deafening explosion filled the ears of those unfortunate enough to have been caught up in the cataclysmic event. Such was the scale of the incident, the explosion was seismically recorded in both the United States and the United Kingdom. To put things into a perspective that can be readily appreciated today, the blast was the equivalent of around ten to thirty megatons of TNT.

Not surprisingly, the Soviet media was quick to report on the almost apocalyptic affair. The *Sibir* newspaper was one of the first to have its reporters hot on the trail. Two days after the calamitous events, staff at the newspaper reported:

"In the N. Karelinski village the peasants saw to the North-West, rather high above the horizon, some strangely bright bluish-white heavenly body, which for 10 minutes moved downwards. The body appeared as a 'pipe,' i.e. a cylinder. The sky was cloudless, only a small dark cloud was observed in the general direction of the bright body. It was hot and dry. As the body neared the ground, the bright body seemed to smudge, and then turned into a giant billow of black smoke, and a loud knocking was heard, as if large stones were falling, or artillery was fired. All buildings shook. At the same time the cloud began emitting flames of uncertain shapes. All villagers were stricken with panic and took to the streets, women cried, thinking it was the end of the world."

Theories abound for what happened at Tunguska on June 30, 1908. Suggestions have been made that the object was a comet, a meteorite, or even perhaps a black-hole. Most intriguing is the theory that an atomic-powered alien spacecraft exploded over the Tunguska landscape.

JULY

ZAPPED BY ALIENS
VALENSOLE, FRANCE

It was shortly before 6:00 a.m. when a French farmer, a man named Maurice Masse, had the shock of his life. It was, quite literally, out of this world. Masse had a profitable farm near Valensole, which included a field of lavender. Like most farmers, Masse was up and at it before dawn broke. Quite naturally, the early morning was still and quiet. For awhile. Suddenly, Masse's attention was drawn to an unusual and out-of-place sound, which was not unlike the whistle of a kettle. He looked behind him and was amazed to see before him a car-sized object of a roughly oval shape and which sported six "legs." Masse tentatively walked over to it.

As he got closer, Masse could see that a hatch into the craft was wide open. He peered inside, noting there were two small chairs. He quickly found out why they were so small. In mere moments, a pair of what he first thought were "small boys" came running over. Boys, they were not.

To his horror, Masse found himself face to face with a pair of roughly four-foot-tall ETs who had armfuls of his lavender plants! Both were dressed in green and had oversized heads and large eyes. Suddenly, one of the green dwarfs pointed a "device" at Masse – which immediately rendered him paralyzed. After a few more minutes of collecting samples from Masse's field, the pair jumped into their craft and took to the skies. Poor, terrified Masse remained in his frozen state for almost twenty minutes. It was a traumatic encounter he never forgot.

AN ANCIENT ALIEN ARTIFACT IN RUSSIA
BENEATH KIEV, RUSSIA

According to data revealed by Russian UFO crash-retrieval investigator Anton Anfalov, in the summer of 1947 during the rebuilding of the city of Kiev, which had been decimated by the Nazis during the Second World War, workers discovered buried underground a "strange object" described as a "silvery, seamless, streamlined cylinder, arrow-shaped object, about 3 to 3.5 meters in diameter and 5 to 6 meters long."

Reportedly, the object was "excavated" and a team of "military field engineers" was brought in to deal with the find. It was subsequently transferred to a location northeast of Moscow that would also house the first Soviet missile research center.

An examination of the object allegedly confirmed that it was not a foreign missile as had been initially assumed, but had possibly been buried underground for up to 5,000 years.

Entry to the device revealed the presence of "2 small chairs for two very small pilots" and an array of "sophisticated equipment." According to Anfalov, "reverse engineering of the alien craft" was undertaken from the 1950s to the 1970s - something that, Anfalov further adds, "promoted Soviet missile and space technology, including the design of metal alloys, instrumental design, control systems and some construction elements."

"THE OBJECT WAS SHAPED MUCH LIKE A DISCUS"
LONGVIEW, TEXAS

"[Moulton B.] Taylor is an aeronautical engineer, and was airport manager at Longview, in charge of an air show that was to be held on the afternoon of 7/3/49, the day of the incident in question," revealed James McDonald, a well-respected authority on UFOs. He added: "A skywriting Stearman was at 10,000 ft at 10:40 a.m., laying down 'Air Show Today,' and hence holding the attention of a number of the personnel already at the airport, when the first of three unidentified objects flew over at high altitude. Alerted by one of the persons who first spotted the object coming from the northwest, Taylor got on the public address system and announced to all persons at hand that they should look up to see the odd object. Many had binoculars, and among the over 150 persons present were police officers, city officials and a number of Longview's leading citizens, Taylor emphasized. The object was observed by a number of experienced pilots; and, according to official file summaries, all agreed that the object was shaped much like a discus. It seemed to have metallic luster and oscillated periodically as it crossed the sky from northwest to southeast until lost in mill-smoke."

UNVEILING THE ROSWELL AFFAIR
ROSWELL, NEW MEXICO

Most researchers of the famous UFO crash outside of Roswell, New Mexico in 1947 agree that the event occurred on July 4:

Independence Day. It was not until July 8, however, that the story reached the press. The front-page story in that day's edition of the *Roswell Daily Record* revealed something amazing. In an article titled *RAAF Captures Flying Saucer On Ranch In Roswell Region*, the newspaper noted the following:

"The many rumors regarding the flying disc became a reality yesterday when the Intelligence office of the 509th Bomb Group of the Eighth Air Force, Roswell Army Air Field, was fortunate to gain possession of a disc through the cooperation of one of the local ranchers and the sheriff's office of Chaves County. The flying object landed on a ranch near Roswell sometime last week. Not having phone facilities, the rancher stored the disc until such time as he was able to contact the sheriff's office, who in turn notified Major Jesse A. Marcel of the 509th Bomb Group Intelligence Office. Action was immediately taken and the disc was picked up at the rancher's home. It was inspected at the Roswell Army Air Field and subsequently loaned by Major Marcel to higher headquarters."

Within twenty-four hours, the military claimed the whole thing was a mistake: nothing stranger than a weather-balloon was the cause of all the fuss. Today, the Air Force asserts that the weather-balloon was actually a Mogul balloon, designed and deployed to monitor for early Soviet atomic bomb detonations. As for the stories of "alien bodies" found at the crash-site, the military dismisses the stories, preferring to conclude that they were "crash-test-dummies" used in high-altitude parachute experiments.

A CRASHED UFO ON THE PLAINS

SAN AGUSTIN, NEW MEXICO

The genesis of the tale that a UFO crashed and was recovered along with its dead crew of alien creatures on the Plains of San Agustin, New Mexico, in early July, 1947 can largely be traced back to L.W. Vern Maltais and his wife Jean, who in turn got the story from their friend, Grady Barney Barnett. The pair approached UFO investigator Stanton Friedman after a lecture at Bemidji State College, Minnesota, in 1978. Friedman, assisted by researcher William Moore, began piecing together Barnett's story from Vern and Jean's testimony; later they would find additional sources.

Barney Barnett was a veteran of the First World War and a solid citizen, well-regarded by all who knew him. In 1947. he was a civil engineer working for the U.S. Soil Conservation Service. So the story went, Barnett stumbled upon the remains of a wrecked saucer and deceased occupants in the desert near the town of Magdalena, New Mexico, specifically on the Plains of San Agustin.

Barnett informed his friends that the saucer was "pretty good sized," and that the bodies of the crew that were scattered around the broken object were small, with "pear-shaped" heads and small eyes, and were all dressed in gray suits. Barnett said he was only at the crash site a short time before he was joined by a group of archaeologists, all of whom wondered what they should do next.

Suddenly the military arrived on the scene and made it clear what they should do next: swear themselves to silence, as the event was one that had a major bearing on U.S. national security.

JULY 6, 1947

"SHERMAN CAMPBELL FOUND A STRANGE OBJECT
ON HIS FARM"

PORTLAND, OREGON

On July 6, 1947, the Portland *Oregonian* reported the following. It has shades of the Roswell story attached to it, with its references to military balloons, tinfoil, and even a rancher:

"Folks in Pickway county, who have been following the 'flying saucer' mystery, became excited Saturday when Sherman Campbell found a strange object on his farm. It was in the form of a six-pointed star, 30 inches high and 48 inches wide, covered with tinfoil. It weighed about two pounds. Attached to the top were the remains of a balloon with a rock 5 inches in circumference. The Fort Columbus airfield weather station at Columbus said the description tallied with an object used by the army air forces to measure wind velocity at high altitudes by the use of radar. Some of the flying discs reported seen in various parts of the country were much larger and flying at terrific speed."

JULY 7, 1947

UFO SIGHTINGS ABOUND

PORTLAND, OREGON

Of the many and varied official documents that have surfaced under the terms of the U.S. Freedom of Information Act, certainly one of the most significant is a December 10, 1948 document which originated with the US Air Force titled *Analysis of Flying Objects in the US*. Unlike so many official documents that have surfaced via FOIA, this one was originally classified Top Secret, which makes it an important and historic one. Indeed, the UFO records that have surfaced via FOIA are, at most, secret in nature, with the majority of them having even lower levels of classification. The report is packed with highly credible UFO reports covering the period 1947-1948, including a report of a cluster of UFO activity on July 7, 1947. An extract from the document states:

"On 7 July 1947, five Portland, Oregon police officers reported varying numbers of disks flying over different parts of the city. All observations were made within a minute or two of 1305 hours. On the same day, William Rhoads of Phoenix, Arizona allegedly saw a disk circling his locality during sunset and took two photographs. The resulting pictures…show a disk-like object with a round front and a square-tail in plan form. These photographs have been examined by experts who state they are true photographic images and do not appear to be imperfection in the emulsion or imperfections in the lens."

JULY 8, 1947

A CLOSE ENCOUNTER IN CALIFORNIA

MUROC, CALIFORNIA

Under the terms of the U.S. Freedom of Information Act, the details of a notable UFO at Muroc Airfield, California have surfaced. The U.S. military has chosen to withhold the name of the witness. Nevertheless, we have his testimony, witnessed by Counter-Intelligence Corps agent Thomas A. McMillan, which reads as follows:

"At 11:50 hours, 8 July 1947, while the undersigned was sitting in an observation truck in Area #3, Rogers Dry Lake, for the purpose of observing a P-82 ejection seat experiment, the following unfamiliarity was observed.

"The undersigned was gazing upward toward a formation of two P-82's and an A-26 aircraft flying at 20,000 feet, preparing to carry out a seat ejection experiment, when I observed a rounded object, white aluminum in color, which at first resembled a parachute canopy. The first impression was that a premature ejection of the seat and dummy dad occurred.

"This body was ejected at a determined height lower than 20,000 feet, and was falling at three times the rate observed for the parachute which was ejected thirty minutes later. As it fell it drifted slightly north of due west against the prevailing wind, toward Mount Wilson…The color was silvery, resembling aluminum painted fabric, and did not appear as dense as a parachute canopy…When the object dropped to a level such that comes into line of vision of the mountain tops, it was lost to the vision of the observer."

JULY 9, 1962

DEAD ALIENS IN NEW MEXICO

SOMEWHERE IN NORTHERN NEW MEXICO

In 1982, Leonard Stringfield published the brief details of a UFO crash somewhere in northern New Mexico, two decades earlier. Specifically, the time was the summer of 1962. The story was brought to the attention of Stringfield by a fellow UFO researcher, Tommy Blann. As Stringfield was informed, Blann had interviewed a retired U.S. Air Force colonel who revealed he was personally at the crash site when the retrieval of the UFO occurred.

Blann's source – given the title of "Colonel X" to protect his identity – said that the craft resembled a pair of saucers placed "end to end." It had a somewhat dullish aluminum color, and a noticeable, dark band around its middle. As for the dimensions of the UFO, it was described as being roughly thirty feet in diameter and twelve feet in height. It was the colonel's assessment that the UFO had "skidded" to a halt after making a not entirely successful attempt to land. Reportedly, eight men were on-site to perform certain, unspecified tasks. All wore gas masks and jump-suits.

The colonel told Blann: "There were two bodies recovered from the craft and they were put in a large unmarked silver van and whisked off. I did not get a good look at the bodies; however, they looked small and were dressed in silver, skin-tight flight suits. They were taken to Holloman AFB as well as the craft, and then sections of the craft were sent to various research labs, including Los Alamos Laboratories. I believe the bodies were also taken to Los Alamos and samples sent to other locations."

JULY 10, 1947

"A CIRCULAR OBJECT FLYING AT HIGH VELOCITY"
HARMON FIELD, NEWFOUNDLAND

A U.S. Air Force document, from the summer of 1947, and which has been released into the public domain as a result of Freedom of Information legislation states the following: "On 10 July 1947, Mr. Woodruff, a Pan-American Airways mechanic reported a circular object flying at high velocity, paralleling the earth's surface and leaving a trail which appeared as a 'burning up' of the cloud formation. The sighting occurred near Harmon Field, Newfoundland. Two other persons also saw the trail: It remained in the sky for about an hour and was photographed by another PAA employee. The resulting photographs support Mr. Woodruff''s observation as far as the sky cleavage is concerned."

NOT A CRASHED UFO, AFTER ALL

BLACK RIVER FALLS, WISCONSIN

Consider the following 1-page FBI report of July 11, 1947, which was sent to the Assistant-to-the-Director, Edward A. Tamm. It was yet another "crashed saucer that never was" case, and investigated by a Special Agent Johnson. The document states:

"SAC Johnson of the Milwaukee Office called to advise he had just received a telephone call from [a] Reserve Officer with the Civilian Air Patrol, Black River Falls, Wisconsin. [He] reported that at 3:30 p.m., July 10…at Black River Falls a large 17" disc [was found] which appeared to have been possibly made out of cardboard painted with silver airplane dope. In the center was a tube and a small motor with a propeller attached to the side. Colonel [name deleted] expressed the opinion that this disc would not be able to fly by itself. He advised it would be taken to the Air Corps Headquarters."

A crashed saucer, it was not.

"I AM BOSCO"

WASHINGTON, D.C.

Declassified US Government files reveal that on a particular occasion in July 1952 – the very month that Washington, D.C. was hit by a veritable tsunami of UFO encounters – a man named Karl Hunrath complained to his local police department about something very weird indeed. Who knows what the cops thought of it all, but it basically went like this: in the early hours of a Sunday morning in July, someone broke into Hunrath's home, injected his arm full of chemicals - which rendered him into a distinctly altered state of mind - and proceeded to tell him that he had been chosen to play a significant role in the alien mission on Earth. A very groggy Hunrath could only look on amazed from his bed as the somewhat foreign-sounding – put perfectly human-appearing – alien told him: "I am Bosco. You have been chosen to enter our brotherhood of galaxies." Typical Space-Brother spiel, in other words.

The files continue that the suit-and-tie-wearing Bosco advised Hunrath the brothers from beyond were deeply worried by our warlike ways, and so action had to be taken against those dastardly elements of the human race that wanted to spoil everyone else's fun. There was not to be any *The Day the Earth Stood Still*-style ultimatum for one and all, however. Nope. The aliens wished to recruit sympathetic humans to aid their righteous cause. Or, more correctly, get someone else to do all their dirty work while they lurked safely in the shadows. And as Hunrath came to quickly realize, he was now one of the chosen few. But there was more. Bosco, via - according to the FBI - "occult techniques," downloaded into Hunrath's mind countless megabytes of data on how to build a terrible weapon that had the ability to destroy aircraft; specifically, the aircraft of the US military, who the Space-Brothers viewed as being just about as dangerous to world peace as the dastardly commies.

"I am Bosco and that will be its name, too," boomed the alleged alien, in reference to the device that he wanted Hunrath to not just build, but also deploy. Far too stunned and drugged to move, Hunrath could only watch in a mixture of befuddlement and shock as Bosco then turned on his heels and left for his – one might be inclined to assume after an experience like that – flying saucer. There was no amazing "Beam me up, Scotty"-type exit for Bosco, however. For an alien, Bosco had a very down to earth means of making good his departure: he pulled back the curtains of Hunrath's bedroom-window, clambered out, and vanished into the depths of the early morning blackness of Hunrath's front-yard!

The curious encounter ended as weirdly as it had begun.

JULY 13, 1968

UFOS AND A CREEPY PHONE CALL
SOMEWHERE IN THE UNITED STATES

It was the night of July 13, 1968 when "Dan O." had the great misfortune to cross paths with a Woman in Black. He was on the phone, speaking with a colleague in the UFO field, when their phone call was suddenly, and mysteriously, interrupted. Dan told UFO authority Brad Steiger: "The third party identified herself as a Mrs. Slago, who, as she said, was accidentally connected with our line. She had been listening to our conversation strictly out of curiosity."

Despite the fact that Mrs. Slago was a complete stranger and had, according to her, intruded upon the conversation by mistake, Dan decided to tell her about his UFO research, since she had at least heard snippets of what he and his friend had been talking about. As the conversation between Dan and Mrs. Slago progressed, however, the likelihood that her intrusion was all a big mistake, and nothing else, quickly evaporated. Dan's words make that extremely clear. He told Steiger that Mrs. Slago suggested investigating UFOs was not a wise thing to do, and that the matter of UFOs possibly being of alien origin was a matter Dan should steer well clear of.

Dan continued: "She also stated that UFO organizations should not attempt to further the investigation and study of UFOs, because as she put it, 'Earth people do not understand.' She suddenly stopped short of what she was about to say, as if she caught herself about to say something that I should not hear."

Things then got even odder, and somewhat troubling: the woman warned Dan that he should cease his UFO investigations, that it was not wise to speak on the phone about such matters, and that her name was not Slago, after all. It was Nelson, and she worked as a "researcher" for the local police. At that point. Mrs. Slago – or Nelson – abruptly left the conversation. The story wasn't over, however, as Dan demonstrated to Steiger:

"When we checked with the police headquarters, the officers told us that they had no knowledge of either a 'Mrs. Nelson' or a 'Mrs. Slago' being connected with any phase of police research. Following this incident, we had a complete check made on our telephone lines, but the check revealed no evidence of wire-tapping or anything of that sort. A check with the telephone company revealed that a misconnection of this type could not possibly have been made."

JULY 14, 1952

"SIX AMBER GLOWING OBJECTS"

NEWPORT NEWS, VIRGINIA

"Another case in which experienced pilots viewed UFOs below them, and hence had helpful background-cues to distance and size, occurred near 8:12 p.m. EST, July 14, 1952'" said James McDonald, PhD. "A Pan American DC-4, en route from New York to Miami, was at 8000 feet over Chesapeake Bay, northeast of Newport

News, when its cockpit crew witnessed glowing, disc-shaped objects approaching them at a lower altitude (estimated at perhaps 2000 feet). First Officer Wm. B. Nash, at the controls for Capt. Koepke (who was not on the flight deck during the sighting), and Second Officer Wm. H. Fortenberry saw six amber-glowing objects come in at high velocity and execute a peculiar flipping maneuver during an acute-angle direction change."

JULY 15, 1963

A CURIOUS CRATER
WILTSHIRE, ENGLAND

It's an odd and near-surreal affair that occurred in the early 1960s. And it's something that most of Ufology has forgotten about. It is, as the title of this article demonstrates, the curious caper of the Charlton Crater. Strange lights were seen in the area late on the night of July 15 – the night on which the mystery began. The location: Manor Farm, Charlton, Wiltshire, England. Leonard Joliffe was the man who kicked off the controversy: he claimed, on the following morning, to have heard a loud explosion some-where nearby in the early hours of the 16th, something which had him puzzled and worried. He was not the only person to suggest something weird was afoot.

A local policeman had seen something unknown and brightly lit crossing the skies over Charlton. Then, when darkness gave way to daylight, a man named Reginald Alexander discovered some-thing not unlike a crater at Manor Farm, in a potato field. *Some-thing* had seemingly crashed to Earth or landed. But what was it? A missile? An aircraft? A bomb? Or…might it have been a UFO?

Alexander quickly told his boss, farm-owner Roy Blanchard,

of what he had found. Blanchard was confronted by a circular area of flattened soil. It was roughly eight-feet in diameter, one-foot deep (and with a deeper depression in the center) and had "lines" coming out of it which created an impression of something resembling a huge bicycle wheel.

A worried Blanchard called the police. They quickly got the Army involved. In no time at all, a bomb-disposal squad was on the scene. So was the media. It was hardly the kind of morning that Blanchard was expecting! Things really took off when Blanchard gave the following statement to the excited press: "There isn't a trace of the potatoes and barley which were growing where the crater is now. No stalks. No leaves. No roots. The thing was heavy enough to crush rocks and stone to powder. I believe that we have received a visit from a spaceship from another world."

The bomb-squad found nothing out of the ordinary, and no viable explanation for the crater was offered; however, the most popular theory was that nothing less than a UFO had landed – and soon thereafter, forever departed.

JULY 16, 1980

"WEITZEL OBSERVED AN INDIVIDUAL DRESSED IN A METALLIC SUIT DEPART THE CRAFT"

PECOS, NEW MEXICO

In December 1980, the Aerial Phenomena Research Association (APRO) received an anonymous letter that described a particular event said to have occurred on this specific day: "On July 16, 1980, at between 10:30 and 10:45 AM, Craig R. Weitzel...a Civil Air Patrol Cadet from Dobbins AFB... visiting Kirtland AFB, NM, observed a dull metallic colored UFO flying... near Pecos, New

Mexico...WEITZEL was with ten other individuals, including USAF active duty airmen, and all witnessed the sightings. Weitzel took some pictures of the object. Weitzel ...observed the UFO land in a clearing approximately 250 yards. NNW of the training area. Weitzel observed an individual dressed in a metallic suit depart the craft and walk a few feet away. The individual was outside the craft for just a few minutes. When the individual returned the craft took off toward the NW."

JULY 17, 1965:

"DIRTY TRICKS AND SINISTER MOTIVES"
WASHINGTON, D.C.

The Inquisitr notes: "Anonymous whistleblowers who claimed to be from the U.S. Defense Intelligence Agency (DIA) began leaking in November 2005 contents of an alleged 3,000-page secret document dating back to the 1970s relating to a secret 1965 alien exchange program, Project Serpo, which the U.S. government allegedly became involved in after the Roswell UFO incident.

"Although the recipient of the body of information, Bill Ryan, later released a statement on March 5, 2007, that the story, allegedly leaked by clandestine CIA and DIA sources, was 'a mixture of disinformation (i.e. truth mixed with added fictional elements) and naturally occurring compounded errors (such as uncorrected audiotape transcripts of the team commander's logs),' he maintained that despite the 'dirty tricks' and sinister motives of the government agents who orchestrated the leak, and inability to get a key witness ('the old man') - reportedly a reserve Serpo astronaut - to tell his story, they were able to verify the core truths of the story."

"THE OBJECT LAY RIGHT OVER THE DAIRY QUEEN"

BAYTOWN, TEXAS

"Baytown, Texas, on Galveston Bay, has a population near 30,000. Several persons evidently saw an interesting object there at about 9:00 a.m.," said ufologist James McDonald. "On 7/18/66. My original source on this case was an article that appeared in the 10/8/66 *Houston Post* from NICAP files. The article, by *Post* reporter Jimmie Woods, represents one of those rare UFO feature stories in which fact is well blended with human interest, as I found when I subsequently interviewed one of the principal witnesses, W. T. Jackson, at whose service station he and assistant Kelly Dikeman made the sighting. Both were inside the station when Jackson spotted the object hovering motionless about 100 yards away. (The *Post* said 1000 yards, but Jackson pointed out that Woods interviewed him while he was waiting on customers at the station and the reporter didn't get all of it correct.) Jackson explained to me that the object 'lay right over the Dairy Queen.' He described it as a white object that 'looked like two saucers turned together with a row of square windows in between,' and he thought it might have been 50 feet in diameter. He called Dikeman over, and they both looked at it for a few seconds and then simultaneously started for the door to get a better look. Almost at that moment it started moving westward," recorded James McDonald.

"A GREENISH GLOWING OBJECT OF NO
DISCERNIBLE SHAPE"

AIKEN, SOUTH CAROLINA

"A rather illuminating multiple-witness case was called to my attention by John A. Anderson, now at Sandia Base, New Mexico, but in 1952 working as a young engineer in the Savannah River AEC facility near Aiken, S.C.," recalled Dr. James McDonald. "After a considerable amount of cross-checking on the part of both Anderson and myself, the date was inferred to be late July, 1952, probably 7/19/52. The circumstance giving a clue to the date was that, at about 10:00 a.m. on the day in question, Anderson, along with what he estimated at perhaps a hundred other engineers, scientists and technicians from his group were outside watching a "required attendance" skit presented from a truck-trailer and commemorating the 150th anniversary of the founding of the DuPont company, July 18, 1802. Anderson indicated that someone less than absorbed in the skit first spotted the unidentified object in the clear skies overhead, and soon most eyes had left the skit to watch more technically intriguing events overhead. A greenish glowing object of no discernible shape, and of angular size estimated by Anderson to be not over a fifth of full-moon diameter, was darting back and forth erratically at very high speed."

GHOST ROCKETS OVER SCANDINAVIA

STOCKHOLM, SWEDEN

In the summer of 1946, Scandinavia was targeted by numerous UFOs. They were referred to as "Ghost Rockets." Reports surfaced from Norway, Denmark, Finland, and Sweden. A number of those reports indicated that at least several of the mysterious rockets crashed and were secretly recovered in July 1946.

On July 11, the US Embassy in Stockholm, Sweden, prepared a secret memo that, in part, reads as follows: "For some weeks there have been numerous reports of strange rocket-like missiles being seen in Swedish and Finnish skies. During [the] past few days reports of such objects being seen have greatly increased... Military Attaché is investigating through Swedish channels and has been promised results of Swedish observations. Swedes profess ignorance as to origin character or purpose of missiles but state definitely they are not launched by Swedes."

On July 19, 1946, the Oslo-based *Aftenposten* newspaper ran an article titled "Did two rocket bombs go down in Mjosa?" The article described the events of the previous night, July 18:

"From a man in Feiring we received this morning a sensational report that two rocket bombs crashed into Mjosa last night. They were shaped like ordinary planes, but quite small with only a 2½-meter wing-span and came between 24 and 0:30 this morning from the west at low height over the southerly part of Feiring, where they were observed by many persons, among them at the Hasselbaken Inn and at the Arnes. The forward one was not lighted.

"People noticed them because they heard a loud whistle and directly after they came flying into sight at terrific speed. They went so low that trees were left swaying after they passed. Nearly midway out in Mjosa, nearer the Feiring side, the water took a big splash and the spray stood many meters high in the air where the objects disappeared.

"Right after we received this report we talked with the sheriff in Feiring and Hurda, who had heard nothing, however. He immediately got into telephone contact with people between Hurdal and Feiring, and was able to report to us some time later that he had gotten confirming reports from many reliable quarters. The place where the planes went down lies 1 mile north from Hinnesund and Mjosa is rather deep here, so it may well be difficult to find them. But the sheriff will notify the Defense High Command immediately so that an investigation can be set in motion."

The result of the investigation? Although the specific wave of encounters continued through July 20, we have nothing but a noticeable, uncomfortable, and enduring silence from the authorities.

JULY 21, 2015

SHATTERED!

ARLINGTON, TEXAS

For me, it's always a good day when I put the finishing touches to a manuscript. And, June 16, 2015 was the date on which I completed the writing of my book, *Men in Black: Personal Stories and Eerie Encounters*. It was all good. Except, that is, for one thing which occurred around 9:45 a.m. That was roughly the time when I made the final change to the manuscript, hit "save," and closed the document. I was ready to email it to my agent, Lisa Hagan, for review.

At the split-second I closed the document, I heard a sudden bang coming from one of the rooms in my apartment. I frowned, stood up, and probably said something to myself along the lines of "WTF?" and, since my home is a relatively compact one, it didn't take long at all for me to find the cause of that bang; seconds, in fact. On walking into my bedroom, I saw that one of the many pictures I have on my walls had fallen to the floor. Despite the floor being carpeted, the black picture frame was broken and the glass had shattered, with pieces and shards all over the carpet.

What was particularly eye-opening, however, was the specific picture which had fallen from the wall. It was a framed letter written back in 1953 by none other than Albert Bender, the man who, arguably, birthed the mystery of the Men in Black, as a result of his traumatic experiences with a trio of glowing-eyed, vampire-like MIB in his hometown of Bridgeport, Connecticut.

When I told a few people about this, they all said it was a sign. But, a sign of what was the thing that no one could agree upon. There were those who viewed it as a warning to me to stay away from the matter of the MIB. Others suggested I was under some kind of dark, demonic attack. And there was one who, in a state of near fear, thought that "the ghost of Albert Bender" was lurking around. Maybe it was.

JULY 22, 1985

"UFOS ARE FROM SOME CIVILIZATION BEYOND OUR PLANET"

MATABELELAND SOUTH, ZIMBABWE

It was in the early evening – shortly before 6:00 p.m. – that a pair of Hawk jet-planes of the Zimbabwe, Africa Air Force encountered a fast-flying UFO in the western part of Matabeleland South. The pilots in question were based out of Thornhill Air Base and encountered what was described as a circular-shaped vehicle with a slight cone-like protrusion on top. Incredibly, when pursued by the jets, the UFO shot from a height of around 7,000 feet to 70,000 feet. Rather notably, Air Commodore David Thorne stated that, "As far as my Air Staff is concerned, we believe implicitly that the unexplained UFOs are from some civilization beyond our planet."

Further words on the extraordinary event came from a source as equally credible as Air Commodore Thorne. Air Marshall Azim Daupota said of the incident: "This was no ordinary UFO. Scores of people saw it. It was no illusion, no deception, no imagination." As the investigation developed it was revealed that were other notable witness, too; they were personal from Bulawayo Airport. The matter was never solved.

(Can we put a little more here? Matabeleland is remote, yes?)

JULY 23, 1995

"24 BRIGHT ORANGE LIGHTS"

SCUNTHORPE, ENGLAND

A very impressive encounter with a squadron of "Flying Triangle"-style UFO encounters took place during the early hours of July 23, 1995. The location was Scunthorpe, England, and the witness was Rob McDonald, who spent twelve years with the British Royal Air Force. As he left a barbecue on West Common Lane, McDonald noticed something in the sky, something very strange:

"The sky was clear and there was no mist. The stars looked very sharp. There were approximately 24 bright orange lights and they were travelling in groups of eight. Each of the lights was joined together with a bar and the lights were mathematically spaced apart. The groups formed a perfect equilateral triangle. They were high up and travelled over West Common Lane in the direction of Polaris. The lights took seven seconds to cross the horizon which means they must have been travelling at nearly 15,000 mph."

JULY 24, 1948

"AT FIRST, THEY THOUGHT IT WAS A JET"

SOMEWHERE BETWEEN HOUSTON AND ATLANTA, UNITED STATES

It's not every day that someone has the opportunity to speak on the UFO subject before the House Committee on Science and Astronautics. But, that's what James McDonald, PhD did on July 29, 1968. In his statement, McDonald a July 24, 1948 case that he considered highly persuasive when it came to the matter of UFOs:

"...one of the famous airline sightings of earlier years is the Chiles-Whitted Eastern Airlines case. An Eastern DC-3, en route from Houston to Atlanta, was flying at an altitude of about 5000 feet, near Montgomery, at 2:45 a.m. The pilot, Capt. Clarence S. Chiles, and the co-pilot, John B. Whitted, both of whom now fly jets for Eastern, were experienced fliers (for example, Chiles then had 8500 hours in the air, and both had wartime military flying duty behind them). I interviewed both Chiles and Whitted earlier this year to cross-check the many points of interest in this case. Space precludes a full account of all relevant details.

"Chiles pointed out to me that they first saw the object coming out of a distant squall-line area which they were just then reconnoitering. At first, they thought it was a jet, whose exhaust was somehow accounting for the advancing glow that had first caught their eyes. Coming almost directly at them at nearly their flight altitude, it passed off their starboard wing at a distance on which the two men could not closely agree: one felt it was under 1000 feett, the other put it at several times that. But both agreed, then and in my 1968 interview, that the object was some kind of vehicle. They saw no wings or empennage, but both were struck by 2 rows of windows or some apparent openings from which there came a bright glow 'like burning magnesium.' The object had a pointed "nose", and from the nose to the rear along its underside there was a bluish glow. Out of the rear end came an orange-red exhaust or wake that extended back by about the same distance as the object's length. The two men agreed that its size approximated that of a B-29, though perhaps twice as thick."

JULY 25, 1998

A CROP CIRCLE SEEN FORMING

WILTSHIRE, ENGLAND

On July 27, 1998, I had the opportunity to meet with a man named Paul Parker. Just two days earlier he had seen nothing less than a Crop Circle formed in a field in Wiltshire, England. It was not one of the huge pictograms, however. Rather it was a single circle, with a diameter of perhaps just fifteen feet or thereabouts.

According to Parker, he was out taking an early morning stroll when he heard a loud buzzing coming from the field he was then passing. Puzzled, he looked to his right and saw a thin column of green light hovering above the field, at a height of around thirty-to-forty feet. As he watched the light, he was amazed to see the corn below him both quickly and uniformly "pushed" to the ground in a perfect circle. Seconds later, the green light winked out of existence, leaving a distinctly confused and amazed Parker wondering what on earth he had stumbled on. He remains both amazed and confused by the event to this very day.

JULY 26, 1952

WASHINGTON, D.C. UNDER ASSAULT

WASHINGTON, D.C.

On the nights of July 19-20, 1952, UFOs were out in force, in the United States' capital. That, however, was nothing compared to an invasion of unknown aerial objects in the Washington, D.C., airspace on July 26; something that prompted the Air Force to prepare a full investigation. The USAF noted:

"This incident involved unidentified targets observed on the radar scopes at the Air Route Traffic Control Center and the tower, both at Washington National Airport, and the Approach Control Radar at Andrews Air Force Base. In addition, visual observations were reported to Andrews and Bolling AFB and to ARTC Center, the latter by pilots of commercial aircraft and one CAA aircraft…"

The report continues:

"Varying numbers (up to 12 simultaneously) of u/i [unidentified] targets on ARTC radar scope…Mr. Bill Schreve, flying a/c NC-12 reported at 2246 EDT that he had visually spotted 5 objects giving off a light glow ranging from orange to white; his altitude at time was 2,200'. Some commercial pilots reported visuals ranging from 'cigarette glow' to a 'light…"

And the deep strangeness only continued, as the USAF revealed:

"…Some commented that the returns appeared to be from objects 'capable of dropping out of the pattern at will'. Also that returns had 'creeping appearance.' All crew members emphatic that most returns have been picked up from time to time over the past few months but never before had they appeared in such quantities over such a prolonged period and with such definition as was experienced on the nights of 19/20 and 26/27 July 1952."

JULY 27, 1997

STAGING AN ALIEN ENCOUNTER
SEDONA, ARIZONA

An example of a case of alleged alien abduction that appears to have been part of a sophisticated military-controlled mind-control operation is described by Alison, a woman from Arizona, who lives on a ranch not too far from the town of Sedona. From the age of twenty-seven to thirty-one, Alison was subjected to at least five kidnappings that bore all the hallmarks of the classic alien abduction scenario.

On each occasion, she was in her livingroom, either reading or watching TV, when her two pet dogs – Lucy and Summer – began to act in a distressed fashion, pacing around the room and whimpering. At that point, things always became a blur, and Alison would later find herself in a different part of the house with several hours of time having passed. She would always awake feeling groggy, and with a pounding headache and dry mouth.

For days after the weird experiences, she would dream of the moment when things would begin to go awry – which always resulted in a complete loss of electricity inside the house, a deep humming noise emanating from outside the large living-room window, and powerful and intensely bright lights enveloping the room.

In her semi-conscious state, Alison would see small shadowy figures scuttling around the room. They would then carry her outside onto a small craft where she was subjected to a gynecological examination and some form of nasal probing. She would then be returned to another part of the house and the aliens would leave. It was only after the aliens had departed that the intense humming noise would cease.

On what Alison believes to have been the fifth abduction, however – July 27, 1997 - the mysterious humming sound abruptly came to a sudden halt, only a few seconds after her cosmic visitors had entered the room. At that point, Alison recalled – significantly, not in a later dream on this occasion but in real time – she began to slowly regain her senses. And, very surprisingly, so did the aliens. In their place was not a group of frail-looking bald-headed, black-eyed "Grays," but a number of large and burly men wearing what looked like suspiciously like black military fatigues – and who quickly exited Alison's home.

This begs an important question: how many more UFO events may have been secretly staged by the military?

JULY 28, 1952

"THEY ARE THE MOST CREDIBLE REPORTS RECEIVED"
WRIGHT-PATTERSON AIR FORCE BASE, DAYTON, OHIO

N.W. Philcox, the FBI's Air Force liaison representative, made arrangements through the office of the Director of Air Intelligence, Major General John A. Samford, to meet with Commander Randall Boyd of the Current Intelligence Branch, Estimates Division,

Air Intelligence, regarding "the present status of Air Intelligence research into the numerous reports regarding flying saucers and flying discs."

Although the Air Force was publicly playing down the possibility that UFOs were anything truly extraordinary, Philcox was advised that "at the present time the Air Force has failed to arrive at any satisfactory conclusion in its research regarding numerous reports of flying saucers and flying discs sighted throughout the United States."

Philcox was further informed that Air Intelligence had set up at Wright-Patterson Air Force Base, Ohio the Air Technical Intelligence Center, which had been established in part for the purpose of "coordinating, correlating and making research into all reports regarding flying saucers and flying discs."

As Philcox listened very carefully to what Boyd had to say on the matter, he noted that the Air Force had placed their UFO reports into three definable categories. In the first instance there were those sightings "which are reported by citizens who claim they have seen flying saucers from the ground. These sightings vary in description, color and speeds. Very little credence is given to these sightings inasmuch as in most instances they are believed to be imaginative or some explainable object which actually crossed through the sky."

Philcox then learned that the second category of encounters proved to be of greater significance: "Sightings reported by commercial or military pilots. These sightings are considered more credible by the Air Force inasmuch as commercial or military pilots are experienced in the air and are not expected to see objects that are entirely imaginative. In each of these instances, the individual who reports the sightings is thoroughly interviewed by a representative of Air Intelligence so that a complete description of the object can be obtained."

The third category of encounters, Boyd advised Philcox, were those where, in addition to a visual sighting by a pilot, there was corroboration either from a ground-based source or by radar. Philcox wrote to Hoover: "Commander Boyd advised that this latter classification constitutes two or three per cent of the total number of sightings, but that they are the most credible reports received and are difficult to explain."

"In these instances," Philcox was told, "there is no doubt that these individuals reporting the sightings actually did see something in the sky." And to demonstrate that Boyd was well acquainted with the UFO issue on a worldwide scale, he confided in Philcox that "sightings have also recently been reported as far distant as Acapulco, Mexico, Korea and French Morocco… the sightings reported in the last classification have never been satisfactorily explained."

<hr>

JULY 29, 1968

"IT IS IMPERATIVE THAT WE LEARN WHERE THE UFOS COME FROM"
WASHINGTON, D.C.

This was the day on which a remarkable statement was submitted to the House Committee on Science and Astronautics at July 29, 1968, Symposium on Unidentified Flying Objects, Rayburn Building, Washington, D.C., by James E. McDonald. For those who may not know, McDonald was the Senior Physicist, Institute of Atmospheric Physics, and professor, Department of Meteorology, at the University of Arizona, Tucson, Arizona.

McDonald said, in a file declassified according to Freedom of Information laws: "I have become convinced that the scientific community, not only in this country but throughout the world, has been casually ignoring as nonsense a matter of extraordinary scientific importance. The attention of your Committee can, and I hope will, aid greatly in correcting this situation. As you will note in the following, my own present opinion, based on two years of careful study, is that UFOs are probably extraterrestrial devices engaged in something that might very tentatively be termed 'surveillance.'"

"If the extraterrestrial hypothesis is proved correct (and I emphasize that the present evidence only points in that direction but cannot be said to constitute irrefutable proof), then clearly UFOs will become a top-priority scientific problem. I believe you might agree that, even if there were a slight chance of the correctness of that hypothesis, the UFOs would demand the most careful attention. In fact, that chance seems to some of us a long way from trivial. We share the view of Vice Adm. R. H. Hillenkoetter, former CIA Director, who said eight years ago, 'It is imperative that we learn where the UFOs come from and what their purpose is.' Since your committee is concerned only with broad aspects of our national scientific program but also with the prosecution of our entire space program, and since that space program has been tied in for some years now with the dramatic goal of a search for life in the universe, I submit that the topic of today's Symposium is eminently deserving of your attention. Indeed, I have to state, for the record, that I believe no other problem within your jurisdiction is of comparable scientific and national importance. Those are strong words, and I intend them to be."

UFOS AND A "TALL THIN MAN"
VICO, ITALY

UFO researcher Gareth Medway reveals…

"Carlo Rossi, who was fishing near Vico, Italy, at the site where he had seen an airborne disc on the 24th, was approached by a tall thin man who asked him about flying saucers, offered him a gold-tipped cigarette, and when it made him ill threw it into the water, then walked off. "Fearing that someone was trying to silence him, Rossi went to the Public Prosecutor's office in the town of Lucca and swore out a statement of his UFO encounter."

A RENDEZVOUS OF THE FLIRTY KIND
MORMON MESA, NEVADA

Truman Bethurum was a Californian, born in 1898. In 1952, Bethurum claimed he had an extremely close encounter with extraterrestrials on Mormon Mesa, in Nevada's Moapa Valley.

On the fateful night, and after the working day was over, Bethurum climbed the mountain, primarily to search for shells. The story goes that Bethurum was rendered into a strange, altered state of mind, during which aliens from another world were suddenly before him; having arrived in a huge, gleaming, flying saucer that quietly descended to the desert floor.

Only around four-feet-five to five-feet tall, the aliens were eerily human-looking and claimed to come from a faraway world: Clarion. Their leader was Captain Aura Rhanes, a woman Bethurum described as being "tops in shapeliness and beauty."

Bethurum's odd story grew at a steady and controversial pace, as did his relationship to the flirty Captain Rhanes. For months, Bethurum and Rhanes had clandestine meetings; usually, late at night. They generally occurred in isolated desert locations in Nevada, where, after Rhanes' huge ship landed, the pair had long and deep conversations about the state of the Earth, the Cold War, and the captain's home world – to which she promised to take Bethurum, one day. She never did.

Fantasy, hoax, or the real thing? While many might find the whole thing unlikely, the FBI was intrigued enough to open a secret file on Bethurum. In the file, one of the Bureau's special-agents refers to Aura Rhanes as "a ravishing space commandant!"

AUGUST

STRANGE LIGHTS OVER A CROP CIRCLE
WILTSHIRE, ENGLAND

Matthew Williams is someone who has played an extensive role in the Crop Circle enigma since the mid-1990s. Welshman Williams has investigated formations, staked out fields late at night, flown over them in his very own microlight and filmed them, and even made them! Williams has also seen mysterious balls of light hovering over Crop Circles in the English county of Wiltshire, where most of the formations are found every year.

Williams and a friend named Paul were deep in the heart of Crop Circle territory when, as they stood at the fringes of a large field in which an equally large formation had been found, the pair was astounded by something wholly unanticipated. It was the sudden appearance of a trio of small balls of light hovering on the fringes of the field. At first, they were clustered together, at heights of between thirty and forty feet, but then they suddenly split up and created a triangular formation, with each ball positioned around sixty feet from the others. Clearly, there was some form of orchestrated intelligence at work. The two men stood still for a few seconds, staring into the dark skies and at the approximately soccer-ball-sized lights, and wondering just what might happen next. They didn't have to wait for too long to find out.

The lights suddenly vanished – and at the exact time that deep and ominous growling, the distinct noises of something large and heavy crunching its way – or their way - along the field, and animal-like screams filled the chilled air. The tables had been duly turned: the Crop Circle investigators were now, themselves, being investigated. But, by what? It was clear to Williams and Paul that whatever the creatures were, that same crunching suggested they were much bigger than the average, wild, English fox, which is largely a non-threatening and even shy animal. And the screams and growls were clearly not those of foxes, either. The two men looked at each other for a moment, and wasted no time in getting the hell out of Dodge, as the old saying goes.

AUGUST 2

CROP CIRCLES AND SORCERY
STAFFORDSHIRE, ENGLAND

Built on land that came into the possession of the Earls of Chester as far back as the end of the 11th Century, Chartley Castle – which can be found in the English county of Staffordshire, where I grew up – is a stone fortress founded in the thirteenth century by Ranulph Blundeville, the then Earl of Chester. Still standing today, the remains are a rare cylindrical keep, with the inner bailey curtain wall flanked by two huge half-round towers, a gatehouse, and angle-tower. A counter-scarp bank and cross-ditch divide the inner and outer baileys, with another ditch and bank encasing the whole castle. Notably, Chartley Castle was to where, on Christmas Eve, 1585, Mary, Queen of Scots was taken before being moved to Fotheringay for execution on February 8, 1586. And, in the summer of 2006, a striking Crop Circle was found in a field directly next to the old castle.

When word got out about the creation, my ex-wife, Dana, and I were in England for three months, and drove out to the site. The Crop Circle was both huge and intricately designed. Not only that, as we clambered down a steep, grassy embankment towards the formation, and made our careful way through thick brambles, lush bushes and a barbwire fence, we could not fail to see something highly strange strewn around the fringes of the Crop Circle: namely, a not inconsiderable pile of large and spectacularly colorful peacock feathers that were laid out in the form of a five-pointed star.

Jane Adams was a student of Wicca who I met back in 1997 – in a Wiltshire-based Crop Circle, as it transpires. An old, wizened and disturbingly odd character with staring eyes and long black hair, Adams had a decidedly unsettling air about her that was detectable to practically anyone and everyone upon first meeting her. When I telephoned Adams from within the Chartley Castle Crop Circle to tell her where we were and what we had found, she surprised me by immediately offering an intriguing scenario to explain the peacock feathers.

According to Adams, the presence of the feathery star-formation at the site was evidence that those people she believed were guilty of making Crop Circles had been using the peacock's "Evil Eye" in "black ceremonies." She added that such ceremonies had been held, under cover of darkness, on a number of occasions within British-based Crop Circles, and ancient stone circles too, and that the people responsible were endeavoring to "create negativity" and conjure up bizarre, life-threatening creatures from darkened realms that co-exist with ours. The reason: to harness the beasts and utilize them in, as she termed it, "psychic assassinations" of people who were either opposed to the activities of the group, or who were trying to expose their actions.

"THE 'FLYING SAUCERS' COULD BE RADIO CONTROLLED GERM BOMBS"

STAMFORD, CONNECTICUT

One particularly fascinating scenario for the sudden appearance of UFOs in the Earth's skies was brought to the attention of officialdom by a little-known, but well respected, source. His name was Edwin M. Bailey. In the summer of 1947, Bailey was living in Stamford, Connecticut. At the time, he was working in the Physics Division of the American Cyanamid Research Laboratories on West Main Street. In the 1970s, the American Cyanamid Company was one of the United States' top 100 manufacturing companies. Its output included antibiotics, vaccines, industrial chemicals, pesticides, and acrylic plastics.

Far more notable is the fact that at the height of the Second World War, Bailey worked at the Massachusetts Institute of Technology (MIT), in Cambridge, Massachusetts. Not only that, the specific branch of MIT to which Bailey was assigned was the Radiation Laboratory. It was a body that played an important role in the development of the atomic bomb, under the overall control of the Manhattan Project. On top of that, Bailey had graduated at the University of Arizona.

The FBI recorded in its files the following: "Bailey stated that the topic of 'flying saucers' had caused considerable comment and concern to the present day scientists and indicated that he himself had a personal theory concerning the 'flying saucers.'"

As to the specific nature of that theory, it was, to say the least, grim. The FBI noted: "Bailey stated that it is quite possible that actually the 'flying saucers' could be radio controlled germ bombs or atom bombs which are circling the orbit of the earth and which could be controlled by radio and directed to land on any designated target at the specific desire of the agency or country operating the bombs."

Disturbing, to say the least.

AUGUST 4, 1987

ALIENS, BLOOD, AND THE MILITARY
BEAUMONT, TEXAS

Brenda was driving late at night to visit family in the southeast Texan city of Beaumont. She arrived fine, but not until the following morning – hours after she should have arrived. Her family was frantic and was all but ready to contact the police when it became clear that something – something deeply worrying – was going down. It was only Brenda's call from a 24-hour gas station, in the early hours of the morning that prevented the authorities from being brought in and a full-scale manhunt initiated.

When Brenda finally reached her family, it was clear she was in a state of deep distress and utter confusion. Concerned that she had been attacked, mugged, or worse, her brother wanted to bring the police in – as in immediately. Brenda pleaded otherwise, and explained what she consciously recalled. It was not much, but it revolved around being taken from her car – by what seemed to be military personnel – who she believed had somehow been able to "prompt" her into exiting the main highway from Houston to Beaumont and down a lonely stretch of heavily wooded road, where she was confronted by a black van, surrounding by a group of four or five men, all dressed in black fatigues. Brenda also recalled being taken, in what she felt was a drugged state, to a small, sub-surface facility, a couple of miles away at the very most, and where she was interrogated in downright hostile fashion by two elderly men that she perceived as being doctors. They were doctors surrounded by several men in military uniforms that befitted the likes of generals.

The two doctors, Brenda says, "…wanted to know, did I know my blood group? Well, yes I did. They took a lot of blood. Vials. They kept asking me about my blood: Did I get a lot of nose-bleeds? Did I have any physical differences? I don't know what that meant. Did I feel like I was on a mission to do things for the aliens? Well, I have *always* thought that and I told them. I remember the doctors looking at each other when I said that."

AUGUST 5, 1952

AN INTRIGUING RADAR-BASED ENCOUNTER
HANEDA AIR FORCE BASE, NEAR TOKYO, JAPAN

From the files of the late James McDonald:

"USAF tower operators at Haneda AFB observed an unusually bright bluish-white light to their NE, alerted the GCI radar unit at Shiroi, which then called for a scramble of an F94 interceptor after getting radar returns in same general area. GCI ground radar vectored the F94 to an orbiting unknown target, which the F94 picked up on its airborne radar. The target then accelerated out of the F94's radar range after 90 seconds of pursuit that was followed also on the Shiroi GCI radar."

AUGUST 6, 1981

"THEY WARNED THE COUPLE TO SAY NOTHING"

MATLOCK, DERBYSHIRE, ENGLAND

"David Ellis and his wife Caroline, who ran The Horseshoes public house outside Matlock, Derbyshire, and had had several recent UFO sightings, were visited at seven in the morning by two men in black with grey suede gloves, 'like twins,' who were revealed to be hairless when they took off their hats, and apparently wore lipstick," says Gareth Medway, UFO researcher and expert on Men in Black.. "They warned the couple to say nothing, made Caroline's signet ring disappear, then drove off in a black Mercedes which had no number plate. The ring soon reappeared. Afterwards they received several telephone calls from a 'somewhat metallic' voice also warning them not to talk."

AUGUST 7, 1953

"AN EGG-SHAPED OBJECT"

FORT POLK, LEESVILLE, LOUISIANA

Sergeant "HJ" saw duty in Korea with the Army's 24th Infantry and claims direct and personal knowledge of a crashed UFO event in Louisiana in the summer of 1953. According to HJ, he was stationed at Fort Polk, Louisiana, at the time and was on maneuvers in the area on a particular day when, at around dusk, "an egg-shaped object" crash-landed close to them in "soft sandy soil."

HJ said that the object was "ovoid," "large," and was surrounded by a fin-like protrusion at its equator. "Top brass and medics" quickly arrived on the scene, recalled the witness, and a small body was removed along with three living creatures, each approximately four feet in height and displaying large heads. After having been placed in isolation, all reportedly died soon afterwards.

"AN UNIDENTIFIED LIGHT IN THE AIR"
COYOTE CANYON, NEW MEXICO

U.S. Air Force documents that have been released under the Freedom of Information legislation describe the following, notable incident:

"On 2 Sept 80, SOURCE related on 8 Aug 80, three Security Policemen assigned to 1608 SPS, KAFB, NM, on duty inside the Manzano Weapons Storage Area sighted an unidentified light in the air that traveled from North to South over the Coyote Canyon area of the Department of Defense Restricted Test Range on KAFB, NM. The Security Policemen identified as: SSGT STEPHEN FERENZ, Area Supervisor, ATC MARTIN W. RIST and AMN ANTHONY D. FRAZIER, were later interviewed separately by SOURCE and all three related the same statement; at approximately 2350 hrs., while on duty in Charlie Sector, East Side of Manzano, the three observed a very bright light in the sky approximately 3 miles North–North–East of their position. The light traveled with great speed and stopped suddenly in the sky over Coyote Canyon. The three first thought the object was a helicopter, however, after observing the strange aerial maneuvers (stop and go), they felt a helicopter couldn't have performed such skills. The light landed in the Coyote Canyon area. Sometime later, three witnessed the light take off and leave proceeding straight up at a high speed and disappear."

BEWARE OF THE OCTOPUS

MARTINSBURG, WEST VIRGINIA

That was the date on which a man named Danny Casolaro was found dead in the shower of room 517 of the Martinsburg, West Virginia-based Sheraton Inn. It appeared that Casolaro had committed suicide: both of his wrists were slashed and there was a suicide note left for his family. But, was it really as tragically straightforward as it seemed? Not for the field of conspiracy theorizing, it wasn't. At the time of his death, Casolaro – an investigative journalist –was chasing down a powerful, secret society that he termed the Octopus – on account of the fact that it appeared to have powerful and influential tentacles that extended across just about the entire planet. And there was a UFO connection, too.

The further Casolaro dug, the more complicated the story got: the Octopus was comprised of numerous powerful people in the worlds of big business, politics, the military, and the Intelligence community. They were somewhat loose-knit and fluid, but they had the power and muscle to influence world events on a massive scale. As Casolaro headed ever deeper into the rabbit hole, he found that the Octopus had played key roles in the 1962 Cuban missile crisis (which brought the world to the brink of nuclear war), the Watergate scandal which brought down President Richard M. Nixon, and the December 1988 destruction of a Boeing 747 Jumbo Jet aircraft over Lockerbie, Scotland. Then things got really weird.

The Octopus, Casolaro discovered, had a significant presence at the world's most famous secret base: Area 51, Nevada. The Octopus was reportedly funding research to create deadly viruses at both Area 51 and at an underground facility in northern New Mexico. Casolaro also made a connection between the Octopus and Majestic 12 – the alleged, secret group that oversees the secrecy surrounding what happened at Roswell, New Mexico in early July 1947. Things then took a strange turn when Casolaro met with a man named Michael Riconosciuto, who had worked in the field of spies, espionage, and intelligence for years, and who advised Casolaro that many assumed UFOs were actually highly advanced, unusual aircraft of the military.

Casolaro's research continued at a phenomenal rate, to the point where he came to see the presence – and manipulative skills – of the Octopus in just about each and every major world event since the end of the Second World War. Of course, it all came crashing down for Casolaro when he was found dead in the tub. But, was it really just a suicide? Many within the field of conspiracy-theorizing cried "No!"

AUGUST 10, 1980

A UFO LANDS IN NEW MEXICO
BELEN AND ALBUQUERQUE, NEW MEXICO

According to the US Air Force:

"On 10 Aug 80, a New Mexico State Patrolman sighted an aerial object land in the Manzano's between Belen and Albuquerque, NM. The Patrolman reported the sighting to the Kirtland AFB Command Post, who later referred the patrolman to the AFOSI Dist 17. AFOSI Dist 17 advised the patrolman to make a report through his own agency. On 11 Aug 80, the Kirtland Public Information office advised the patrolman the USAF no longer investigates such sighting unless they occur on a USAF base."

WEIRDNESS ON THE RADIO
NEW YORK, NEW YORK

In August 2015, I was on Steve Warner's *Dark City* show, in which we discussed the MIB. During the interview, Steve experienced something very weird, involving the lights in his home. Namely, they were repeatedly turning on and off. I don't mean flickering on and off as they might during a storm. Rather, Steve - sat in front of his computer – could hear the light-switches being *turned* on and then off – albeit by invisible hands. It was something which actually became a part of the interview! When I mentioned this in a two-part online article at *Mysterious Universe*, it generated a few replies, including one from "Rob from Rigel VII," who wrote: "You may not believe this, but as soon as I pulled up part 2 of this article, the power went out at work, which is a large office building. The UPS boxes started beeping and then the power all came back. Eerie!"

A FLYING WOMAN IN VIETNAM
DA NANG, VIETNAM

One of the strangest, and undoubtedly, creepiest of all encounters with something truly out of this world occurred at the height of the Vietnam War, and specifically in Da Nang, Vietnam. It was in August 1969 that a man named Earl Morrison, along with several comrades, had the shock of his life. It was, very appropriately, in the dead of night when the menacing event occurred – and as the men were on guard-duty, keeping a careful look out for the

Vietcong. Everything was quiet and normal until around 1:30 a.m. That's when the atmosphere changed, and an eerie form made its presence known to the shocked men of the US 1st Division Marine Corps.

Despite being somewhat reluctant to speak out publicly, Morrison eventually changed his mind and, by 1972, was comfortable about discussing the incident, even if he wasn't comfortable with what he encountered. His story makes for incredible reading:

"We saw what looked like wings, like a bat's, only it was gigantic compared to what a regular bat would be. After it got close enough so we could see what it was, it looked like a woman. A naked woman. She was black. Her skin was black, her body was black, the wings were back; everything was black. But it glowed. It glowed in the night, kind of greenish cast to it. She started going over us, and we still didn't hear anything. She was right above us, and when she got over the top of our heads she was maybe 6 or 7 feet up. We watched her go straight over the top of us, and she still didn't make any noise flapping her wings. She blotted out the moon once – that's how close she was to us. And dark – looked like pitch black then, but we could still define her because she just glowed. Real bright like. And she started going past us straight towards our encampment. As we watched her – she had got about 10 feet or so away from us – we started hearing her wings flap. And it sounded, you know, like regular wings flapping. And she just started flying off and we watched her for quite a while."

One of those who took a great deal of interest in the story of the flying woman of Da Nang was a UFO researcher named Don Worley. His personal interview with Morrison revealed additional data, such as the fact that the woman's hair was black and straight, that the wings may have had a slight furry quality to them, that she "rippled" as she flew by, that she appeared to lack bones in her body, and that her wings seemed to be directly "molded" to her hands and arms.

"THE PRESENCE OF HOSTILE INTELLIGENCE"

KIRTLAND AIR FORCE BASE, ALBUQUERQUE, NEW MEXICO

In the same time frame that strange and unsettling UFO activity was afoot at Kirtland Air Force Base, New Mexico throughout August 1980, a strange incident occurred on the 13th of the month, as official Air Force documents reflect:

"On 13 Aug 80, 1960 COMM Sq Maintenance Officer reported Radar Approach Control equipment and scanner radar inoperative due to high frequency jamming from an unknown cause. Total blackout of entire radar approach system to include Albuquerque Airport was in effect between 1630-2215 hrs. Radar Approach Control back up system also was inoperative.

"On 13 Aug 80, Defense Nuclear Agency Radio Frequency Monitors determined, by vector analysis, the interference was being sent from an area (V-90 degrees or due East). On DAF map coordinates E-28.6. The area was located NW of Coyote Canyon Test area. It was first thought that Sandia Laboratory, which utilizes the test range was responsible. However, after a careful check, it was later determined that no tests were being conducted in the canyon area. Department of Energy, Air Force Weapons Laboratory and DNA were contacted but assured that their agencies were not responsible.

"On 13 Aug 80, Base Security Police conducted a physical check of the area but because of the mountainous terrain, a thorough check could not be completed at that time. A later foot search failed to disclose anything that could have caused the interference. On 13 Aug 80, at 2216 hrs, all radar equipment returned to normal operation without further incident.

"CONCLUSION: The presence of hostile intelligence jamming cannot be ruled out. Although no evidence would suggest this, the method has been used in the past. Communication maintenance specialists cannot explain how such interference could cause the radar equipment to become totally inoperative. Neither could they suggest the type or range of the interference signal. DNA frequency monitors reported the interference beam was wide spread and a type unknown to their electronical equipment. Further checks of the area were being conducted by Technical Services, AFOSI."

AUGUST 14, 1971

ETS AND A MONSTER

LOCH NESS, SCOTLAND

According to Swedish Jan-Ove Sundberg, twenty-three at the time, on August 14, 1971, and at some point between 8:30 and 9:30 a.m., he was in a section of woodland above Foyers Bay, Loch Ness, Scotland, when he came across something staggering. No, not a fully-grown Nessie roaming around. Sundberg near-stumbled upon a landed UFO and its presumed extraterrestrial crew! The craft was situated in a clearing, giving the impression that its pilots had chosen the site deliberately, since it gave them the opportunity to land and hide their presence – that is, until Sundberg inadvertently foiled their plan.

The craft was, to say the least, a decidedly odd one. It was around thirty feet in length, dark gray in color, and cigar-shaped. It had a significantly sized section on top that reminded Sundberg of a large handle. The overall image was that of a giant iron used for getting the creases out of clothing. Amazement turned to concern when, out of the trees, came a trio of figures: all humanoid in shape, of approximately human proportions, and dressed in outfits that closely resembled the outfits worn by divers. In fact, at first, Sundberg assumed they *were* divers, from a then-active team that was searching the depths of Loch Ness for the monster. It became apparent the three were not divers, however, when they entered the odd-looking craft via a panel and the craft took to the skies, vertically, for about sixty feet. After which it began to move horizontally over the hills and in the direction of nearby Loch Mhor.

AUGUST 15, 1955

A GUN-FIGHT WITH ALIENS

KELLY, KENTUCKY

Kelly, Kentucky is, a small, rural town that is situated just short of ten miles from Hopkinsville. They are the kinds of places where people keep themselves to themselves, and nothing of a particularly sensational matter ever happens – apart, that is, from the fateful night of August 15, when absolute chaos broke out. It all went down at the farmhouse of the Sutton family, who had visitors in from Pennsylvania: Billy Ray Taylor and his wife. It was roughly 7.00 p.m. when Billy Ray left the farmhouse to fetch water from the family's well. And what a big mistake that was.

In mere minutes, Billy Ray was back, minus the water. Terrified Billy Ray told the Suttons and his wife that as he headed towards the well he saw a significantly sized, illuminated, circular-shaped object come to rest in a nearby gully. As the group tried to figure out what on earth (or off it…) was going on, they mused upon the possibilities of shooting stars, meteorites, and good old leg-pulling. By all accounts, it was none of those. In just a few minutes, the Suttons' dog began to bark, growl, and snarl in an aggressive, uncontrollable fashion – after which it raced for cover underneath the porch. Clearly, something strange was going down. Exactly how strange, soon became very apparent.

Intent on making sure they were in control of the situation, Elmer Sutton and Billy Ray Taylor armed themselves with a shotgun and headed out into the darkness. In no time, they were confronted by something terrifying: a small, silvery, creature – in the region of three feet tall – that was scurrying towards them with its long, ape-like, arms held high in the air. Sutton did what most folk might do when confronted by a strange, dwarfish thing after sunset: he blasted the beast with his shotgun. To the consternation of both men, the gun had no effect, aside from causing the creature to do a quick, impressive backflip, after which it disappeared into the darkness – for a while. The creatures were soon back, something which ultimately led one and all to flee the house and contact the police. Despite a quick response by the police, the strange creatures were nowhere to be seen. A legend was born.

AUGUST 16, 1957:
ALIENS AND THE CHUPACABRA
HILLS OF CANOVANAS, PUERTO RICO

In July 2004, I traveled to Puerto Rico with Jon Downes, a good friend and a full-time monster-hunter. While there, we heard a story of a UFO crash in the hills of Canovanas in 1957, one which reportedly, and quickly, led to gross, physical mutations in the local populace when an alien virus found its way into the local water-supply. It was not a stand-alone story, however. On his first trek around the island, in 1998, Jon, himself, was given no less than five, independent accounts of this August 16, 1957 event. One of Jon's sources was a man named Reuben, a Puerto Rican brought up in New York, but who returned to the island as an adult. Arguably, Reuben was Jon's most significant source, since he personally took Jon to the very spot in Canovanas where, he claimed, the craft from another world slammed into the ground, back in 1957.

Jon told me that they came to a big clearing where the path became narrow, and, on one side, disappeared altogether, into a huge saucer-shaped arena. This, according to what Reuben had to say, at least, was where the UFO had crashed. Admittedly, there was a huge indent in the side of the mountain, said Jon. No trees grew there, and it did look as if some huge object had crashed into the mountain, scooping out trees and vegetation and leaving a bare area intermittently covered with patchy grass.

AUGUST 17, 2016

THE STRANGE CASE OF A VANISHING CAR

NORTHERN ENGLAND

In this particular incident, the witness, Jim Wilson, who lived in the north of England, saw an unidentified – but not overly-fantastic – light in the sky, and was later blessed with a visit from a pair of suit-wearing characters flashing ID cards that demonstrated they came from the British Ministry of Defense. The two suggested to the man that he had merely viewed a Russian satellite – Cosmos 408 – and that he should forget all about the experience.

That would indeed have been the end of things, were it not for the fact that the witness found to his concern that, on a number of occasions and shortly after the visit occurred, his home seemed to be under some form of surveillance by two men sitting in a black Jaguar – which is the preferred mode of transport in most British Men in Black cases. The police were called, and, across the course of several nights, stealthy checks of the immediate vicinity were made.

After seeing the car parked outside the man's home on several occasions, and then managing to get a good look at his license plate – which the police were quickly able to confirm as being totally bogus – they carefully closed in, with the intention of speaking with the pair of MIB and finding out the nature of their game.

Unfortunately, they never got the chance to do so: as two uniformed officers approached the vehicle and prepared to knock on one of the windows, the black Jaguar melted away into nothingness. There was, not surprisingly, a deep reluctance on the part of the officers to prepare any written report alluding to such an event in the station logbook!

AUGUST 18, 1983

A SPOTTED UFO

FLORENCE, ITALY

"18 Aug 83 Florence – Unidentified flying object seen by crew. Large black object, balloon shaped with large white spot on it, observed 10 NM SE of Firenza. No attachments to object. SUPP. INFO.: Italian CAA replied no met [meteorological] balloon could possibly have been present at the indicated place or time."

Prepared by the staff of the UK's Civil Aviation Authority in the summer of 1983, this particular report, although brief, clearly demonstrates something very unusual was seen in the skies of Florence. Precisely what was seen, however, remains unknown.

AUGUST 19, 1949

UFO CRASH IN A MONTANA LAKE

HEBGEN LAKE, MONTANA

A little-known, and seldom seen, US Air Force document of August 1949 details the reported crash of not just one UFO, but two, in Hebgen Lake, Montana. In a one-page *Incoming Message* from Great Falls Air Force Base, Montana, to the Air Materiel Command at Wright-Patterson Air Force Base, Ohio, dated 17 August 1949, the incident is as follows:

"This office advised on 9 August 49 that 7 flying discs had been sighted at Hebgen Lake, Montana at 0930 hours that date. 2 of the discs were alleged to have crashed, 1 on the lake, and the other on the opposite shore in a wooded area. 2 agents of this office dragged the lake with negative results. Informant and only actual eyewitness, while absolutely trustworthy, is prone to exaggeration.

"He stated discs were all little larger than an auto tire, of a grayish color, and either having a hole in the center or being painted dark in the center. Informant was not capable of estimating speed but agents estimated from description that discs were traveling in excess of 1000 miles per hour. Objects were reported traveling in South Westerly direction. A check of winds aloft for period revealed a generally South Easterly direction and of a maximum velocity of 24 knots per hour.

"No unusual atmospheric phenomena were evident on 9

August, sky conditions were clear and visibility unlimited. Informant described sound of object as being similar to a siren. Request advice of detailed report desired."

As well as having dragged the lake, the military undertook additional inquiries in and around the area. They came up with nothing but a definitive mystery, something which leaves us with an intriguing possibility: that at least one of the UFOs might still be buried in the mud of Hebgen Lake. Such a thing is not impossible, as the lake is fifteen miles long, four miles wide – plenty of room to hide a tire-sized flying saucer.

AUGUST 20, 1957

THE SOUND OF A SAUCER
QUILINO, ARGENTINA

Sightings of UFOs in the skies of our planet have been reported for decades – and perhaps, even, for hundreds, and maybe thousands, of years. But what about the sound of a UFO? Interestingly, there are numerous accounts on record where UFOs have reportedly emitted deep, resonating, humming noises that seem to exert some form of both physical and mental influence over the witnesses. Not only that, such encounters have also left eyewitnesses feeling distinctly ill and disorientated. As a perfect example, consider the following:

It was the night of August 20, 1957 when a guard was standing watch near a US Air Force aircraft that had crashed near Quilino, Argentina. Suddenly, he heard an "eerie hum" and was amazed to see above him a large, seemingly metallic, disc-shaped UFO. In stark terror, he attempted to draw his pistol, but with the humming sound becoming deeper and deeper, he found himself unable to do so and was certain that his very self-will was under extreme threat. Most fascinating of all, the guard then had an overwhelming sensation that his mind was being "flooded" with information from an intelligence aboard the UFO that revolved around mankind's misuse of atomic energy – something that he perceived was of great concern to those inside the craft.

AUGUST 21, 1986

A CIGAR-SHAPED UFO AND AN OFFICIAL DOCUMENT
BELGRADE, ENGLAND

The following is extracted from a notable file on UFOs prepared by the UK's Civil Aviation Authority in the 1980s:

"21 Aug 86 Belgrade – Non UK Airmiss missile type object passed 500 feet above on reciprocal track A/C heading 290 MAG at FL 390. Object was black, cigar shaped, without wings. Belgrade radar informed on RTF. CAA closure – foreign authority advised."

The case remained unresolved.

AUGUST 22, 1980

COYOTE CANYON LIGHTS
COYOTE CANYON, NEW MEXICO

On this particularly intriguing case, UFO Evidence says: "Three other unnamed Security Guards observed a light over Coyote Canyon that behaved in a similar manner as the one seen on 8 August. Coyote Canyon is part of a large restricted test range used by the Air Force Weapons Laboratory, Sandia Laboratories, the Defense Nuclear Agency, and the Department of Energy."

AUSTRALIA'S MYSTERIOUS "SILVER DART"

NEW GUINEA

From Mr. T.P Drury – none other than the Director of Civil Aviation on New Guinea – had an extraordinary UFO encounter, along with his wife and children. Such was the amazing nature of the encounter, Drury went public with his story:

"I was standing on the coast road overlooking the flying boat base at Port Moresby. It was about 11:00 a.m....My wife noticed a wisp of cloud appear from nowhere in the blue sky and start to build up...I watched it slowly building up into a thick white mass of cumulus. There was no other cloud in the sky and nothing to account for it...

"Suddenly an object like a silver dart shot out of the cloud. It was elongated like a bullet and subtended about one inch at arm's length. It shot out of the cloud upwards at an angle of forty-five degrees. It was metallic and flashed in the sun. It was very clear cut. It was sharp in front, but apparently truncated behind, though the tail may have been hidden by the vapor trail. No wings or fins were visible...

"If anyone in the Territory had the qualifications to identify an unknown aircraft I had. It is my business to know what is in the air."

But, not on this occasion: the mysterious matter was never resolved.

ALIEN CRASH IN ICELAND?

NORTHEASTERN ICELAND

A two-page document prepared by the 468th Counter Intelligence Corps (CIC) Detachment for the Air Force Office of Special Investigations, Washington, D.C., describes an intriguing event that occurred in northeastern Iceland in 1954. According to the document, titled *Unidentified Flying Object*:

"On 1 September 1954, information was received by this command to the effect that an unidentified flying object had been sighted at approximately 2050 hours, 24 August 1954, in the vicinity of Egilsstadir by an individual at Hjardarbol, a farm located near the junction of the Lagarfljot ad Jokula Rivers, in Northeastern Iceland.

"The eyewitness, who was located approximately 3000 feet from the line of flight of the object, described it as being approximately the length of a man's arms (2 to 2 ½ feet long), approximately 4 to 5 inches in diameter, cylindrical in shape and dark gray in color. The object, emitting a loud whizzing sound, reportedly crossed the sky from the Northwest and traveled a level course to the Southeast at a rapid rate of speed. The object continued its level flight for some time and then lost speed and fell into a sandbar in the Lagarfljot River."

Despite the fact that the river was extensively searched and dragged, nothing was found. Officially, at least…

MEXICO'S VERY OWN ROSWELL

CHIHUAHUA, MEXICO

Longstanding rumors suggest that a UFO crashed to earth in Chihuahua, Mexico late on the night at issue. Monitored and tracked on radar by both Mexican and US military personnel, the UFO catastrophically collided with a small passenger plane, bringing both down on the desert terrain. Mexican authorities were quickly on the scene, intent on recovering the mysterious object. Things got even more dramatic when the retrieval team reached the crash site. The pilot of the aircraft was clearly killed and his plane was all but destroyed. As for the UFO, it escaped with nothing more than an approximately 1-foot-square hole in its side. It was a full-blown flying saucer, albeit one that was only around sixteen-feet in diameter.

Mexican troops quickly loaded the UFO onto a military transporter vehicle, intent on taking it to the nearest military installation. It didn't work out like that. At some point in the journey, the retrieval team was overcome by either a fast-acting "alien virus," or something akin to a powerful chemical-warfare agent. American authorities, realizing that something very disturbing had occurred, took steps to dispatch their own retrieval team, before a second Mexican unit had time to arrive.

U.S. personnel succeeded in grabbing the small saucer and flew it to the United States by helicopter. The final destination of the UFO: the Center for Disease Control (CDC) in Atlanta, Georgia; the ideal place to deal with what could have been a lethal pathogen of extraterrestrial origins.

AUGUST 26, 1953

"THE WERE SHOWN THE BODIES"

WHITE SANDS PROVING GROUND, NEW MEXICO

Mailed to the National Investigations Committee on Aerial Phenomena organization in April 1964, the following letter describes an event that - according to the writer, K.A., a student at Bob Jones University - occurred in New Mexico on an undetermined date in 1953. It reads:

"Here at school there is an instructor, who during the Korean conflict was an adjutant to an Army Air Corps General at one of our New Mexico proving grounds. I got the following story from him. In 1953 a flying saucer crash-landed near the proving grounds. Air Force personnel immediately rushed to the area and found the saucer, unharmed and unoccupied, with doors open. Upon searching the surrounding area they came upon the bodies of the saucer's four occupants, all dead.

"Shortly after this, certain top level personnel were given the true saucer story by Air Force officials. In his capacity my source was included in this. They were shown the bodies of the four occupants of the ship, which he described as from three to four feet tall, hairless, and otherwise quite human in appearance. An autopsy had been performed on one of them to determine the cause of death. No cause for their deaths was ever found. Also at this time, they were shown three saucers which the Air Force has. He described them as ovoid, with a length of twenty-five feet and a width of thirteen feet. They were shown the interior as well, and there were no visible means of control, no visible means of propulsion. He told me that since that time, the Air Force has been working intensely, though unsuccessfully, at trying to discover the means of propulsion."

A MILITARY VETERAN SPEAKS
BECKENHAM, KENT, ENGLAND

An event occurred at Beckenham, Kent, England, in late August 1963 that bore all the hallmarks of an encounter with one of the famous Foo Fighters of the Second World War. And, notably, the witness had a military background: he had served during the hostilities of 1939-45 with an anti-aircraft detachment and until 1961 was attached to a territorial unit of the British Army.

As Mr. W. Hooper informed the Air Ministry:

"At 0150 hours on Tuesday the 27th August I was awakened by my wife to see what appeared to be something in flames falling from the sky, slightly N.W. of my house. This object appeared to be a ball of incandescent gas, red and black and was about a foot in diameter, and gave the impression of intense heat. It dropped like a stone from approximately 1000 to 500 feet, then stayed still for about 2-3 seconds, then started moving at an incredible speed in a Northerly direction and was out of sight in a matter of about 4 seconds. As it went away the wind brought a slight humming sound to us and the red and black appearance turned slightly yellow."

He continued: "I would be grateful if you could throw any light on the matter for me and would like especially to know if you had anything showing on your radar screens at the time I have stated. I am convinced that the object was powered as it travelled against the wind, and think what we saw may have been some sort of exhaust gas or flame."

Possibly anticipating that Whitehall would offer a totally down-to-earth explanation for what occurred, Mr. Hooper closed his letter thus: "I hope you will not try and persuade me that the object was a meteorological balloon as these as far as I know could not possibly travel against the wind."

In this particular case, Air Intelligence once again asserted that a solution had been found. Mr. Hooper, came back the conclusion, had been fooled by a "fireball." That the UFO had hovered in the air for two to three seconds was ignored by Air Intelligence; as was the fact that Mr. Hooper's anti-aircraft work during the Second World War would have given him first-class observational skills.

AUGUST 28, 1977

UFOS AND THE POLICE
CUMBRIA, ENGLAND

Shortly after midnight on Sunday, August 28, 1977, a large object – that fits the description of a specific type of UFO that has become known as the Flying Triangle – was seen by more than ten police officers and several members of the public in and around the Windermere area of Cumbria, England.

Sergeant James Trohear described the "triangular or slightly diamond-shaped" nature of the craft, while another officer commented that it "resembled the shape of a stingray fish." Meanwhile, Constable David Wild added that it was "very large and solid in construction."

It, like so many other sightings of a similar nature, was classified as unexplained.

"THEY FOUND THEMSELVES OUT IN A FIELD WITH NO MEMORY"

COLUMBUS, MISSISSIPPI

On This Day reveals the following: "At around 7:00 p.m. two soldiers in the air traffic control tower at the Army Air Corps Flying School in Columbus, Mississippi observed the rapid descent of two red round glowing objects that demonstrated extreme maneuverability and then hovered over the woods at the end of the runway. They next experienced an episode of missing time as well as sensory dislocation: they found themselves out in a field with no memory of how they got there."

CATTLE MUTILATION CONSPIRACIES

DENVER, COLORADO

There can be very few people – if, indeed, any – with an interest in UFOs, conspiracies, cover-ups, and strange and sinister goings-on of a distinctly weird nature who have not heard of the so-called "black helicopters" or "phantom helicopters" that seem to play an integral – albeit admittedly unclear – role in perceived UFO-connected events. And one of the biggest misconceptions about this deeply weird phenomenon is that those same mysterious helicopters are lacking in official documentation. Actually, not so at all. In fact, exactly the opposite. If you know where to go looking.

The FBI's now-declassified files on cattle-mutilations in 1970s America make for fascinating reading and demonstrate the Bureau had a deep awareness of the presence of the enigmatic helicopters in affairs of the mute kind. On August 30, 1975, Floyd K. Haskell, Senator for the State of Colorado, mailed an impassioned letter to Theodore P. Rosack, Special Agent in Charge of the FBI at Denver, Colorado, imploring the FBI to make a full investigation into the cattle mutilations, in an attempt to resolve the matter once and for all.

Haskell said: "For several months my office has been receiving reports of cattle mutilations throughout Colorado and other western states. At least 130 cases in Colorado alone have been reported to local officials and the Colorado Bureau of Investigation (CBI); the CBI has verified that the incidents have occurred for the last two years in nine states. The ranchers and rural residents of Colorado are concerned and frightened by these incidents. The bizarre mutilations are frightening in themselves: in virtually all the cases, the left ear, rectum and sex organ of each animal has been cut away and the blood drained from the carcass, but with no traces of blood left on the ground and no footprints."

The grisly mystery was never resolved – nor was the presence of those mysterious helicopters.

AUGUST 31, 1945

PERIL IN THE SKY
IWO JIMA, JAPAN

A particularly intriguing UFO report came from the late Leonard Stringfield, who, during the Second World War and its immediate aftermath, was attached to the US 5th Air Force in a military-intelligence capacity. On August 29, 1945, and while flying in a C46 over Iwo Jima, Japan at around 10,000 feet, Stringfield and the rest of the crew encountered a trio of teardrop- shaped UFOs that adversely affected the engines and navigation equipment of the aircraft and almost resulted in violent death for all aboard. Fortunately, as the UFOs exited the area, the pilot was able to regain control of the aircraft and disaster was averted.

It was this experience that led Stringfield to devote much of his post-military life to trying to unravel the complexities of the UFO mystery. Although Stringfield chiefly focused his investigations on reports of crashed UFOs held by the US Government, he continued to ponder on, and champion, his own encounter until his passing in 1994.

SEPTEMBER

SEPTEMBER 1, 1965

IMPELLED BY AN ALIEN

HUDANUCO, PERU

Around 5:00 a.m., a man named Serge Bourbot had a very weird encounter in Hudanuco, Peru. He witnessed a classic flying saucer-shaped UFO land on a private airstrip owned by a localrich businessman, whose spacious home stood adjacent to the small airstrip. As Bourbot stood frozen to the spot, and stared in wide-eyed fashion, a human-sized entity exited the craft. Human-sized except for one thing: its head, which was massively out of proportion.

When the creature saw Bourbot, it began waving its arms and pointing with its fingers – something which led to believe it was trying to communicate with him. Eventually, the thing gave up and returned to its craft. It was immediately bathed in a bright light and shot skywards in a vertical fashion.

Rather notably, Gordon Creighton – who, for many years, was the editor of *Flying Saucer Review* magazine - noted of this affair: "The interesting point is that, beforehand, the man had experienced a strange sensation which seemed to impel him to go to the spot where the craft landed."

A case of alien mind-control, perhaps?

SEPTEMBER 2, 2016

SKINNY AND SINISTER

GREENSBORO, NORTH CAROLINA

The Slender Man is a fictional character created in June 2009 by Eric Knudsen (using the alias of "Victor Surge," at the forum section of the *Something Awful* website), who took his inspiration from the world of horror fiction. The Slender Man (also spelled as Slender Man) is a creepy creature indeed: tall, thin, with long arms, a blank (faceless, even) expression, and wearing a dark suit, it sounds almost like a nightmarish version of the Men in Black of Ufology. While there is no doubt that Knudsen was the creator of what quickly became a definitive, viral, meme, people have since claimed to have seen the Slender Man in the *real* world.

In other words, so the theory goes, it's a case of believing in the existence of the Slender Man and, as a result, causing it to actually exist – which is very much akin to the phenomenon of the Tulpa. An entity is envisaged in the mind, and the imagery becomes so powerful and intense that it causes that same, mind-based imagery to emerge into the real world, with some degree of independent existence and self-awareness. Such a scenario may well explain why people are now seeing something that began as a piece of fiction.

One such witness is Martine, who encountered the Slender Man in her home in North Carolina in September 2016. It was late at night when Martine was disturbed in her sleep by what she described as a tall, thin, pale-faced man dressed in a black suit and who ominously whispered, "I can see you all the time," before vanishing into the darkness.

SEPTEMBER 3, 1987

A SLOW-MOVING "MISSILE"
NAVAN, IRELAND

The Connolly family of England, on vacation in Ireland, reported to the local police that while strolling through the green and pleasant hills of the country they caught sight if what they described as "a ten foot [long] missile" flying very slowly, around seventy feet from them, and at an extremely slow speed. The object was light brown in color and was, they thought, around fifteen to twenty feet in length. The report was taken very seriously, but not a single answer was forthcoming. The military were not missing any sophisticated aircraft. It didn't sound like what, today, we would call a typical drone. And no one else saw the strange craft, and nothing untoward came of the sighting. The mystery remained a mystery.

SEPTEMBER 4, 2016

A UFO WITH A HALO
YORKSHIRE, ENGLAND

On this day, the UK's *Sun* newspaper reported:

"A family out walking on a Yorkshire moorland claim to have captured a Star Trek-shaped UFO flying overhead. The dark grey object, which appears to have a halo around it, was snapped by Nicole Smith, 19, on her smartphone during a family day out to Bronte waterfalls, in West Yorkshire. She was with her parents Catherine and Shane at the time and was shocked when she discovered the UFO on one of her photos. Her mum Catherine, 49, from Normanton, said:

"'We went for a day out in Haworth and decided to drive to the moor and parked near a footpath leading to Bronte waterfalls. It was a good two and a half mile walk from where the car was parked. My daughter was taking random pictures of the sheep and scenery on our way back from the falls. It was around 5:30 p.m. when she took the picture on her mobile phone. It was only when we were on our way home she was scanning through the photos she had taken, she noticed the object in the picture.'"

SEPTEMBER 5, 2011

"YOU KNEW I WOULD COME"

NOVA SCOTIA, CANADA

Marc, who lives in Nova Scotia, had a strange encounter on the night at issue with an entity that sounds very much like the Slender Man encountered by Martine on September 2, 2016. He was in bed, awoken from his sleep, and terrified. The only difference: Marc's Slender Man was one-dimensional, like a shadow. It, too, however, spoke to Marc, saying in a low voice: "You knew I would come."

SEPTEMBER 6, 1994

BEWARE OF THE HAT MAN

LEONMINSTER, MASSACHUSSETS

The Hat Man is a Man in Black-type being that appears in shadowy form (not unlike the infamous Shadow People – to whom the Hat Man is almost certainly related, even if we're not sure why). On many occasions, however, the Hat Man appears in regular, human form, sporting a black beard and a black suit, and wearing a long overcoat or a cloak – almost always black, too. Most noticeable about this creepy figure is, of course, his hat. Sometimes, it's a fedora, other times it's an old style top hat. Occasionally, it's more like a cowboy hat. But, regardless of the kind of hat, it's always present. Many of the encounters occur while the victim is in a distinct altered state – that of sleeping.

Angie had just such an encounter in Leominster, Massachusetts, on September 6, 1994. Very much like those people unfortunate enough to be confronted by the Slender Man, Angie was sleeping when the foul thing disturbed her sleep by manifesting in her bedroom and staring at her with a menacing grin on its pale, ghoulish face. For a few moments, Angie was unable to move. As she finally broke the spell of paralysis, however, the Hat Man was gone.

SEPTEMBER 7, 1971

A BLUE GLOBE AT OKANAGAN LAKE

OKANAGAN LAKE, BRITISH COLUMBIA

In the same way that UFOs have been seen over monster-infested Loch Ness, Scotland, they have also been seen over Okanagan Lake, British Columbia. The witnesses were the Shelley family from New Hampshire who were actually at the lake hoping to catch a sight of the legendary monster. Instead, they encountered something very different but no less amazing.

As they scoured the lake with binoculars for Ogopogo, they were amazed to see a large ball of blue light race across the stretch of lake in front of them, at a very low level above the surface of the water. Most amazing of all, as they continued to watch the blue globe, it suddenly plunged into the water, never to be seen again.

SEPTEMBER 8, 1957

UFO FRAGMENTS UNDER THE MICROSCOPE

UBATUBA NEAR SAO PAULO, BRAZIL

Midway through 1957, Brazil's *O Globo* newspaper reported on the mid-air explosion of a UFO over a beach near Ubatuba, Sao Paulo, Brazil. The letter-writer said that the flying saucer-shaped craft "…disintegrated into thousands of fiery fragments, which fell sparkling with magnificent brightness... most of these fragments, almost all, fell into the sea. But a number of small pieces fell close to the beach and we picked up a large amount of this material, which was as light as paper... I am enclosing a sample of it..."

UFO investigator John Harney said: "The material was given a spectrographic analysis and the report merely indicated that this showed the presence of magnesium of a high degree of purity and absence of any other metallic element...A second spectrographic test confirmed the first result. Other samples were later analyzed using more refined techniques."

Harney adds that researchers came to the conclusion "... the magnesium was of a higher degree of purity than could be obtained by any refining processes known at that time."

Were the fragments from an exploded UFO, a military missile, aircraft, or something akin to a meteorite? The answers still elude the UFO research community. We'll close with the words of Jim and Coral Lorenzen of the Aerial Phenomena Research Organization: "That the material is not 100 percent pure magnesium does not lessen the impact of the case, for we still have to explain how that magnesium got to a remote beach area at that time. What manner of machine was the shiny disc-shaped object that exploded?"

SEPTEMBER 9, 1960

"WE ARE NOT ALLOWED TO RELEASE INFORMATION"
NEWCASTLE, ENGLAND

On this night, a UFO − described as a "triangular formation of lights with a red light in the center" − was viewed by various people in and around the city of Newcastle, England. Leslie Otley stated that he and his wife, along with two neighbors, saw the strange craft sometime after 9:00 p.m.

After having been firmly pressed by the *Newcastle Evening Chronicle* newspaper for a comment, a spokesperson for the Royal Air Force admitted that he had received a pair of reports of the UFO seen over Newcastle and confirmed they had been dispatched to the Air Ministry at London for scrutiny.

In a slightly conspiratorial fashion, he added: "I have no further information about this, and even if I had, we are not allowed to release information."

SEPTEMBER 10, 1982

ENDANGERED SPECIES
ON DEMAND

Directed and co-written by Alan Rudolph, *Endangered Species* hit cinemas in the United States on this day. It focuses on one Ruben Castle (actor Robert Urich). He's a Big Apple-based police-officer. He has a major drink problem. And, his relationship with his daughter, Mackenzie (Marin Kanter) is rocky, to say the least. So, something has to give. And it does. Castle decides that the best thing he can do is to get out of New York for a while, quit the bottle for good, and try and mend fences with his daughter. It doesn't quite work out like that, however.

After arriving in a small Colorado town, specifically one where an old friend in the world of newspapers, Joe Hiatt (played by Paul Dooley) lives and works, both Castle and his daughter cause problems for the local police.

In no time at all, Castle learns that something very strange is going on in town and in the surrounding fields of local farmers.

Cattle have been found killed under very strange circumstances. Organs are removed with what appears to be expert precision. Incisions seem to have been achieved by nothing less than lasers. Everyone in town is on edge. Ranchers are angry and outraged. That's hardly surprising, given that there is talk of UFOs skulking around in the dead of night.

I won't spoil things by revealing the outcome, and who – or what – is really mutilating cattle in Colorado and elsewhere. And why. I will, however, say that this is a well-made, largely engrossing, movie.

SEPTEMBER 11, 1976

MAN IN BLACK TERROR
ORCHARD BEACH, MAINE

That was the decidedly ill-fated evening upon which the Orchard Beach, Maine, home of a certain Dr. Herbert Hopkins was darkened by a nightmarish MIB – an event that was soon followed by the appearance of a very odd woman. Vampire-like scarcely begins to describe the terrible thing that descended on Hopkins' home on that fraught night. When Hopkins opened the front door, he was confronted by a pale-faced, skinny, bald ghoul; one that was dressed in black, had dark and hostility-filled eyes, and sported the de rigueur Fedora hat.

The MIB made it very clear, and extremely quickly, that if Hopkins knew what was good for him he would immediately cease all of his then-current research into the life and experiences of a reported alien abductee: David Stephens, who lived in nearby Oxford. Hopkins, frozen to the bone, didn't need telling twice. Just for good measure, the undeniably malevolent MIB – in monotone fashion – told Hopkins to take out of the right pocket of his pants one of the two coins that was in there and hold it in the open palm of his hand. Hopkins didn't even think to wonder how the MIB knew the coins were there; he just did as he was told.

With a detectable threat in his robotic voice, the MIB ordered Hopkins to keep his eyes locked on the coin, which he did. To Hopkins' amazement and horror, something terrifying happened: the coin transmuted. It turned blue in color, shimmered slightly – as if in a mini heat-haze – and then, in a second or so, became 100 percent vaporous. After a few moments the vapor was gone. The MIB implied that he could do exactly the same thing to Hopkins' heart. Hopkins got the message. The MIB shuffled his curious way to the door and vanished – as in *literally* – into the chilled night.

SEPTEMBER 12, 1952

A MONSTER, A UFO, AND A FRIGHTENED TOWN
FLATWOODS, WEST VIRGINIA

Within the domains of Cryptozoology and Ufology the saga of the so-called Flatwoods Monster, or Braxton County Monster, of 1952 has become legendary. It's a story that has been extensively investigated by Frank Feschino. In his 2004 book, *The Braxton County Monster: the Cover-Up of the Flatwoods Monster Revealed*. Feschino noted: "On the night of September 12, 1952, a shocked American public sought answers when strange unidentified objects were seen flying through the sky over Washington, DC, and the eastern United States."

He continued: "One of the strange objects crash-landed on a rural hilltop in Flatwoods, West Virginia." Feschino also noted that a group of schoolboys were witness to the descent of the device and, with two adults, "headed off to look for the object."

According to the witnesses, however, far more than a UFO was seen. A definitive monster, estimated to be around twelve feet tall, was about to put in an appearance. UFO authority Kevin Randle said: "What they saw was not an animal, but some sort of creature, at least in their perception…They could see no arms or legs, but did see a head that was shaped like an ace of spades. That was a description that would reoccur with all these witnesses. No one was sure if there were eyes on the creature, or if there was a clear space on the head, resembling a window, and that the eyes were somehow behind the that window and behind the face."

Not surprisingly, the group fled, terrified to their collective core. And although a veritable posse returned to seek out the beast from the dark skies, it had utterly vanished. The legend, however, most certainly remains, nearly sixty years later. The people of Flatwoods have not forgotten that trauma-filled night in September 1952.

SEPTEMBER 13, 1966

"BURNT MARKS AND TAPERED HOLES"
NAVAN, IRELAND

Think About It says: "Young Randy E. Rotenberger was waiting for the school bus outside his home when he saw 'some flashing lights,' then an object. 'It looked like two bowls put together,' the witness told an AP reporter. He saw three 'pegs' on the bottom and antennae projecting from the top. Later, 'some burnt marks' and tapered holes were found at the scene, each about a foot in diameter and five inches deep."

SEPTEMBER 14, 2015

A READER SPEAKS

DALLAS, TEXAS

One of the people whose MIB experiences feature in my *Men in Black* book is a friend of mine named Steve Ray. After reading the book, just a few days after it was published, Steve experienced something weird, too. In his very own words: "I read the whole Kindle version of the book Sunday and Monday. Monday night I came home and found two black cars parked – headlights out – in non-assigned spaces directly facing my assigned parking space. When I came upstairs, I found my living-room lamp had been switched from its normal setting to the spookier black-light setting – which I have no memory of doing, and I was the last one here."

I told Steve I was not surprised. He was not comforted by my words; not at all. He wasn't meant to be: I tell it as it is, good, bad or dangerous.

SEPTEMBER 15, 1962

A UFO AND A MONSTER

AVEBURY, ENGLAND

The witness to this particularly weird case was a middle-aged lady who had lived in the small village of Avebury, England all of her adult life and who was fascinated by archaeological history. A "spinster," (as the now-declassified British Royal Air Force files describe her) she would often stroll among Avebury's famous Stonehenge-like formations at night, marveling at their creation and musing upon their history. It was on the night in question that she had been out walking at around 10:30 p.m. when she was both startled and amazed to see a small ball of light, perhaps two-feet in diameter, gliding slowly through the stones – a definitive UFO. Transfixed and rooted to the spot, she watched as it closed in on her at a height of about twelve feet. The ball then stopped fifteen feet or so from her, and small amounts of what looked like liquid metal slowly and silently dripped from it to the ground. Then, in an instant, the ball exploded in a bright, white flash.

For a moment she was blinded by its intensity and instinctively fell to her knees. When her eyes cleared, however, she was faced with a horrific sight. The ball of light had gone, but on the ground in front of her was what she could only describe as a monstrous, writhing worm.

The creature, she said, was about five feet long, perhaps eight or nine inches thick, and its skin was milk-white. As she slowly rose to her feet, the creature's head turned suddenly in her direction and two bulging eyes opened. When it began to move unsteadily towards her in a caterpillar-like fashion, she emitted a hysterical scream and fled the scene. Rushing back home, she slammed the door shut and frantically called the airbase, after having been directed to them by the less-than-impressed local police.

The Royal Air Force's Provost and Security Services dispatched an officer early the next day to interview the woman – amid much hilarity on the part of the man's colleagues, all of whom thought that the story was someone's idea of a joke. On returning, however, the officer colleague had a very serious and grim look on his face. Whatever had taken place, it was definitely no hoax.

SEPTEMBER 16, 1963

"I AT FIRST TOOK IT TO BE A PLANE BUT THE LIGHT WAS TOO BRIGHT"

COUNTY DURHAM, ENGLAND

On this date, Flight Lieutenant A.J. Brown of RAF Middleton St. George, near Darlington, England received details of an encounter with an unidentified aerial intruder reported by one O. Filon of County Durham. Undercover of a "Restricted" memorandum forwarded to Whitehall, London, Flt. Lt. Brown mailed a copy of Mr. Filon's report, which read thus:

"At approximately 10.25 p.m. last night (sun. 15th) my son called me into his bedroom. He pointed out a light looking exactly like a star. It was moving towards us in what appeared a very slow fashion. I at first took it to be a plane but the light was too bright and it appeared to be at a great height. The light then appeared to be zig zagging. Not as an aircraft would, i.e. with a bank or curve at each new leg of flight, but with an immediate change of direction.

"When almost overhead the light underwent a course change of approx. 90 degrees. The line of flight was again constant and it headed away in an E.S.E. direction. After a short time it appeared stationary. This was for maybe three to four minutes. The light suddenly appeared to go out, then just for a fraction of a second it seemed to be dark blue, then it was gone.

"The only conclusion I can make out is that it was moving outwards! The whole thing lasted for approx. 15 mins. and was seen by my wife, my son and myself."

And there was also this: "I would like to point out that during the war I was a radar operator, a trained supervisor, one of six selected for the whole of the M.E. Command."

NATO, THE CIA, AND UFOS

KENT, ENGLAND

In September 1952, NATO held a large-scale military exercise in the North Sea and English Channel. Its name: Mainbrace. During the week long exercise numerous UFO sightings were made by military personnel. One of those was William Maguire, whose encounter occurred on September 17. At the time, he was stationed at RAF Sandwich, Kent. Maguire speaks of his memories of how staff at the base tracked on radar the movements of a gigantic UFO hovering over the sea:

"My memory was that everything was in a complete flap. Normally, in a military situation everything is ordered, regular and set out. But here was a situation that was plainly out of control. Mechanics were flying about all over the place.

"The mechanics were being blamed for not calibrating the instruments properly; we were being blamed for not interpreting the readings correctly. Every single instrument on the base was showing this enormous object sitting up at an unbelievable height. It was the size of a warship and it just stood there."

Now we move on to the world of the CIA: As part of their monitoring of foreign press agencies, the CIA obtained a copy of a newspaper clipping concerning another incident that occurred on September 18. Published in a Harstad, Norway newspaper, a CIA translation of the article reads as follows:

"On 18 September, at 1400 hours, three forestry workers who were working right outside Kirknes, noticed a flat, round object hovering motionless at about 500 meters altitude. The object appeared to have a diameter of 15-20 meters. After the workers had observed the object for a while, it suddenly flew away at great speed in a northwesterly direction. It appears that only these workers saw the object; they swear, however, that their report is true."

SEPTEMBER 18, 1954

GREEN FIREBALLS IN THE SKIES

NEW MEXICO, COLORADO, TEXAS

In his classic book, *The Report on Unidentified Flying Objects*, Captain Edward J.Ruppelt, of the U.S. Air Force's UFO program, Project Blue Book, wrote: "At exactly midnight on September 18, 1954, my telephone rang. It was Jim Phalen, a friend of mine from the *Long Beach Press-Telegram*, and he had a 'good flying saucer report,' hot off the wires. He read it to me. The lead line was: 'Thousands of people saw a huge fireball light up dark New Mexico skies tonight.'

"The story went on to tell about how a 'blinding green' fireball the size of a full moon had silently streaked southeast across Colorado and northern New Mexico at eight-forty that night. Thousands of people had seen the fireball. It had passed right over a crowded football stadium in Santa Fe, New Mexico, and people in Denver said it 'turned night into day.' The crew of a TWA airliner flying into Albuquerque from Amarillo, Texas, saw it. Every police and newspaper switchboard in the two-state area was jammed with calls.

"One of the calls was from a man inquiring if anything unusual had happened recently. When he was informed about the mysterious fireball he heaved an audible sigh of relief, 'Thanks,' he said, 'I was afraid I'd gotten some bad bourbon.' And he hung up.

"Dr. Lincoln La Paz, world-famous authority on meteorites

and head of the University of New Mexico's Institute of Meteor-
itics, apparently took the occurrence calmly. The wire story said he
had told a reporter that he would plot its course, try to determine
where it landed, and go out and try to find it. 'But,' he said, 'I don't
expect to find anything.'

"When Jim Phalen had read the rest of the report he asked,
'What was it?'"

"It sounds to me like the green fireballs are back," I answered.

"What the devil are green fireballs?"

"What the devil *are* green fireballs? I'd like to know. So would
a lot of other people. The green fireballs streaked into UFO history
late in November 1948, when people around Albuquerque, New
Mexico, began to report seeing mysterious 'green flares' at night."

They continued to perplex the Air Force, the government,
and the media for more than a year.

SEPTEMBER 19, 1961

THE WORLD'S MOST FAMOUS ALIEN ABDUCTION

A HIGHWAY IN NEW HAMPSHIRE

On the night of September 19, 1961, Betty and Barney Hill, a
New Hampshire couple, were driving home from vacationing
in Canada when they were subjected to a terrifying experience.
Despite viewing some form of unusual aerial object in the night
sky, and what appeared to be living entities that could be seen
through the craft's portals, until their arrival back home, the Hill's
had little indication that there was far more to the encounter than
they realized.

It later transpired, however, that approximately two-hours of
time could not be accounted for.

After months of emotional distress, sleepless nights, and strange dreams pertaining to encounters with unusual, otherworldly beings, the couple finally sought assistance from Benjamin Simon, a Boston-based psychiatrist and neurologist. Subjected to time-regression hypnosis, both Betty and Barney recalled what had taken place during that missing 120-minutes or so.

Significantly, they provided very close accounts of encounters with apparent alien creatures that took the pair on-board some form of alien vehicle and subjected them to a series of physical examinations – a number of which were highly distressing in nature.

The experience of the Hill's later became the subject of John Fuller's now-classic book, *The Interrupted Journey* and a 1975 movie of the same name. Although claims have been made that the phenomenon long pre-dates the Hill affair, it was certainly this incident that paved the way for the massive interest in abductions and missing time phenomena that ultimately developed in the 1980s and 1990s.

SEPTEMBER 20, 1957

"ESPECIALLY INTRIGUING"

GULFPORT, MISSISSIPPI, THROUGH LOUISIANA AND TEXAS

According to UFO researcher James McDonald: "An Air Force RB-47, equipped with ECM (Electronic Countermeasures) gear, manned by six officers, was followed over a total distance in excess of 600 miles and for a time period of more than an hour, as it flew from near Gulfport, Miss., through Louisiana and Texas, and into southern Oklahoma. The unidentified object was, at various times, seen visually by the cockpit crew (as an intense white or red light), followed by ground-radar, and detected on ECM monitoring gear aboard the RB-47. Simultaneous appearances and disappearances on all three of those physically distinct 'channels' mark this UFO case as especially intriguing from a scientific viewpoint."

SEPTEMBER 21, 1951

A SHIP-SIZED UFO CAUGHT ON RADAR
FORT MONMOUTH, NEW JERSEY

An FBI document of September 21, 1951, and captioned "Flying Saucers," reads as follows: "On September 20, Andrew J. Reid G-2 [Army Intelligence] Ft. Monmouth, NJ, provided following report of unconventional aircraft observed by radar at above Army installation. On Sept 10, fifty one [sic], an AN/MPG-1 radar set picked up a fast moving low flying target, exact altitude undetermined at approximately 11:10 a.m., southeast of Ft. Monmouth at a range of about twelve thousand yards. The target appeared to approximately follow the coastline, changing its range only slightly but changing its azimuth rapidly. The radar set was set to full aided azimuth tracking which normally is fast enough to track jet aircraft, but in this case was too slow to be resorted to. Target was lost in the N.E. at a range of about fourteen thousand yards."

The story gets even more controversial, as the next part of the report makes very clear: "This target also presented an unusually strong return for aircraft [,] *being comparable in strength to that usually received from a coastal ship* [italics mine]. The operator initially identified target as a ship and then realized that it could not be a ship after he observed its extreme speed. September 10, fifty one [sic] an SCR–584 radar set, at 3:15 p.m., tracking a target which moved about slowly in azimuth north of Ft. Monmouth at a range of about 42,000 yards at extremely unusual elevation angle."

In no time at all, a second radar operator was tracking the movements of the "coastal ship"-sized UFO. The file states: "Both sets found it impossible to track the target in range due to it speed and the operators had to resort to manual range tracking in order to hold the target. The target was tracked in this manner to the maximum tracking range of 32,000 yards. The operator said the target to be moving at a speed several hundred mph higher than the maximum aided tracking ability of the radar sets. The target provided an extremely strong return echo at times even though it was the maximum range. However, echo signal occasionally fell off to a level below normal return. These changes coincided with maneuvers of the target."

The strange and sensational affair received nothing in the way of a satisfactory explanation.

SEPTEMBER 22, 1952

MY FATHER (ALMOST) ENCOUNTERS A UFO

NORFOLK, ENGLAND

Like the majority of young men in Britain in the 1950s, my father was required to serve a three-year-term in the military under British National Service regulations (the Draft, in the U.S.). Because of his keen interest in aviation, he chose the Royal Air Force. During his service with the RAF (after which he returned to his regular job as a carpenter), he was posted to various RAF stations. By far the most memorable experience of his career, however, occurred near the East Coast of England at a base called RAF Neatishead, Norfolk. It was September 1952 and my father was working as a radar mechanic.

He told me that during a September 1952 NATO exercise

– *Mainbrace* – several UFO incidents occurred over the course of three nights. And, as a radar mechanic, he was brought in to check there were no problems with the sets; problems that might have led to false readings. It turns out there were no problems at all: they were all working fine. All was normal until the early hours of September 20. We're talking about somewhere between 4:00 a.m. and 5:00 a.m. Something was picked up on the radar moving fast; as in extremely fast, and at a height of around 50,000 feet. It was flying parallel to the English coastline.

Although the object was clearly out of the ordinary, the first thought was that it had to be a sneak penetration of British airspace by the Russians. This would have made sense, as the Reds were surely keen to keep a careful watch on *Mainbrace*, given that it was a huge exercise, involving thousands of personnel from numerous NATO nations. My father recalls that an official report on the incident went up the chain of command, but he was not told of the conclusion reached – if, indeed, *any* conclusion was reached. Things didn't end there, however: there were other invasions of British airspace across the following two nights. And, when the story was told to me, as a young boy, I was instantly hooked.

SEPTEMBER 23, 1981

A SWAYING UFO

BRIXHAM, ENGLAND

The Bakewell family of Woodbridge, Suffolk, England were on vacation in the Devon, England town of Brixham when they saw a UFO off the coastline, hovering at a height of around a couple of hundred feet above the cliffs on which they were standing. It was circular in shape, silver in color, and swayed from side to side.

Although the UFO was only in sight for a few moments – it quickly vanished into the clouds above – it was there long enough for the entire family to conclude they saw an alien spacecraft.

SEPTEMBER 24, 1949

"THE OBJECT OFFERED AN ECHO SIMILAR TO THAT OF A LARGE PASSENGER OR FREIGHT SURFACE VESSEL"

KENT, ENGLAND

Operation Bulldog – held in September 1949, and overseen by the UK's Fighter and Bomber commands – was a show of strength to the Soviets. It demonstrated that the West could take swift and decisive action in the event the Russians flexed their muscles a bit too much. And, for good measure, the operation also involved the air-forces of the United States, Belgium, France, and Holland. The Soviets took careful and concerned notice, which was the whole point. It appears it was not just the Russians that kept a beady eye on the military maneuvers. Just possibly, entities from another world did likewise.

At the time Bulldog was held, the late J.R. Oliver was a radar-operator at a British Royal Air Force base called Sandwich, which was situated in the English county of Kent. Oliver said: "Even so long ago, it was almost impossible to fly a glider across the [English] Channel without it being plotted. The exercise was structured in such a way that the technical resources and personnel of the defensive screen were stretched to the limit."

Oliver added that the staff of RAF Sandwich "were fully skilled and right on top of their job. Two watches were kept, A and B, on alternate twelve-hour shifts for the duration of Bulldog." According to Oliver on one particular night, around midnight, "things had gone slack," and his group was told it could "take a break." It was a break that didn't last for long, as Oliver noted:

"Within about fifteen minutes, the PBX operator came in, approached the Duty Controller and advised him that Beachy Head radar was passing a plot to us on a large flying object and would we track it?" They did exactly that. It became very clear, and very quickly, that this was no ordinary aircraft. Oliver recalled: "Reaching a position out to sea off the 'heel' of Kent, it abruptly turned north and as it approached the Thames estuary we passed it on to Martlesham radar, with whom we had been in contact."

Oliver offered something remarkable: "Flying at close to 50,000 feet, the air speed of the object we had observed and plotted in accordance with RAF standard procedures was assessed at very nearly 3,000 miles per hour. The general consensus regarding its size, among the very best experienced radar personnel engaged in the operations, was that the object offered an echo similar to that of a large passenger or freight surface vessel, something in the region of 15,000 or 20,000 tons."

In typical British understatement, Oliver said there was "quite a bit of buzz about this."

SEPTEMBER 25, 1999

A TERRIFYING VISION
HOUSTON, TEXAS

Houston, Texas was the location on which Bill Rice, who worked as a private detective and who was in town on business, had a strange encounter while driving along a stretch of highway around 10:00 a.m. As he headed along the highway, the view before him suddenly changed. Instead of seeing the regular city in front of him, it was briefly replaced by a horrific image of the city destroyed, the sky dark, and a huge atomic mushroom cloud looming ominously in the background. World War Three had clearly begun. Strangest of all, squadrons of flying saucers soared across the sky, like furious bugs, and which added to the apocalyptic imagery by zapping the irradiated survivors with laser-like weaponry. In seconds, however, Rice's vision was over and normality was restored. To this day, Rice believes he saw a brief glimpse of the future; a dark glimpse of a nuclear war involving aliens.

SEPTEMBER 26, 1963

"THEY WERE THEN SEEN TO ORBIT OVERHEAD FOR SOME TEN MINUTES"

PETERBOROUGH, ENGLAND

On this day, a UFO incident took place at Peterborough, England, that involved both civilian and military witnesses. The facts were set forth in a two-page Restricted report from Sergeant T.G.M. Kendall at RAF Wittering, Northants., who graphically relayed to the Air Ministry what took place; and since this particular report is of some significance, I reproduce its contents in total:

"Sir, I have the honor to report the following facts for your consideration. I was NCO in charge [of the] Operations Room at 2240 hours on 26th September, 1963 when I received a telephone call from Mr. STRICKSON of [witness's address] who, in company with Mr. QUANTRELL of the same address, saw what he considered to be two unidentified flying objects. The objects were in view in the first instance from 2000-2100 hours.

"During that time two orange colored balls of light travelled from the South to the East in a zig-zag fashion, then were seen again moving from West to East. They were then seen to orbit overhead for some ten minutes during which time three or four objects left the two first mentioned and then rejoined them. Mr. Strickson was not able to estimate the range or the altitude of the sightings, but considered them to be higher than an aeroplane but lower than a star."

SEPTEMBER 27, 1994

A MYSTERIOUS CRASH
BOSCOMBE DOWN, ENGLAND

In the early hours of the morning, all hell metaphorically broke loose when an unusual vehicle crash-landed on the runway at the UK Government's highly sensitive Boscombe Down facility. As rumors began to circulate among the UFO research community and the media, numerous theories were put forth attempting to explain the case: that the object was a UFO, that it was some form of next-generation Stealth aircraft; or that it was one of the so-called Flying Triangles that have been reported throughout the planet for the last several decades.

Unusual things had been afoot in the immediate vicinity of Boscombe Down in the build-up to the crash of 26 September. Only weeks before, the *Salisbury Times* newspaper reported the following concerning an incident practically on the doorstep of Boscombe Down:

"A green flying saucer hovered beside the A303 road at Deptford last week – according to a lorry driver who rushed to Salisbury Police Station in the early hours of the morning. The man banged on the station door in Wilton Road at 1.30 a.m. on Thursday after spotting the saucer suspended in mid-air. 'He was 100 per cent convinced it was a UFO,' said Inspector Andy Shearing.

"The man said it was bright green and shaped like a triangle with rounded edges. Other drivers had seen it and were flashing their car lights at him. A patrol car took the lorry driver back to the spot but there was no trace of the flying saucer. Inspector Shearing said police had been alerted about similar sightings in the same area in the past."

Neither the crash-landing at Boscombe Down or the encounter on the A303 road has ever been explained – at least, not publicly.

SEPTEMBER 28, 1984

"TOO AMAZED TO BE SCARED"
ADELAIDE, AUSTRALIA

Adelaide, Australia was the site of a profoundly odd encounter reported by Sam. As she walked home from a late shift at the restaurant she worked for at the time, she almost stumbled into what she described as a "little man," about two feet tall, who raced across the quiet road and who was dressed in a silver, one-piece suit – and a large helmet. He vanished into a nearby alleyway. Sam says she was "too amazed to be scared" by the weird experience.

SEPTEMBER 29, 2015

A "TELEPHONE POLE"-STYLE UFO
BROWN MOUNTAINS, NORTH CAROLINA

While on vacation in North Carolina, Dawn Todd, an Irish woman, saw what she described as a "rocket" flying impossibly slowly across the Brown Mountains, which at the time she was hiking along, on what was a pleasant morning. Even though the rocket-like thing made absolutely no noise at all, Todd felt suddenly, and eerily, compelled to look up. On doing so she saw the object – somewhere in the region of twenty-feet in length – directly above her. She described it as a "telephone pole on its side," and said that it was in sight for just a few seconds, after which it shot away at high speed and vanished into the distance.

SEPTEMBER 30, 1972

DEAD ALIENS OR A LOYALTY TEST?
WRIGHT-PATTERSON AIR FORCE BASE, DAYTON, OHIO

On this day, Marion – a resident of Dayton, Ohio – confided in her sister that her husband, who worked at nearby Wright-Patterson Air Force Base, came home from work the previous night looking pale and in a near-panic state. When Marion finally got her husband to open up, he claimed that he had been shown photographs of three dead aliens held in a vault-like room deep below the base. All three bodies were small and had large heads. The bodies were very badly damaged, as if they had been in a violent accident. Oddly, the man's superior officer merely told him to think about the photos and nothing more. Whether the photos were the real deal, some strange loyalty test, or a bizarre operation to see if the man could keep his mouth shut, Marion never knew – and neither did her husband.

OCTOBER

OCTOBER 1, 1997

ANIMAL MUTILATIONS AND A UFO IN THE SEA
LYME BAY, EXMOUTH, ENGLAND

It all began on October 1, 1997, as the journal of a British UFO investigator and good friend, Nigel Wright, makes very clear:

"Approximately three weeks ago two young men were swimming in Otter Cove [Lyme Bay, Exmouth, England]. As darkness drew in, they decided to make for the shore and change to go home. As they got changed, one of them looked out to sea. He saw what he described as a 'greenish' light under the surface. He called to the other young man and they both watched as this light 'rose' to the surface of the water. The next thing they knew there was a very bright light shining into their faces. They turned the scene and fled."

Meanwhile, on the top of the cliffs, equally strange things were afoot. The two young men raced for the car of a relative and breathlessly explained what had happened. Incredibly, she, too, had seen something highly unusual in precisely the same time frame on the road leading to Otter Cove: a strange animal that she likened to "an enormous cat." Whatever the origin of the beast, however, she was certain of one thing: it was, to quote her, "all lit up" – glowing almost.

On the following day, a dead whale was found washed upon the beach below the cliffs. This did not appear to have been merely a tragic accident, however. Rumors quickly circulated that the culprit was the monstrous–glowing, cat-like thing. On receiving reports that a whale had been found in precisely the area that anomalous lights and a strange creature were seen, Wright launched an investigation.

"The first thing that struck me as I looked on at this scene," recalls Wright, "was how perfect the carcass was. There was no decay or huge chunks torn from it. Then, as I wandered around it, I noticed that there was only one external wound: in the area of the genitals a round incision, the size of a large dinner plate, was cut right into the internal organs of the mammal. The sides of this incision were perfectly formed, as if some giant apple corer had been inserted and twisted around. From the wound hung some of the internal organs."

Wright continues: "I quizzed the official from English Heritage, who was responsible for the disposal of the carcass. He informed me that no natural predator or boat strike would have caused this wound. As I looked at this sight, the first thing that came into my mind was how this looked just like the cattle mutilation cases of recent times."

OCTOBER 2, 1961
"IT APPEARED AS A BICONVEX METALLIC GRAY OBJECT"
CENTRAL UTAH

From the files of James McDonald:

"A private pilot, Mr. Waldo J. Harris, was taking off on Runway 160 at Utah Central Airport at almost exactly noon on 10/2/61 when he noted what he at first idly viewed as a distant airplane. He noted it again in the same area just after becoming airborne, once more after gaining some altitude, and then became somewhat puzzled that it had not exhibited any appreciable change of position. About then it seemed to tilt, glinting in the noonday sun, and exhibiting a shape unlike any aircraft. To get a better view, Harris climbed towards the southeast and found himself at its altitude when he was somewhat above 6000 feet. By then it appeared as a biconvex metallic gray object, decidedly different from conventional aircraft, so he radioed back to the airport, where eventually seven persons were taking turns viewing it with binoculars. I have interviewed not only Harris, but also Jay W. Galbraith, operator of the airport, who, with his wife, watched the object, and Robert G. Butler, another of those at the airport. As Harris attempted to close in, he got to a minimal distance that he thought might have been approximately two or three miles from the object, when it abruptly rose vertically by about 1000 feet, a maneuver confirmed by the ground witnesses."

OCTOBER 3, 1980

ALIENS DOWN IN THE ANDES

PIEDRA DEL AQUILA, NEUQUEN PROVINCE, ARGENTINA

Bob Pratt uncovered intriguing data on a UFO crash in the Andes in late 1980; around 1,400 miles from the site of the Bolivian UFO crash of May 1978. In this case, the country was Argentina. Pratt said of this particular event:

"This one was near Piedra del Aguila in Neuquen Province. Witnesses for three hundred miles around saw what appeared to be a fireball come down and explode about seven o'clock at night on October 3, 1980. One witness said it was saucer-shaped. People close to the area said the object flew low and slowly in perfect circles, almost hitting a hill, something a meteor wouldn't do.

"Two minutes later, an explosion was heard and one man said his furniture shook. A second explosion occurred a minute or two later and a tall column of white smoke rose into the sky. Newsmen who flew over the area reported seeing two fires about five hundred yards apart, with a bluish-green circular area between the two.

"Captain Carlos Lima, then head of the Space Research Division of the Argentine Air Force, officially investigated the incident. He first flew over the area in a plane and then went there in a helicopter. He found four burned spots, each almost circular and ten to eighteen meters in diameter that appeared, in Captain Lima's words, 'to be the product of combustion originated by liquid fuel or some sort of material with a very high temperature. Even with the rare vegetation in the area, which has a very soft soil like sand, the ground was completely burned to a depth of about two centimeters.'"

In his official report on the incident, Captain Lima wrote: "What they observed was a fiery object appearing to be about forty centimeters in diameter that was discharging black smoke and moving at great speed. It went into a cluster of clouds and when it came out it looked smaller and left a trace of white smoke. About three minutes later, there was a loud explosion and the echo shook the ground and windows in all the houses around."

Interestingly, Pratt added: "Captain Lima took soil samples from the burned area but the results of any analyses have never been released."

OCTOBER 4, 1972

A UFO AND STRANGE DREAMS
STAFFORDSHIRE, ENGLAND

British Royal Air Force Provost and Security Services files – now officially in the public domain – tell a strange story of the Morris family that was driving near the Staffordshire, England village of Barton-Under-Needwood, at some time after 11:00 p.m. They claimed to have seen a small, metallic-looking UFO that was hovering in the road in front of them at a height of about three or four feet. They were forced to bring their car to a quick halt, and stared, amazed, as the object silently floated before them – at least, for around twenty seconds, after which the UFO shot into the sky.

Notably, all of the family had strange dreams the night following the incident – George Price having dreamed of being taken aboard a UFO and his wife, Sheila, having a nightmare of seeing a creepy, small, humanoid creature standing by the car. Deeply repressed memories of an alien abduction? Very possibly.

OCTOBER 5, 1996

THERE'S SOMETHING IN THE SKY
SKEGNESS, ENGLAND

It was in the early hours of the morning that an extraordinary radio conversation occurred between police at Skegness, England, personnel based at Royal Air Force Kinloss, and the crew of a North Sea tanker, the *Conocoast*. Transcripts of the conversation have been officially declassified via the UK's Freedom of Information Act and tell an intriguing story.

At 3:14 a.m., Skegness Police said: "We can see a strange red-and-green rotating light in the sky directly south-east from Skegness. It looks strange as it is stationary and there is no aircraft sound in the area."

Then, at 3:46 a.m., the crew of the *Conocast* reported the following: "We have these lights on visual. Now they are flashing red, green and white. Cannot identify it as an aircraft as it looks stationary and it is approximately one mile high."

Seven minutes later, RAF Kinloss had the following to say: "Well, Neatishead and Northwood report that there is no transponder on this object and therefore no means of interrogation. It is obvious that whatever it is it does not want anyone to know that it is there."

"It is still stationary and flashing red, green, blue and white. It looks very high, north of us, and there is no engine noise," stated the captain of the *Conocoast* at 4:08 a.m.

"Neatishead are running a trace on this and cannot explain it," noted RAF Kinloss at 5:21 a.m. "If they are helicopters they are fast approaching the end of their endurance as it is well over two hours since the first report, let alone how long they have been up there before they were actually sighted."

The mystifying evens continued, but with no definitive answer in sight.

OCTOBER 6, 1953

A FROG-LIKE ALIEN
ASHEVILLE, NORTH CAROLINA

Asheville, North Carolina was the location of a very strange encounter that involved a truck-driver, who reported the incident to staff at Fort Bragg. The story is only mentioned as an aside in available records, but reveals that the agitated driver claimed to have seen an approximately four-foot-tall entity − resembling a person in shape but with a frog-like head − standing by the edge of a road as he exited town in the early hours of the morning. The man claimed that his headlights clearly lit up the creature, something which left him in no doubt about what he encountered. Of interest, the man claimed that only seconds after he passed the strange entity, he saw a blue streak cross the sky directly in front of his truck.

"INFORMATION CONCERNING BEINGS FROM
OUTER SPACE"

DALLAS, TEXAS

An intriguing 1960s-era UFO case – the details of which surfaced via FOIA and that has undoubted Contactee overtones to it – can be found in the now-declassified UFO files of the FBI. Dating from October 10, 1967, the report – prepared by a special-agent of the FBI – reads as follows and describes the contents of a statement the woman prepared on October 7, two days earlier:

"A young while female, who refused to give her name, appeared at the Dallas [Texas] FBI Office on October 9, 1967. She stated she is interested in Unidentified Flying Objects (UFOs) and has received a quantity of information concerning beings from outer space. She stated she will not reveal her identity as she would feel like a fool if the information is not true. She stated if it is true, however, she will meet with interested officials and furnish all the information she has, provided nothing is done to endanger her safety.

"She stated in July 1967, she met a being from another planet who had assumed earthly form. He gave her certain information; he was picked up and departed from the earth on August 21, 1967. She stated she then received messages from non-earthly sources in a manner she refused to discuss. She stated these sources told her of the following:

"1. An anti-missile missile was fired at a UFO over America on May 22, 1962, but the UFO was protected by its 'force field'.

"2. A UFO was detected 22,000 miles from earth by radar about August 6, 1967.

"3. A UFO was detected over Antarctica August 20, 1967.

"4. A UFO was detected over the 'Dewline' in the past week and was shot down, and beings from outer space are trying to recover it.

"Informant would furnish no further details. She stated if this information is true, she will know other information she received is true, and will furnish full details. This will include information regarding the destruction of a moon explorer vehicle by beings from outer space, and how those beings shot down the Russian Cosmonaut.

"She stated she fears for her life if it becomes known she contacted officials, as persons who saw UFOs have died mysteriously in the past. She stated if Air Force officials want to contact her she can be reached by a message to a telephone number she has given an FBI agent, and she will meet officials at the Dallas FBI Office only."

There is no doubt that this case is absolutely rich in Contactee–like data. For example, there is the reference to the woman having "received a quantity of information concerning beings from outer space." She advised the FBI that contact had been made with "a being from another planet who had assumed earthly form." And, subsequent to the departure of the alien, she had been the recipient of "messages from non–earthly sources" that had come to her attention via "a manner she refused to discuss."

A NOTABLE NEWS STORY
COLORADO SPRINGS, COLORADO

On this day, Ted Hubbard, a journalist with the Lemoore, California *Advance* newspaper, wrote an article titled "Air Academy Text Book Urges More Study of UFO Sightings." The following is a notable extract:

"Students at the U.S. Air Force Academy at Colorado Springs are being taught to stop scoffing at the mention of UFO's or 'flying saucers' and to keep an open mind on the subject. This was made clear last Thursday in an interview given by Major Stewart Kilpatrick, deputy Director of Public Information of the Air Force Academy, Colorado Springs, to *The Lemoore Advance* in a lengthy and exclusive phone interview.

"The 'National Enquirer,' a country-wide journal, which claims the 'largest circulation of any weekly paper in America,' headlined this following statement, 'Air Force Academy Textbook Warns Cadets That UFO's May Be Spacecraft Operated by Aliens From Other Worlds,' in its October 11 issue. Because so many of our readers are interested personally in aircraft, *The Advance* sought to verify what appeared to be exaggerated claims and somewhat on the unbelievable side. This despite the reported sightings of some strange craft over Lemoore by several witnesses a few weeks ago.

"Major Kilpatrick, as second ranking officer in public affairs at the Air Academy, is in a position to speak authoritatively for the Air Force. He admitted at once that Plebes are taught from a text entitled 'Introductory Space Science, Volume II' and an entire Chapter 33 deals entirely with UFO considerations. He quoted from page 455, that '50,000 virtually reliable people have reported sighting unidentified flying objects. This leads us with the unpleasant possibility of alien visitors to our planet,' the 14-page chapter continues, 'or at least alien controlled UFOs.'"

OCTOBER 9, 1995

"IT WAS A WELL-GROOMED, OFFICIAL LOOKING WOMAN"
MANCHESTER, ENGLAND

The Women in Black are the female counterparts of the menacing MIB. There is a sub-category of the WIB known as the Bogus Social Workers. Paul Meehan, who has researched the British BSW phenomenon, says: "A typical case occurred on the morning of October 10, 1995 [actually October 9], when Mark Dunn was alone in his home in Manchester, his wife and children out of the house, and a visitor came to the door. It was a well-groomed, official looking woman of about 35, who claimed to be a social worker with the Manchester City Council investigating alleged mistreatment of his younger child. When Mr. Dunn demanded to see her identification, the woman told him she had to retrieve it from her car. Dunn observed her retreat to a parked car in which two men were waiting. The woman then got in and the car raced off."

Meehan adds: "Another BSW case occurred in Leigh, Lancashire, when a well-dressed couple came to the door of one Mrs. Carter, a local nurse who had two daughters. The man, who had the air of a petty bureaucrat, produced a photo ID that identified him as a worker with the community's social services department, while the woman wore a scarf emblazoned with the words, 'Child Protection.' The 'social workers' claimed they were there to investigate reports that Mrs. Carter was not feeding her children properly."

After the weird duo checked the family's food supplies – by obsessively ferreting through the pantry, no less – and demanded to physically examine the children, Mrs. Carter decided enough was well and truly enough and sent the pair packing. They got the hint and hurried out of the house – and into a large van parked outside. Somewhat ominously, it contained several others of their weird breed.

OCTOBER 10, 1973

THE SAGA OF THE ABDUCTED FISHERMEN
PASCAGOULA RIVER, MISSISSIPPI

On the night in question, two men – Charles Hickson and Calvin Parker – were fishing on the banks of Mississippi's Pascagoula River. That is, until approximately 9:00 p.m. rolled around. Parker and Hickson suddenly noticed a light in the distance. It was following the river and appeared to be coming in their direction.

As the light got closer, they could see it was actually a brightly lit, somewhat egg-shaped craft, from which came a deep, throbbing hum. Such was the intensity of the hum, it provoked intense nausea in both men. Confusion quickly followed. The pair watched in horror and amazement as what was described as a "hatch" opened and a trio of very strange-looking creatures exited the hovering object. Even stranger, the three things floated from the craft, across the waters of the river, and towards Hickson and Parker.

This particular breed of E.T. was described as humanoid, with mask-like faces, and heads from which three carrot-style points protruded. On top of that, they had large crab-like or lobster-like claws.

When the things from another world were practically on top

of terrified Parker and Hickson, both men were rendered into a state of paralysis. Suddenly, the entities seized the pair, who were manhandled onto the UFO. Like most abductees, Hickson and Parker were quickly reduced to the equivalents of lab rats. When the trauma-filled encounter was over, the pair was dumped back on the edge of the river.

OCTOBER 11, 1966
"NO-ONE COULD REMEMBER HIS NAME"
WANAQUE RESERVOIR, NEW JERSEY

"Several witnesses to a glowing object over the Wanaque Reservoir, New Jersey, including a policeman with an unlisted phone number, received phone calls, before they had reported to anyone, warning them to keep quiet," said Men in Black authority, Gareth Medway. "Later, several witnesses were gathered in a High School auditorium by an Air Force officer who derided them about the sighting. No-one could remember his name, and afterwards the Air Force denied all knowledge of the case."

OCTOBER 12, 1950
"NO REASONABLE EXPLANATION"
OAK RIDGE, TENNESSEE

An FBI teletype of October 13, 1950 refers to the detection of a definitive squadron of unknown objects tracked over the Oak Ridge installation at 11:25 p.m. on October 12. The documentation states: "USAF radar installation at Knoxville…picked up indications of eleven objects and perhaps more traveling across controlled area of Atomic Energy installation at Oak Ridge." The report continued: "Altitude of objects varied from one thousand to five thousand feet…and density from reading made by light aircraft equal in size to C-47, speed from one hundred to one hundred twenty-five miles per hour…"

Then we have the following from the same document: "No reasonable explanation for radar readings yet developed although operators are experienced reliable personnel and radar set is in perfect operating condition. Bureau will advise of further developments." Four days later, the FBI received the details of yet another alarming incident, this time involving the visual sighting of a UFO over Oak Ridge. The witnesses were a trio of military personnel. In a report of October 16, signed by Troopers Lendelle Clark and Hank N. Briggs, it was reported…

"…at approximately 2:55 p.m. Trooper [John L.] Isabell stopped us at this installation and showed us an object in the north that was traveling toward the northwest. It looked to be about 2,000 feet in the air and a white-silver looking color, rotating in a counter clockwise manner. It was round in shape and going in a rather fast motion. This object was at a high altitude and seemed to come in sight and then disappear. It looked about the size of a ball and round at every angle we looked at it."

OCTOBER 13, 1998

A SOCCER-BALL-SIZED UFO

DEVIZES, ENGLAND

Bob Anthony says that while driving past fields near the English village of Devizes, he saw a small UFO hovering over one specific field that was the site of a recently appeared Crop Circle. The object was only in view for a few seconds, but he was sure of what it was that he saw: an approximately soccer-sized ball that looked like "shiny aluminium" and which shimmered as it swayed slightly over the circle.

OCTOBER 14, 1967

"AN UNIDENTIFIED FLYING OBJECT EXPLODED"

CONGO, AFRICA

Under the terms of the Freedom of Information Act, the CIA has declassified a practically illegible 11-page report titled *Fragment, Metal, Recovered in the Republic of the Congo, Origin Believed to be an Unidentified Flying Object.* Despite the poor condition of the document, one discernible portion makes for intriguing reading:

"The purpose of this report is to present the results of the exploitation of a metallic fragment recovered near the town of [illegible] in the Republic of the Congo. Fragment recovery was the result of a ground-level search which was coordinated after an unidentified flying object exploded and fell to earth in the area. The sighting and recovery took place sometime between 10 and 15 October 1965 [later documentation showing that the date was October 14]. Other than a reported east-to-west direction of flight for the UFO specific observation and recovery details are lacking."

Also lacking is any further data of discernible value and interest, primarily due to the exceptionally poor quality of the document at issue. Nevertheless, direct reference to a "UFO" that "exploded and fell to earth" and that was the subject of CIA "exploitation" suggests that this case may potentially be of profound significance. To date, the incident has barely been investigated by the UFO research community.

MEN IN BLACK IN SCOTLAND
LOCH NESS, SCOTLAND

In 1968, Alistair Baxter – who had a lifelong interest in stories and folklore relative to Irish and Scottish lake monsters – travelled to Loch Ness and spent nine weeks armed with a camera and binoculars quietly and carefully monitoring the loch for any unusual activity of the long-necked and humped variety. Baxter never did see the elusive beast of Loch Ness, but he was able to speak with numerous people who *had* seen it.

After being at the loch-side almost constantly for five weeks, however, an unusual event occurred. Baxter was awoken in the middle of the night by a curious humming sound that was emanating from a bright, small, ball of light about the size of a football that – at a height of around fifteen feet from the ground – was slowly and carefully making its way through the surrounding trees that enveloped Baxter's modestly sized tent.

Suddenly, and without warning, the ball of light shot into the sky to a height of several hundred feet and hovered in deathly silence over the still waters of Loch Ness. For reasons that Baxter was at a loss to explain, he felt an overwhelming urge to go back to sleep and the next thing he knew it was daybreak. But the strangeness had barely begun.

Shortly after breakfast three men in black suits appeared outside of Baxter's tent seemingly out of nowhere and proceeded to ask him if he had seen anything unusual during the night. He replied that he hadn't, at which point one of the three men turned to his two colleagues and made what Baxter said was "a strange smile." He turned to face Baxter. "We might return," said one of the mysterious men in black and all three departed by simply walking off into the woods. They never did return, which was perhaps very fortunate for Baxter!

SEX AND SAUCERS IN SOUTH AMERICA

FRANCISCO DE SALES, BRAZIL

It was on February 22, 1958 that a young Brazilian farmer named Antonio Villas Boas prepared for a Dr. Olavo Fontes – both a respected gastroenterologist at the National School of Medicine in Rio de Janeiro and a highly dedicated flying saucer investigator – a remarkable, and undeniably sensational, document that told of his, Villas Boas', close encounter with an alien only eight days earlier.

But, this was no sterile "take me to your leader"-style experience involving bug-eyed, spindly creatures. Nope. According to the twenty-three-year-old farmer, he went where, quite possibly, no man had ever gone before. So Villas Boas told Fontes, he did nothing less than get it on with a hot babe from the great and mysterious beyond.

According to Villas Boas, on the night in question he was kidnapped from his family's farm - situated near the town of Francisco de Sales, in the state of Minas Gerais, close to the border with the state of Sao Paulo - by a group of ETs and taken on-board nothing less than a flying saucer. Initially terrified, Villas Boas very quickly, and very understandably, became highly enthused by the cosmic kidnapping.

After getting nabbed by aliens, taken on-board their craft, and hosed down like a muddy, old car, Villas Boas was rewarded after that traumatic experience with a fine and tasty piece of extraterrestrial ass. A metal door opened, and in walked a woman, butt-naked as the day she was born. At this stage, it's perhaps best to get the lowdown from the man of the hour:

"Her hair was fair, almost white, smooth, not very abundant...her eyes were large and blue, more elongated than round, being slanted outwards...the cheekbones were very high...her lips were very thin, hardly visible...her body was much more beautiful than that of any woman I have ever known before. It was slim, with high and well-separated breasts, thin waist and small stomach, wide hips and large thighs...another thing that I noted was that her hair in the armpits and in another place was very red, almost the color of blood."

And it was what he tactfully referred to as "another place" that Villas Boas had his sights set on. He didn't have to wait long, however. Nor did he have to break the ice with a bit of meaningless chatter. The seemingly real-life Barbarella was decidedly proactive and on him in a flash – in animalistic fashion, no less.

Although Villas Boas admitted to being not exactly enamored by the woman's loud grunts, he clearly considered himself to be quite the stud-muffin. One can almost imagine him in his recliner with brandy and cigar in-hand as he proudly told Fontes: "That was what they wanted of me – a good stallion to improve their own stock."

OCTOBER 17, 1947

"UNKNOWN MISSILE" IMPACTS IN MEXICO
GUADELOUPE, MEXICO

Found by me, in 2001, within the now-declassified files of the White Sands Proving Ground, New Mexico (now the White

Sands Missile Range) that are housed at the National Archives and Records Administration, Maryland, is the following document that references the crash of an "unknown missile" on Mexican territory in October 1947. Prepared by a Mr. Roddy, for the Director of Research & Development Office, Deputy Chief of Staff, the document is dated October 17, 1947 and titled *Unknown Missile in Mexico*. It reveals the following:

"Investigation of the unknown missile which landed near Guadeloupe on 11 October 1947 has failed, so far, to identify it as a V-2, GAPA or other type of guided missile. Careful check by USAF, Ordnance, and Navy indicates that no missiles were fired from Alamogordo Special Range or White Sands Proving Ground on 12 October 1947. Army Ground Forces has eliminated possibility of an anti-aircraft target having gone astray.

"Negotiations with the Mexican Government for the Long Range Proving Ground for guided missiles, which have been started through the State Department, may be jeopardized if Mexico is dissatisfied with the investigation. It is understood that newspaper statements that fragments of a V-2 have been identified are disturbing the Mexican Government."

Whatever the curious object was, it was fully confirmed that nothing of U.S. origin had gone astray – from any arm of the military. Intriguingly, the story died a quick death, suggesting that whatever the true nature of this UFO, some form of secrecy veil encompassed the entire affair. Whether orchestrated by Mexican authorities or the United States, however, remains unknown.

A NEAR-COLLISION IN THE SKIES

MANSFIELD, OHIO

One of the most notable UFO encounters ever recorded occurred shortly after 11p.m. on October 18, 1973. That the prime witnesses were serving members of the U.S. Army Reserve only added to the credibility of the report. Having departed from Port Columbus, Ohio, their UH-1H helicopter was headed for its home base at Cleveland Hopkins Airport. Aboard were Captain Lawrence J. Coyne; Sergeant John Healey, the flight-medic; First Lieutenant Arrigo Jezzi, a chemical engineer; and a computer technician, Sergeant Robert Yanacsek. All seemed normal as the crew climbed into the air and kept the helicopter at a steady 2,500 feet altitude.

But approximately ten miles from Mansfield, they noticed a "single red light" to the west that was moving slowly in a southerly direction. Initially they thought the object might be an F-100 aircraft operating out of Mansfield. Nevertheless, Coyne advised Yanacsek to "keep an eye on it." These were wise words, as suddenly the unidentified light changed its course and began to head directly for them.

Captain Coyne immediately swung into action, putting the helicopter into an emergency descent, dropping 500 feet per minute. Equally alarming was the fact that radio contact with Mansfield Tower could no longer be established, and both UHF and VHF frequencies were utterly dead, too.

When it seemed that a fatal collision was all but imminent, the red light came to a halt, hovering menacingly in front of the helicopter and its startled crew. At that close proximity to the object, Captain Coyne and his team were able to determine that this was no mere light in the sky. Coyne, Healey, and Yanacsek agreed that the object before them was a large, gray-colored, cigar-shaped vehicle, which they described as being somewhat "domed," and with "a suggestion of windows." They could now see that the red light was coming from the bow section of the object.

Then, without warning, a green "pyramid shaped" shaft of light emanated from the object, passed over the nose of the heli-copter, swung up through the windshield, and entered the tinted, upper window panels. Suddenly the interior of the helicopter was bathed in an eerie green light. A handful of seconds later the object shot off toward Lake Erie. But the danger was still not over.

To the crew's concern, the altimeter showed an altitude of 3,500 feet and a climbing ascent of 1,000 feet per minute, even though the stick was still geared for descent. The helicopter reached a height of 3,800 feet before Captain Coyne was able to safely and finally regain control of the helicopter. Shortly thereaf-ter, all radio frequencies returned to normal and Coyne proceeded on to Cleveland Hopkins Airport without further problems.

OCTOBER 19, 1966

"THEY HAD A SLIGHT SLANT TO THEIR EYES"
ELIZABETH, NEW JERSEY

"George Smyth of Elizabeth, New Jersey, went to visit two teenag-ers who had seen a mysterious green entity," says Gareth Medway. "The boys were surrounded by a crowd. He noticed two men emerging from a large black car, leaving a third behind the wheel. They had a slight slant to their eyes. Later, when *Saucer News* inves-tigators went to visit one of the lads, Smyth noticed the same black car parked nearby, and the same two men get out and watch the house while the interview was going on. Two weeks later he received a phone call telling him to give up UFO investigation."

"A PILOT OF CONSIDERABLE EXPERIENCE"

WARWICKSHIRE, ENGLAND

One of the most fascinating of all UFO encounters – an incident that almost resulted in a mid-air collision between a UFO and a *Meteor* jet – occurred over Royal Air Force Gaydon, Warwickshire, England, on the night of October 21, 1957. Less than a week later, the UK media was chasing down the story. Describing RAF Gaydon as "one of the RAF's top V-bomber stations," the *Sunday Express* newspaper stated that the Air Ministry (today, the Ministry of Defense) had taken rapid steps to get to the heart of the mystery.

Reportedly, the UFO was seen visually by the pilot and tracked by ground-radar personnel – and only a few minutes apart. Questions, unsurprisingly, were quickly being asked: could the UFO actually have been a Soviet spy-plane? It was certainly a scenario that the Air Ministry felt important enough to address. Although – as will become apparent – the description given by the pilot did not sound like that of the average Russian aircraft. Plus, six days after the event occurred, Air Ministry staff were still scratching their heads.

The *Sunday Express* revealed something notable: "The Air Ministry is awaiting the report of a senior intelligence officer who has visited Gaydon and other stations concerned. This is the first time that an unidentified flying object – as the Air Ministry calls them – has been detected both from the air and the ground."

The facts were as follows: At 9:18 p.m. on the night in

question, Flying Officer D.R. Sweeney – who was described as "a pilot of considerable experience" – was flying a *Meteor* on a training mission from RAF Station North Luffenham. All was normal until Sweeney reached a height of approximately 28,000 feet. As he flew in a westerly direction, Sweeney "almost collided" with an unidentified object. Whatever the nature of the craft, Sweeney was only sure of three things: (A) the UFO was illuminated by six lights; (B) it was flying at a very slow speed; and (C) he was directly over RAF Gaydon when the encounter occurred, and where "atom-bomber crews train in *Valiants*."

The matter was quietly closed down by the Air Ministry, who grudgingly admitted the case remained unresolved.

OCTOBER 21, 1978

VANISHED WITHOUT A TRACE
MELBOURNE, AUSTRALIA

Frederick Valentich was just twenty years of age when he vanished into oblivion over Australia's Bass Strait. The mystery began when Valentich took off from Moorabin Airport – located in the Australian city of Melbourne – at around 6:19 p.m. in a Cessna aircraft. The planwas a simple one: leave the airport, fly approximately 130 miles, and then land at King Island, Victoria. If only it had been that easy

Approximately forty-five minutes into the flight, Valentich contacted staff at Moorabin to inquire if there was "any known traffic below five thousand feet." Radar personnel were puzzled, as their screens failed to show anything anomalous or out of place. Valentich continued to insist that he was not alone, referring to the accompanying object as a "large aircraft."

Valentich's anxiety levels began to rise when, as the object got closer, he realized its configuration and colors of lights did not match what one would expect to see on an aircraft. He told Moorabin: "He's flying over me two to three times at speeds I could not identify."

Things got even more hazardous: "Melbourne, it seems like it's chasing me. What I'm doing now is orbiting and the thing is just orbiting on top of me, also. It's got a green light and sort of metallic. It's all shiny."

Valentich was determined to make it to King Island. He failed. His last words were: "It is hovering and it's not an aircraft." Then, nothing but a strange sound, and, finally, silence. Contact was lost and neither Frederick Valentich, nor his aircraft, was ever seen again. The case remains one of Australia's most baffling aviation mysteries.

OCTOBER 22, 1947

A UFO IN PARADISE

PARADISE VALLEY, ARIZONA

The first indication that something of a crashed-UFO nature might have occurred at Paradise Valley, Arizona, in October 1947 surfaced from Silas Newton. He was a convicted con man from Colorado who would also become one of the central players in the tale of the alleged UFO crash event at Aztec, New Mexico in 1948. Possible corroboration for the reality of the Paradise Valley affair was brought to light in 1987 by British researcher Timothy Good. Good, the author of *Above Top Secret*, interviewed a man named Selman Graves, who claimed to have witnessed aspects of the retrieval of a strange object at Paradise Valley.

According to Graves, he briefly witnessed seeing in the sand at Paradise Valley (and in the correct time frame) a large, circular shaped object that was more than thirty feet in diameter. Graves knew little more than that; and the details provided by Silas Newton to author Frank Scully (published in his book *Behind The Flying Saucers*) are very brief indeed.

To date, additional evidence concerning this particular report has failed to surface into the public domain.

OCTOBER 23, 1986

BLOWING THE WHISTLE ON UFOS

WRIGHT-PATTERSON AIR FORCE BASE, DAYTON, OHIO

The British UFO investigator, Jenny Randles, made an intriguing comment with regard to an offer of alleged Top Secret documents on crashed UFOs that had been made to her on this date in 1986 by a British Army source that she calls "Robert." According to Randles, Robert had then recently left the military and had personal access to certain UFO files that had been surreptitiously removed from Wright-Patterson Air Force Base, Dayton, Ohio, and provided to the British Army by a source at Wright-Patterson.

From there, sources in the Army were determined to forward this documentation on to Randles for circulation and dissemination to the public. The transfer of the classified material to Randles never occurred, however, and to this day she remains unsure of what motivated this bizarre episode. Her comments on this strange, cloak-and-dagger episode are notable, however, and highly relevant to alleged film footage showing an alien autopsy.

Within the files that Robert described to her in 1986 were photographs that sound very much like images that had been lifted directly from the notorious Alien Autopsy film: "Bear in mind," Randles said, when I interviewed her specifically on the matter in 1997, "1986 was years before the Autopsy film surfaced. In fact, the connections with the Autopsy film and with what Robert told me are chillingly similar. One of the impressions that you get from viewing the Alien Autopsy footage is that the body is very human-like; and is around five foot in height. I have to say, it struck me as soon as I saw the footage that this was *very* similar to what Robert had described."

OCTOBER 24, 1973

"HE WARNED HER NEVER TO DISCUSS HER CLOSE ENCOUNTER"

PASADENA, CALIFORNIA

"Pauline" had a very strange encounter with a Man in Black back in October 1973, when she was living in California. It's notable, and probably relevant, for me to remind readers that a major UFO wave was going on at that time, and all across the United States. While hiking in the California hills one Sunday morning, Pauline encountered a classic, silver-colored flying saucer-style UFO which, at first, at least, was high in the sky. Suddenly, it dropped to around fifty or sixty above her, hanging there in an odd, wobbling fashion. Amazed, Pauline could only stare as the silent craft bobbed around – like a boat on churning waters – and then shot away at high speed.

Pauline raced home and excitedly told her family of what had just taken place. They, apparently, weren't the only ones who knew what had occurred on the fateful morning in 1973. Three days later, and after sunset, Pauline had a visitor. Not a welcome

one, I should stress. It was a Man in Black, a skinny – almost ema-
ciated – old man, dressed in a shabby black suit, looking pale and
ill, and wearing an old, 1950s-style fedora hat.

Pauline said that she felt her mind was briefly enslaved, as the
MIB near-hypnotically asked her to invite him into her home.
In a slight daze, and to her eternal cost, she did exactly that. She
retreated to the couch, stumbling slightly and feeling ice-cold. The
old man followed her, and stood in the living-room, looming over
her, as he warned her – in no uncertain terms – never to discuss
her close encounter again. Ever. The MIB then turned around and
headed to the door. At that exact same moment, Pauline felt her
mental faculties return to normal and she raced after him, just as
he exited the door and closed it behind him. Pauline threw the
door open wide, only to find the old Man in Black gone.

OCTOBER 25, 1973

A UFO, BIGFOOT, AND AN OMINOUS MESSAGE
FAYETTE COUNTY, PENNSYLVANIA

That was the night when all hell broke loose in the heart of Fayette
County, Pennsylvania – just one day after Pauline's encounter with
a Man in Black. The primary player in the story was one Steve
Palmer who was both amazed and frightened to see a brightly
illuminated UFO hovering over local farmland, around 9.00 p.m.
But that wasn't all that Palmer encountered: a pair of immense,
ape-like animals with very long and muscular arms surfaced out of
the shadows of the dark field and proceeded to walk right towards
Palmer himself. He wasted no time and blasted them with a salvo
of bullets.

Very weirdly, the bullets appeared to have no effect – at all

– on either creature, and they retreated into the darkness. The UFO did likewise, vanishing in an instant. That was not the end of the affair, however. Approximately four hours later, things took on even stranger, and far more terrifying, proportions.

It was roughly 1.00 a.m. when Stan Gordon arrived on the scene, having been alerted to the Palmer encounter by a local police officer, one who had been apprised of the facts. Along with Gordon were fellow investigators Dennis Smeltzer, Fred Pitt, David Smith, and George Lutz. They met with Palmer, who proceeded to tell them of his unearthly encounter with the two Bigfoot and the UFO. Then, quite out of the blue, something horrifying occurred: Palmer's breathing changed, to the extent that he was literally panting heavily and deeply, and he broke into a deep, guttural growl and knocked both his own father and Lutz to the field floor. And that was only the start of things.

Pitt found himself unable to breathe properly, Smeltzer felt faint, and Palmer fell to the ground, having apparently passed out. A powerful, rotten odor of brimstone suddenly dominated the cold night air. The terrified group knew that it was vital they get out of the field – and quickly, too – before things got even worse. Later, when Palmer regained consciousness, he told Gordon and his team that he, Palmer, while in his passed out state, had seen before him a sickle-carrying, dark-robed figure that warned him the Human Race was on the verge of destroying itself – and would do exactly that unless it curbed its violent instincts.

SCOTLAND'S ROSWELL?
ISLE OF LEWIS, OUTER HEBRIDES, SCOTLAND

That was the day on which something exploded over the Scottish Outer Hebrides, specifically in the area of the Isle of Lewis. Witnesses spoke of seeing unusual aerial activity, and there were tales of the military organizing a hasty operation to recover something unknown from the harsh Highland waters.

"At first," said witness Norman MacDonald, "I thought it was a firework. Then I saw three flashes and heard two further bangs. I rushed into a local shop and took the staff and customers aside. They also saw the dense smoke spiral. That was about 4:10 p.m."

The coastguard confirmed that numerous reports had been filed – to the extent that the military launched an intense search of the area. It was a search that cost no less than 200,000 English pounds, and which covered an area in excess of 300 square-miles. A Royal Air Force *Nimrod* aircraft, packed with sophisticated detection equipment, scoured the vicinity for around ten hours, but with no success. A Royal Air Force helicopter from RAF Lossiemouth did likewise. And an absolute flotilla of boats and ships took to the waters.

Officially, nothing was found. Unofficially, however, the story was very different: rumors revolved around the crash of a UFO, or possibly a highly classified aircraft of the U.S. military known as *Aurora*. Whatever the truth, it still has yet to surface.

OCTOBER 27, 1957

"HE WOULD SEE SOMETHING UNUSUAL"

RANTON, ENGLAND

Researcher Gavin Gibbons wrote in 1957 that one October evening in 1954, a Dutchman living in England named Tony Roestenberg returned home to find his wife, Jessie, "in a terrified state." According to Jessie: earlier that day nothing less than a flying saucer hovered over their isolated farmhouse in Ranton, England. In addition, Jessie could see peering down from the craft two very "Nordic"-like men that could have stepped right out of the pages of the controversial Desmond Leslie-George Adamski tome, *Flying Saucers Have Landed.*

Their foreheads were high, their hair was long and fair, and they seemed to have "pitiful" looks on their faces. The strange craft reportedly circled the family's home twice, before streaking away. Curiously, on the following Sunday, Tony Roestenberg had a "hunch" that if he climbed on the roof of his house "he would see something unusual," which he most certainly did. It was a high-flying, cigar-shaped object that vanished into the clouds.

Gavin Gibbons, who investigated the case personally, stated: "When I visited the Roestenberg's house almost three weeks after the sighting…Jessie Roestenberg appeared. She seemed highly strained and nervous and her husband, coming in later, was also very strained. It was evident that something most unusual had occurred."

HELICOPTERS OR UFOS?

LORING AIR FORCE BASE, CASWELL, MAINE

In 1975, there occurred across much of the northern portion of the United States numerous encounters with what were – at first, at least – perceived as unidentified helicopters, but that were later interpreted as UFOs. The helicopter theory was a reasonable one, since military personnel described seeing craft that could hover and fly backwards, just like a helicopter. Files show, however, that the helicopter theory was an assumption, rather than fact. One particular document, of October 28, 1975, serves to demonstrate the weirdness that went on during that particular night. Titled *Unidentified Helicopter Sighted at Low Level Over Loring AFB*, it provided the following:

"On 28 Oct 75, Lewis…advised that the a/c [aircraft] was first observed by Clifton W. Blakeslee, Sgt. [deleted] and William J. Long, SSgt., both assigned to the 42 SPS, who were on duty at the storage area. The initial sighting took place at approximately 1345. The a/c was observed approximately 1,000 meters north of LAFB. The a/c was subsequently observed by Lewis and others intermittently for the next hour and a half. Subsequent to the sighting by Long and Blakeslee, the a/c did not come nearer to the northern perimeter of LAFB than approximately 3 miles. Lewis observed a flashing white strobe light and red navigation lights on the a/c. The operator of the a/c either turned the lights off periodically or the a/c flew below a point from which the lights could be observed. The a/c disappeared from view and did not reappear. A search of the vicinity of the northern perimeter of LAFB by 42 SPS personnel met with negative results."

The unsettling affair was nowhere near over:

"On 28 Oct 75, Commander, 42 8 W, advised that he responded to the area from which the unidentified a/c was observed. He arrived at approximately 1955. The a/c bore a white flashing light and an amber or orange light. The speed and movement in the air suggested that the a/c was a helicopter. From 1345-2020, the a/c was under constant observation. Subsequent to that time the a/c would appear and disappear from view. The a/c definitely penetrated the LAFB northern perimeter and *on one occasion was within 300 yards of the munitions storage area perimeter* [emphasis mine]. Efforts to identify the a/c through Maine State Police and local police departments were not successful."

The matter of the mysterious "helicopters" of October 28, 1975 was never resolved.

OCTOBER 29, 1948

"THE OBJECT DISAPPEARED AT A TERRIFIC SPEED"
NEUBIBERG AIR BASE, BAVARIA, GERMANY

European newspapers reported: "Five U. S. Air Force pilots observed a mysterious, silvery object similar in appearance to a so-called flying saucer hanging high over Neubiberg Air Base in Bavaria. The object disappeared at a terrific speed after having remained over the air base more than 30 minutes. A similar object had been seen days before by another group of American pilots."

OCTOBER 30, 199

A KITE-LIKE UFO

RANTON, ENGLAND

Ranton, England was the location of a sighting made by two young boys, who claimed to have seen a large, black, triangular-shaped UFO as they walked home from school. It was described as "looking like a big black kite," but which was clearly far more substantial than a kite. It flashed across the sky, only in view for moments, but long enough for the lads to be certain that they had encountered something amazing – and maybe even other worldly.

OCTOBER 31, 1994

"DO THEY THINK WE ARE MAD AROUND HERE?"

COTSWOLDS, ENGLAND

According to residents of Church Lench and Norton, just north of the Cotswolds, England, onOctober 31, 1994 a "barrel-like object" was seen to descend at speed into a field at nearby Hepton Hill. The military quickly sealed off the area and issued stern warnings to dissuade those who might try to uncover the truth surrounding the event. With great speed, the unidentified object was loaded aboard a Royal Navy truck, which departed for destinations unknown. Questions were put to the Royal Air Force and the Fleet Air Arm. Both issued strong denials of involvement in either the crash or recovery of the unknown object at Hepton Hill.

One witness who was able to confirm the reality of the crash, however, was Paul Brooke of Norton, who likened the object to a "forty-gallon drum."

"There were several fire engines and lots of police here,"

Brooke said. "The area was cordoned off and people were stopped from entering the field. Then at about eight that night [the object] was taken away by a Royal Navy vehicle with a police escort at the front and back."

Perhaps the most carefully phrased statement came from Inspector Mike Rowlands of the Eversham Police: "I can't categorically say that it did not happen, but my investigations have revealed that it was a bale of straw that was on fire and which was put out by the fire brigade. The reports of something falling from the sky may either be hoaxes or somebody may have seen something and come to the wrong conclusion."

To which Paul Brooke countered: "Do they think we are mad around here?"

NOVEMBER

NOVEMBER 1, 1985

SOMETHING LANDS IN A TEXAS FIELD

PARADISE, TEXAS

This particular case is made notable by the fact that no UFO or alien entity was seen, heard or encountered. But something else was encountered. The location was the Texas town of Paradise, which is a relatively short drive from the city of Fort Worth. The story comes from a local rancher who, on November 1, awoke to find something very strange in one of his fields. As he went to feed his cows, the man came across three large depressions in the ground. They were circular depressions, in a triangular fashion and were so deep that the rancher concluded that something large and heavy had quietly descended on his land at some point in the very early hours of the same morning. By daybreak, the object was clearly long gone.

NOVEMBER 2, 1966

THE WEIRD SAGA OF INDRID COLD

PARKERSBURG, WEST VIRGINIA

Mothman authority Andy Colvin notes that a man named Woodrow Derenberger "…claimed to have had a series of strange adventures beginning on November 2nd, 1966. While driving home from Parkersburg, West Virginia to his suburban home in Mineral Wells, he suddenly found the highway blocked by a large gray object. Someone emerged from the object and walked to the passenger side window of his car. The man introduced himself as 'a searcher,' and offered words of comfort to Derenberger."

After noting that he would come again, the "spaceman," who

called himself "Indrid Cold," stepped back into the object and it rose out of sight. Woody Derenberger went home and told his story to his wife. He then called the police and the press. Soon after, other witnesses came forward to say that they, too, had seen Cold talking to Derenberger by the side of the road. (In time, several locals would have their own encounters with Cold.)

Two days later while driving in his car, Derenberger began to receive telepathic communications from Cold, who described himself as from the "galaxy of Ganymede." Cold also supplied some information about his life, including the observation that people on his planet (Lanulos) lived to be 125 to 175 of our Earth years.

Over the next weeks, other stories would accumulate that substantiated other parts of Derenberger's story, including independent UFO sightings on November 4th. An initial investigation concluded that Derenberger was not a fraud or hoaxer, and was mentally and psychologically sound.

Throughout this period, Derenberger's direct contacts with Indrid Cold continued. He learned much about Cold's people and their desire for friendly contact. In 1967, Cold took Derenberger for a ride in his spaceship. Strangely, they visited the oilfields of Iraq and Afghanistan, as well as Cold's lush, jungle planet, which was populated by beautiful humanoids wearing no clothes.

Derenberger told his story frequently over the next few years, and his story was given extended treatment by Fortean researcher John A. Keel.

NOVEMBER 3, 1948

"THE POSSIBILITY THAT THE REPORTED OBJECTS ARE
VEHICLES FROM ANOTHER PLANET HAS NOT BEEN IGNORED"
WASHINGTON, D.C.

On this day, the U.S. military recorded: "All information that has been made available to this headquarters indicates that the discs, the cigar shaped objects, and the 'balls of light' are not of domestic origin. Engineering investigation indicates that disc or wingless aircraft could support themselves in flight by aerodynamic means. It is probable that the problems of stability and control could also be solved for such aircraft. However, according to current aerodynamic theory in this country, aircraft with such configurations would have relatively poor climb, altitude and range characteristics with power plants now in use. The possibility that the reported objects are vehicles from another planet has not been ignored. However, tangible evidence to support conclusions about such a possibility is completely lacking. The occurrence of incidents in relation to the approach to the earth of the planets Mercury, Venus and Mars have been plotted. A periodic variation in the frequency of incidents, which appears to have some relation to the planet approach curves is noted, but it may be purely a coincidence."

NOVEMBER 4, 1989

A UFO CRASH IN CANADA
CARP, CANADA

Midway through November 1989, a document – prepared by a still-unknown source – was circulated to a number of researchers within the field of Ufology, including Leonard Stringfield. It detailed the alleged landing – or crash-landing - of a UFO in the Canadian town of Carp, which is located near Ottawa. Although there was talk of the entire issue being a hoax, Stringfield felt the case was either (a) genuine or (b) "an orchestrated disinformation ploy, designed to 'muddy the waters." Pertinent parts of the document are detailed below:

"Canadian and American Security Agencies are engaged in a conspiracy of silence to withhold from the world the alien vessel seized in the swamps of Corkery Road, Carp, in 1989. UFO sightings in the Ontario region had intensified in the 1980's, specifically around nuclear power generating stations. On November 4, 1989 at 20:00 hours., Canadian Defense Department radars picked up a globe shaped object traveling at a phenomenal speed over Carp, Ontario. The UFO abruptly stopped, and dropped like a stone.

"Canadian and American Security Agencies were immediately notified of the landing. Monitoring satellites traced the movements of the aliens to a triangular area, off Old Almonte and Corkery Roads. The ship had landed in deep swamp near Corkery Road. Two AJ-64 Apaches and a UH-60 Blackhawk headed for the area the following night. The helicopters carried full weapon loads. They were part of a covert American unit that specialized in the recovery of alien craft.

"Flying low over Ontario pine trees, the Apache attack choppers soon spotted a glowing, blue, 20 meter in diameter sphere. As targeting lasers locked-on, both gunships unleashed their full weapon loads of eight missiles each. All sixteen were exploded in proximity bursts ten meters downwind from the ship. The missiles were carrying VEXXON, a deadly neuroactive gas which kills on contact. Exposed to air, the gas breaks down quickly into inert components. Immediately after having completed their mission, the gunships turned around, and headed back across the border.

"Now the Blackhawk landed, as men exploded from its open doors. In seconds, the six-man strike-team had entered the UFO through a seven meter, hatchless, oval portal. No resistance was encountered. At the controls, three dead crewmen were found. With the ship captured, the United States Air Force, Pentagon, and Office of Naval Intelligence were notified. Through the night, a special team of technicians had shut down and disassembled the sphere. Early the next morning, November 6, 1989, construction equipment and trucks were brought into the swamp. The UFO parts were transported to a secret facility in Kanata, Ontario."

Truth or disinformation? It all very much depends on who you ask.

NOVEMBER 5, 1983

PURSUED BY A UFO
LEOMINSTER, MASSACHUSETTS

Leominster, Massachusetts played host to a small, diamond-sized UFO that was white in color and that was seen by a young man driving home from a friend's party on a Saturday night. As he negotiated a winding tree-shrouded stretch of road, the man was both amazed and scared when the roughly four-foot-long object suddenly appeared. It dropped from above, and kept pace with the car – next to the passenger-side window - for a frightening thirty seconds or thereabouts and then shot away into the woods – not to be seen again.

A DAZZLING UFO NEAR LOCH NESS

INVERNESS, SCOTLAND

The outskirts of the town of Inverness, Scotland were the location of a UFO encounter reported to me personally in 2016. The witness had read my book, *Nessie*, which focuses on the long and rich history of paranormal phenomena recorded in and around Loch Ness and nearby Inverness. According to the witness, Roger Carter, while heading out of town for a long, work-based drive to the English city of Bristol, his car was suddenly enveloped in a near-blinding light – to the extent that he was forced to slam on the brakes, fearing that he would slam into the surrounding trees.

Carter leapt out of the car and looked up. Such was the brilliance of the light, he could not make out anything at all – beyond the light itself. And, particularly puzzling, absolutely no noise could be heard either. In seconds, the light was gone – as was its source. A shaken Roger Carter continued on his journey, keeping a careful look at the skies above for the next few miles.

HELICOPTERS OR UFOS?

LEWISTOWN, MONTANA

On this date, there occurred a strange wave of activity that had weird, UFO-tinged angles attached to it, as the following official reports of the US Air Force show:

"On 7 Nov 75 an off duty missile launch officer reported that unidentified aircraft resembling a helicopter had approached and hovered near a USAF missile launch control facility, near Lewistown. Source explained that at about 0020, 7 Nov 75, source and his deputy officer had just retired from crew rest in the Soft Support Building (SSB) at the LCF, when both heard the sound of a helicopter rotor above the SSB. The Deputy observed two red-and-white lights on the front of the aircraft, a white light on the bottom, and a white light on the rear.

"On 7 Nov 75, Roscoe E. III, Captain, 341 Strategic Missile Wing, advised that during the hours of 6-7 Nov 75, two adjacent LCFs, approximately 50 miles south of aforementioned LCF, reported moving lights as unidentified flying objects (UFO). During this period there were no reports of helicopter noises from personnel at these LCFs.

"This office was recently notified of a message received by security police MAFB, MT., detailing a similar nocturnal approach by a helicopter at a USAF weapons storage area located at another USAF base in the Northern Tier states. Local authorities denied the use of their helicopters during the period 6-7 Nov 75."

NOVEMBER 8, 1966

"HER DAUGHTER HAD BEEN IN A DISTRESSED CONDITION"
SHREWSBURY, ENGLAND

In a detailed document, a Corporal R.A. Rickwood, of the British Royal Air Force's Provost and Security Services, Special Investigation Section, related to his superiors the facts of an amazing and disturbing UFO event:

"On 10th November 1966 a telephone message was received from Flight Lieutenant Williams, RAF Shawbury, reporting that a Mrs. Foulkes of [address deleted] Shrewsbury, had complained that his daughter had been frightened by an object in the sky whilst she had been driving along the A5 road near Great Ness at 2355 hours on 8th November 1966.

"This object had emitted brilliant lights and radiation beams. On arriving home her daughter had been in a distressed condition and she had discovered marks on the car, which she considered were burn marks.

"On 14th November 1966, Miss Diane Foulkes, aged 22 years, a typist employed in Shrewsbury was seen at her home in the presence of her parents. She stated that she had received a letter dated 11th November 1966 from RAF Shawbury signed by a Flight Lieutenant Penny informing her that no service aircraft had been flying in that area at the time of the incident. She was now satisfied that the incident was in no way connected with the Royal Air Force or the Armed Forces.

"She could see rays of light shooting from the object which had again appeared to keep station with her car until she arrived home. At one time during the journey the object travelled near her and the rays seemed to come towards the right hand side of her car.

"She felt a bump against that side as if they had struck it. At this moment she felt as if she had received an electric shock and had felt a severe pain in her neck. The left-hand side headlight of the car also went out. This made her extremely frightened. When she got home, she felt very ill and had complained to her parents."

"IT WAS ABOUT TWENTY FEET WIDE"
GLASGOW TO EDINBURGH, SCOTLAND

One of the most intriguing, but also baffling, UFO encounters occurred in Scotland on the day in question, as ufologist Jenny Randles reveals:

"The witness, Robert Taylor (then sixty-one-years-old) at this time worked for the forestry department of the local development corporation. One of his tasks was to patrol an area of woodland not far from the M8 Glasgow to Edinburgh motorway.

"He had just finished his coffee break and driven his van to the edge of the particular spot he was to check for stray animals. He continued on foot, with his dog (a Red Setter called 'Lara') running loose nearby sniffing happily at the various local smells.

"Bob turned into a clearing and suddenly, unbelievably, he was standing just feet away from a dome-shaped (or possibly spherical) object that was just sitting quietly on the ground. It was about twenty feet wide and a dull grey metallic color, with a rim near to the base from which sprang several vertical antennae or propellers. There was neither sound nor sign of life."

Then, things got even weirder: a pair of spherical, spiky objects exited the vehicle, surrounded Taylor, and sprayed a noxious gas in his direction, which caused him to pass out. When he awoke, the spheres and the craft were gone.

FLYING INTO OBLIVION

GARDINA COUNTY, CALIFORNIA

It was a clear morning when a pair of UFO researchers, Karl Hunrath and Wilbur Wilkinson, took to the sunny skies in a small plane – containing about three hours' worth of gas - rented from Gardina County Airport, California. The purpose of their flight, was to rendezvous at a remote stretch of Golden State desert with fantastically advanced beings from another world. The two had recently contacted these visitors via what they were calling "mechanical contractions." The pair was not seen nor heard of again. And neither was the aircraft.

No skeletal, ragged remains turned up. No tell tale wreckage was found. *Ever*. Hunrath and Wilkinson were - for all intents and purposes - gone, vanished. In the immediate aftermath of their disappearance, L.A.-based saucer sleuths began to suspect that they were *really* gone. Like *up there* gone.

Ten days later, the *Los Angeles Mirror* highlighted their disappearance in its pages – as well as the attendant theory that their vanishing act was the work of aliens. Suddenly, and not surprisingly, pretty much the entirety of the city's media descended on the Wilkinson home, as Contactee George Hunt Williamson noted. When the press arrived, said Williamson, they found that:

"Wilkinson's den was lined with flying saucer pictures, weird signs and formulas, which Mrs. Wilkinson said were supposed to be the new interplanetary language. 'Of course, I don't quite go for all the flying saucer talk, but Karl convinced Wilbur they actually existed,' said Mrs. Wilkinson. She then said, 'Karl had tape recordings of conversations with men from other planets who landed here in Saucers.' She showed reporters messages tacked on the wall of the den which were supposedly received by radio from the interplanetary visitors. One was from Regga of the planet Masar."

The photos, said Williamson, were actually some of those taken by the world's most famous Contactee, George Adamski, while the strange formulas and signs "were received by our group working in Northern Arizona, starting in early August, 1952. The tape recordings that Hunrath had were taken during receptions of the Arizona research group."

Was it true? Were Hunrath and Wilkinson really invited to take a one-way trip to another, far-away world by benevolent Space-Brothers, as some of their friends and families suspected? Did they stage the whole thing, to start new lives elsewhere? Those questions are still being asked.

NOVEMBER 11, 1954

ALIENS AMONG THE TREES
FOUKE, ARKANSAS

U.S. Air Force files reveal that on this day, a report of a strange encounter came in from Fouke, Arkansas of a local woman who saw a pair of long-haired people, dressed in silver, one-piece outfits and walking through an area of woodland on the fringes of town. Both were female, pale and tall – in excess of six-feet and probably closer to six-and-a-half feet. As they got closer, both women smiled and nodded at the awestruck witness. She continued to watch for a minute or so, after which the pair became enveloped in a denser part of the woods and were not seen again.

With hindsight, and although no UFO was seen, they sound very much like the kinds of humanlike ETs reported throughout the 1950s by such UFO "Contactees" as George Adamski, Orfeo Angelucci, Dana Howard and George Van Tassel.

NOVEMBER 12, 1967

UK-SOVIET FLYING SAUCER RESEARCH
LONDON, ENGLAND AND MOSCOW, RUSSIA

As incredible as it may sound, in 1967 – which, bear in mind, was still the height of the Cold War – British authorities made a secret approach to the highest echelons of the former Soviet Union's military. It was an approach that revolved around nothing less than Unidentified Flying Objects. In fact, the British Government came straight to the point: they wished to clandestinely discuss the possibility of establishing a joint UK–Soviet UFO study-program. Sounds near-unbelievable? Yes, it does. But, it's one hundred percent verifiable.

Thanks to the provisions of the US Freedom of Information Act (FOIA), documentation has surfaced from the Defense Intelligence Agency that reveals at least significant parts of the story. According to the DIA: "In early 1967 (exact date believed to be 10 Nov) Moscow TV presented a program on Unidentified Flying Objects. On 12 Nov 67 a Reuters release in the UK (believe article was in *Daily Telegraph*) reported the TV program."

The essence of both the Soviet television show and the Reuters story, noted the DIA, was that "...the Russians had recently set up a commission to study UFOs." The chairman of the commission, the DIA learned, was a retired Soviet Air Force (SAF) Major General A.F. Stolyarov, a former Technical Services Officer. Not only that, the project had at its disposal no less than 18 astronomers and SAF officers and "200 observers."

There was a dramatic development in the story – and, probably, a wholly unforeseen development. The DIA uncovered information to the effect that, "…on 12 December 1967, the British Embassy was directed by London to further investigate the subject with a view to cooperating with the Russians in observation teams for UFOs." There may have been a very good reason for the actions of the Brits. Between the seven-year-period of 1959-1966, documentation now declassified by the British Ministry of Defense reveals, British authorities received a combined total of 446 UFO reports. In 1967, alone, however, the MoD was inundated with no less than 362 reports – averaging at almost one report per day.

NOVEMBER 13, 1952

"SEVERAL OF THOSE FIERY OBJECTS LANDED CLOSE TO ME"
FRIONA, TEXAS

The documentation, declassified under the terms of the Freedom of Information Act, dates back to 1952, was prepared by the Air Force's Office of Special Investigations, and is titled "*Unconventional Flying Objects Sighted; And Portions Recovered by* [first name deleted] *McLean, Friona, Texas.*" It's a deeply weird file that is suggestive of one of three things: (a) that the witness may have been suffering from a degree of dementia; (b) something highly unusual really *did* occur; or c) maybe it was a bit of both.

The basics of the story can be found in the "Synopsis" section of the Air Force dossier, which reads as follows: "Special Agent in Charge, Dallas, Texas, Texas Field Division, FBI, advised this district that McLean of Friona, Texas, had reported seeing flying saucers at an unnamed point in New Mexico; had recovered three fragments which landed close to him; and had notified the Pentagon but hearing nothing had sold a portion of one object to a Russian scientist from the USSR Embassy."

Well, that's quite a summary: UFOs, physical evidence, and the Russians, no less! But was it true? That's where things get pretty murky. While the circumstances are unclear, the file reveals that the FBI somehow got its hands on a letter that 71-year-old McLean wrote to a friend in Amarillo, Texas on the subject of his find, and which the FBI then shared with Air Force Intelligence.

McLean's very own words — as contained in the aforementioned letter — go like this: "To get back to flying saucers that are real, recently I was camped on a mountain in New Mexico and saw a dim light at first circling around up high. It circled in a mile across cycle but kept descending. First the light was white but as it got lower it turned green and exploded, showering light objects in all directions. Several of those fiery objects landed close to me, most of them were buried in the ground, but I gathered up three that were only partly buried and brought them home with me."

McLean continued: "I notified the Pentagon in Washington what I had saw fall. I heard nothing from them but a Russian scientist from the U.S.S.R. Embassy did come and buy one half of one of those objects. It was so hard we had to use a sledgehammer to break into. In the center was a round hole or vacuum filled with fine powder. This scientist scraped every bit of the dust up and put it in a bottle. He claims the object was uranium and other unknown minerals."

ETS AND RABBITS!

LA SPEZIA, ITALY

La Spezia, Italy was the site of a very strange UFO encounter on this particular day. A rancher saw a brightly illuminated, missile-shaped UFO land on his property, out of which came a trio of roughly three-to-four-foot-tall creatures, all attired in identical silver, one-piece outfits. As the amazed and worried farmer watched from behind a clump of bushes, he noticed the ETs immediately focused their attentions on a number of rabbits that the farmer had in a series of cages. They clearly were interested in the animals, as they suddenly started babbling in a language that wasn't Italian – or indeed, any terrestrial language, so far as he could tell.

Worried that the rabbits would become the central part of what we might call a "cosmic kidnapping," the farmer quietly and stealthily made his way back to his nearby home and grabbed his rifle. On returning, he could see the small aliens were still there and still staring intently at the rabbits. So, he decided to blast the creatures back to wherever it was they came from. At that point, something weird happened: his rifle failed to fire. And it became inexplicably heavy, to the point where the farmer was forced to let it drop to the ground. Worse, the man was suddenly rendered into a state of paralysis – something which gave the aliens the opportunity to seize the rabbits and take them to their craft. Within seconds of the vehicle taking to the skies, the man was able to move again.

Renowned UFO investigator Jacques Vallee says that the man "told his story to his close friends only, but it soon spread. The witness is known as sober and reliable."

MOTHMAN IN THE UK?

HYTHE, KENT, ENGLAND

Midway through November 1963, one of the most chilling and eerie of all monster encounters on record occurred in the dark and shadowy environment of Sandling Park, Hythe, Kent, England. It was an encounter that, in terms of the description of the creature, provokes Mothman-style imagery – even though the latter, famous creature did not hit the headlines in and around Point Pleasant, West Virginia until 1966. Although Sandling Park was certainly shrouded in overwhelming darkness at the time of the beastly event, it was hardly the sort of place where one would expect to encounter nothing less than a fully-fledged monster. Amazingly, however, and according to a group of terrified witnesses, that is exactly what happened.

John Flaxton, aged seventeen on the night that all hell broke loose, was accompanied by three friends, including eighteen-year old Mervyn Hutchinson. As they walked along a lane running by the park – after returning from a local Friday night dance – the group of friends became aware of a bright object moving over-head, which they at first took to be nothing stranger than a star. How very wrong they turned out to be.

The teenagers were amazed, and more than a bit scared, by the object's presence, as they watched it hover and then drop out of sight behind a group of trees. The boys decided to leave the area with haste, but the light soon loomed into view again. It hovered around ten feet from the ground, and at an approximate distance of two hundred feet, then once again went out of sight.

"It was a bright and gold oval," one of the boys reported.

"And when we moved, it moved. When we stopped, it stopped." That was not necessarily a good sign.

Suddenly, the boys heard the snapping of twigs from a nearby thicket, and out from the wooded area shuffled a creature of horrendous appearance. "It was the size of a human," reported Mervyn Hutchinson. "But it didn't seem to have any head. There were wings on its back, like bat wings."

The group fled, perhaps understandably not wanting to hang around and see what developed next. Matters didn't end there, however. Five night later, one Keith Croucher saw an unusual object float across a nearby soccer field. Forty-eight-hours after that, one John McGoldrick, accompanied by a friend, checked out the location and stumbled upon unusual impressions in the ground, which gave every indication that something solid and significant had landed there.

The impressions were never conclusively identified and the mysterious entity failed to make another appearance.

NOVEMBER 16, 1989

THE BELGIAN MILITARY GETS CONCERNED
LIEGE, BELGIUM

Officially, the U.S. Government got out of the UFO issue in 1969 when the Air Force's Project Blue Book closed its doors. Of course, that doesn't mean that agencies have not taken an interest in UFOs post-1969. They certainly have. A perfect example is the so-called Flying Triangle phenomenon. It took off in the early-to-mid 1980s and reached its peak in the following decade. Although, a careful study of the history of Ufology demonstrates that the large, black, triangular-shaped UFOs have, in fact, been reported since the 1940s – although, admittedly, not on the scale they were reported in later years.

One of the more interesting documents that demonstrates post–1969 interest in the UFO puzzle focuses on those strange Flying Triangles – specifically over Belgium in the 1989-1990 time-frame. It originates with the US Department of Defense and is titled "Belgium and the UFO Issue." Circulated widely among the US Intelligence community, it reveals the following: "Numerous UFO sightings have been made in Belgium since Nov 89. The credibility of some individuals making the reports is good… Investigation by BAF [Belgian Air Force] continues."

We're then provided with the story of a very credible source: "[Deleted] related a similar UFO sighting which apparently happened to a Belgian Air Force officer in the same area near Liege during November 89. The officer and his wife were allegedly blinded by a huge bright object as they were driving on the autoroute. They stopped their car, but were so frightened they abandoned the vehicle and ran into the woods…The BAF is concerned to a point about the UFO issue and is taking action to investigate information they have…The USAF did confirm to the BAF and Belgian MOD that no USAF Stealth aircraft were operating in the Ardennes area during the periods in question."

NOVEMBER 17, 1958

ALIENS OF THE GIANT-SIZED KIND
BALMORAL, SCOTLAND

On this particular day a bizarre UFO encounter occurred in the wilds of Scotland, and involved two members of the British Territorial Army. As part of their training, an Aberdeen-based unit of the TA had been dispatched to an area near Balmoral to take part in weekend maneuvers. During the exercise, two from the group were deployed to guard a small hilltop and, fully-equipped, set about digging themselves a trench for cover.

In the early hours of the morning, both men heard what they described as a strange "gurgling" sound. It was coming from a nearby group of trees, a couple of hundred meters from their position. Somewhat curious, they set out to investigate, when two huge figures emerged from the shadows and proceeded towards them. Both witnesses were horrified to see that the creatures were more than seven feet in height.

Naturally overcome with terror, the Territorials hastily retreated. As they ran, they heard a "swishing noise," and, glancing over their shoulders, saw a gigantic, disc-shaped object in the sky that appeared to be following them. Reportedly "pulsating," the UFO swooped low over their heads and disappeared trailing a shower of sparks. They chose not to tell the officer in charge of the operation of their extraordinary experience.

NOVEMBER 18, 1957

AN ALIEN MATERIALIZES
BIRMINGHAM, ENGLAND

Around 3:00 p.m., Cynthia Appleton, who lived in the city of Birmingham, England, had an extraordinary encounter in the family home. As she went upstairs to check on her baby, Mrs. Appleton "sensed an oppressiveness like that preceding a thunderstorm," said Charles Bowen, a noted UFO investigator of that era. Then, out of the blue, the form of a man materialized – first blurry and then completely clear. At the same time, a high-pitched whirring was heard.

Perhaps recognizing the terror on Mrs. Appleton's face, the entity seemingly had the ability to calm her mind. Now relaxed, she could see that the man was dressed in a one-piece, tight-fitting outfit that resembled a "plastic raincoat" in quality and texture. The man apparently spoke to Mrs. Appleton in telepathic fashion, claiming to be from another word, and asking odd questions about titanium.

Charles Bowen, who took a particular interest in this odd affair, said: "The visitor also conveyed to her by some mysterious process involving his hand, a picture of a saucer-type craft with a transparent dome, and also a larger 'Master' craft. He indicated that he came from a world of peace and harmony."

NOVEMBER 19, 1973

THE SONS OF SATAN AND MYSTERIOUS MUTILATIONS
UNITED STATES

Since at least 1967, reports have surfaced throughout the United States of animals – but, chiefly, cattle – slaughtered in bizarre fashion. Organs are taken and significant amounts of blood are found to be missing. In some cases, the limbs of the cattle are broken, suggesting they have been dropped to the ground from a significant height. Evidence of extreme heat, to slice into the skin of the animals, has been found at mutilation sites. Eyes are removed, tongues are sliced off, and, typically, the sexual organs are gone.

While the answers to the puzzle remain frustratingly outside of the public arena, theories abound. They include extraterrestrials, engaged in nightmarish experimentation of the genetic kind; military programs involving the testing of new bio-warfare weapons; and government agencies secretly monitoring the food-chain, fearful that something worse than "Mad Cow Disease" may have infected the U.S. cattle herd – and, possibly, as a result, the human population, too. Then, there is the matter of the Sons of Satan; a secret cult that engaged in the sacrifice of cattle to their lord and master, the Devil himself.

The story concerns an inmate of the Federal Penitentiary in Leavenworth, Kansas. The year had barely begun when one of the prisoners at Leavenworth – a man named A. Kenneth Bankston - penned a letter to a well-known UFO investigator, Jerome Clark. Bankston's reasoning for contacting Clark was simple enough: one year earlier, in 1973, Clark wrote an article on the cattle mutilation puzzle for *Fate* magazine. So, Bankston was looking for someone with whom he could share his story – a story focused on what he termed the Sons of Satan.

Bankston's story was as eye-opening as it was controversial. The Sons of Satan was a powerful, very well hidden group, said Bankston, that had seemingly endless funding and manpower and which was led by a mysterious character only referred to as "Howard." The secret group was determined to provoke "hell on earth." And the sacrificial rites were a way to ensure that Satan would aid in the group's efforts to create hellish mayhem.

NOVEMBER 20, 1952

AN ENCOUNTER IN THE DESERT
PARKER, ARIZONA

Greg Bishop, who has carefully studied the life and ufological claims of George Adamski – one of the most controversial of all the so-called "Contactees" – reveals the details of Adamski's life-changing, initial encounter: "...Adamski left his Palomar

[California] mountain retreat at 1:00 a.m. on Thursday November 20, 1952 along with his lifetime secretary Lucy McGinnis and Alice Wells… At about 8.00 a.m. they met with Al Bailey and his wife Betty, and George Hunt Williamson [a fellow-Contactee, and about who more imminently] and his wife, Betty, in Blythe, [California] just west of the Arizona / California border."

As they reached Parker, Arizona, something amazing happened: a UFO loomed into view. Back to Greg Bishop: "Williamson understatedly asked: 'Is that a space ship?', as Betty Bailey tried to set up a movie camera, but couldn't because 'she was so excited.' According to Adamski, they were anxious not to attract attention to the object, so they didn't point at it and alert other passing cars to this event."

"Someone take me down the road, quick! That ship has come looking for me and I don't want to keep them waiting!" Adamski yelled, as he jumped into the car with McGinnis and Mr. Bailey. About a half-mile down the road, with the craft shadowing them, Adamski told McGinnis to turn off the road. Adamski soon saw a figure waving to him and walked towards it.

Adamski said of the encounter, "I fully realized I was in the presence of a man from space – a human being from another world! The entity identified himself as Orthon and claimed to come from the planet Venus. After some warnings about atomic weapons and wars, and a refusal to be photographed, Orthon returned to his ship and sailed away."

A MYSTERY ON THE MOORS

HARWOOD DALE, NORTH YORKSHIRE, ENGLAND

On this particular night, three Englishmen – Frank Dickenson, Frank Hutton and Fred Taylor – were driving from a Harwood Dale, England mill with Dickenson behind the wheel of the car. As they closed in on an area of moorland called Reasty Bank, all three noticed a red light falling from the skies and seemingly crash-landing on nearby, hilly ground. It was moorland very close to Royal Air Force Fylingdales, a military installation that has been implicated in numerous UFO incidents since the mid-1960s. Dickenson brought his car to a screeching halt.

Taylor opened one of the back doors, leaped out, and headed up the hills to the area where it appeared the UFO had come down. Taylor was fortunate enough to stumble on the object, after about five or ten minutes spent searching the area. It was saucer-shaped, roughly 18 inches in diameter, and weighed around 50 to 60 pounds – which was a surprisingly heavy weight for its relatively small size. Due to the weight of the object, Taylor headed back down the hill to inform his friends what he had found. They drove as close as was conceivably possible to the crash site. Having done so, the trio then headed across the dark moors to the site of the crash.

Despite the fact that Taylor was sure they were in the right area, the UFO could no longer be located – to the consternation of all three. It had vanished as mysteriously as it had appeared, and in a period of no longer than fifteen minutes. Given the fact that the temperature was freezing and the entire area was by now enveloped in darkness, they elected to come back the following day. No luck: the object still could not be found.

It did turn up later on – apparently on a shelf of a local fish and chips shop, no less! – but quickly vanished again, amid claims that it was either a genuine UFO of mini-proportions, some sort of classified weapon of the British military, or possibly even a portion of a Soviet space satellite. The matter remains enigmatically unexplained.

NOVEMBER 22, 1963

A PRESIDENT KILLED BECAUSE OF HIS UFO KNOWLEDGE
DALLAS, TEXAS

It's fair to say that within the field of Ufology, there are more than a few people who believe – or suspect – that JFK was whacked to prevent him from blowing the lid on his knowledge of the UFO phenomenon. I've written about aspects of this highly controversial issue before, and it's worth noting just how many connections there are between UFOs and the killing of JFK.

Fred Crisman was one of the key figures in the notorious UFO saga of Maury Island, Puget Sound, Washington State. It's a bizarre story which pre-dates, by a few days, Kenneth Arnold's famous flying saucer encounter of June 24, 1947. It's a case which involves the deaths of two members of the military – Lt. Frank Brown and Capt. William Davidson – and threats from a Man in Black-type character. Then there are claims of secret surveillance of the central players in the odd story. On the other hand, many within Ufology believe the whole thing was nothing but a tragic hoax.

As for Crisman and the JFK assassination, author Kenn Thomas tells us: "In 1968, New Orleans district attorney Jim Garrison subpoenaed Fred Crisman as part of his investigation into the JFK assassination, which became the subject of Oliver Stone's

1992 *JFK* movie. Garrison believed that Crisman was the infamous grassy knoll shooter. And he's the central figure in the 'Mystery Tramp' photo of the Dallas rail yard hobos."

While there is a great deal of dispute about who shot JFK, there's no doubt about who killed Lee Harvey Oswald. It was Dallas strip-club-owner and Mob-buddy, Jack Ruby. Journalist Dorothy Kilgallen was deeply interested in the circumstances surrounding the JFK affair, and particularly so Ruby's links – to the extent that she managed to secure an interview with him. Back in 1955, the following words of Kilgallen appeared in the pages of the *Los Angeles Examiner*: "British scientists and airmen, after examining the wreckage of one mysterious flying ship, are convinced these strange aerial objects are not optical illusions or Soviet inventions, but are flying saucers which originate on another planet."

Kilgallen claimed her information came from a British official of Cabinet rank. Some suggest Kilgallen's death on November 8, 1965 was not the result of an accidental overdose of booze and pills. They see a far more sinister explanation.

One day before his death, JFK spoke at the dedication ceremony of the Aerospace Medical Health Center at Brooks Air Force Base, San Antonio, Texas. The base had been chosen to conduct groundbreaking work in the field of space-medicine; figuring out how to keep astronauts free from deadly radiation, learning more about how gravity-free environments can affect the human body, and so on. While at Brooks, Kennedy met with personnel from Wright-Patterson Air Force Base, Ohio (the alleged home of the legendary "Hangar 18"). JFK also met with staff from Fort Detrick, Maryland. For years, rumors have circulated to the effect that Fort Detrick has been the home of classified research into "alien viruses."

And the strange list, linking UFOs and the JFK assassination, goes on and on.

FROM INTERCEPTION TO MISSING IN ACTION

SKIES OVER LAKE SUPERIOR, UNITED STATES

The so-called "Kinross Case" focuses upon the strange – and still-unresolved - disappearance of a US Air Force F-89C jet fighter that was scrambled late on the night of November 23, 1953, on an "active air defense mission" to intercept an "unknown aircraft" over Lake Superior. Kinross Air Force Base, which was closest to the scene where the "unknown" was initially tracked, quickly alerted the 433rd Fighter Interception Squadron at Truax Field, Madison, Wisconsin, and the F-89C gave immediate chase.

Available USAF records demonstrate that the F-89 was vectored west-northwest, then west, climbing to 30,000 feet. While on its westerly course, the crew received permission to descend to 7,000 feet, turning east-northeast and coming steeply down on the target from above. Alarmingly, as the aircraft closed-in on the "unknown" it subsequently vanished into oblivion, along with its two crew-members. The last radar contact placed the interceptor at 8,000 feet, 70 miles from Keeweenaw Point, and about 150 miles northwest of Kinross AFB, which, today, is called Kincheloe AFB.

An extract from the official USAF Aircraft Accident Report outlines further details of the official story:

"Aircraft took off at 2322 Zebra 23 Nov 53 on an active Air Defense Mission to intercept an unknown aircraft approximately 160 miles Northwest of Kinross Air Force Base. The aircraft was under radar control throughout the interception. At approximately 2352 Zebra the last radio contact was made by the radar station controlling the interception. At approximately 2355 Zebra the unknown aircraft and the F-89 merged together on the radar scope. Shortly thereafter the IFF signal disappeared from the radar scope. No further contact was established with the F-89. An extensive aerial search has revealed no trace of the aircraft. The aircraft and its crew are still missing."

For both ufologists and the Air Force, the matter of the Kinross affair remains wide open.

NOVEMBER 24, 1948

"PUBLICITY OF THIS NATURE IS UNDESIRABLE"

THE PENTAGON, WASHINGTON, D.C.

Declassified Air Force memoranda prepared on this date demonstrates the approach that the military took when it came to the matter of UFOs and the American media. In part, the document states: "Mr. Stanley Shallet, a member of the staff of the *Saturday Evening Post*, has been directed to write an article for the Post dealing with the 'flying saucer' incidents. Mr. Shallet has approached the Director of Intelligence for assistance in the preparation of this article.

"It is the opinion of the Directorate of Intelligence that publicity of this nature is undesirable but, if such articles are written, they will be less harmful to the national interest if a degree of guidance in their preparation is exercised by the Directorate of Intelligence.

"Sufficient unclassified data is on hand in the Air Intelligence Division, D/I, to assist in the preparation of an article on the 'flying saucer" incidents. Project officers to give guidance to Mr. Shallet are available within the Air Intelligence Division."

NOVEMBER 25, 1991

ALIENS OR DEMONS?
WASHINGTON, D.C.

On this particular day, a Nebraskan priest named Ray Boeche had a clandestine meeting with a pair of physicists working on a top-secret program for the US Department of Defense. Both men were deeply worried and were looking for advice and guidance from Boeche on the project in which they were immersed.

The classified operation, Boeche was told, revolved around attempts by certain elements of the DoD to contact what were termed "Non-Human Entities," or NHEs. Most people might call them extraterrestrials, aliens, or in terms of the field of Ufology and popular culture – "the Grays." For a while, the DoD referred to them in those terms, too. But not for long. As Ray Boeche listened carefully to what his Deep Throat sources told him, he came to realize that the Pentagon was dabbling in decidedly dangerous areas.

The scientists explained to Boeche that the contact with the NHEs was not achieved on a face- to-face basis, but, rather, in mind-to-mind fashion. Telepathy, ESP, and channeling were the primary ways via which interaction occurred. But, as the program progressed, something ominous occurred: it was as if a dark cloud descended on all those tied to the program. Bad luck, illness, and even death, blighted the team. Such was the extent of the negativity that surrounded the operation the DoD came to a startling and disturbing conclusion.

Although the DoD had initially assumed the entities they

were dealing with were extraterrestrial, Boeche was informed that over time that view changed significantly and dramatically. Indeed, the scientists on board eventually came to believe that they were not dealing with aliens from far away galaxies, after all, but with highly dangerous, deceptive, manipulative demons – as in literal demons from a literal Hell.

The group still exists to this day, still deeply worried by what it sees as a deadly, deceptive phenomenon doing its utmost to disrupt and destroy the human race.

NOVEMBER 26, 1952

"FOUR DISCS HANGING IN THE SKY"
BOUAR, CENTRAL AFRICAN REPUBLIC

Father Carlos Maria was an Argentinian missionary who spent time working in Africa, specifically in and around Bouar. It was while being given a ride to his destination by a truck-driver named Lasimone that Father Maria encountered something incredible in the skies above: a squadron of UFOs.

The missionary reported that he saw "four discs hanging in the sky to the left of the road. We could see them quite clearly, though it was impossible to judge their distance. There were two above and two below, and they were not in contact. When they came to a standstill they were pale silver in color, like the moon. I had several opportunities of seeing them in motion ad had a strong idea that the lower pair only were revolving. Just before morning, they blazed up as bright as the sun. Then they seemed to arrange themselves in a group that proceeded to describe circles before returning to their starting point. When they stopped, the bright blaze died down to the original dull silver."

Father Maria added: "When they were on the move they looked slightly oval, but I could not say for certain whether that was because they actually changed shape or because they were viewed from a different angle. Whatever the reason, the same conformation and the same blaze-up marked every change of position. We were watching them from 10:00 to 10:20 p.m. After their final circling movements, they remained motionless for several minutes. Then they departed and disappeared in the opposite direction to ours, still keeping to the left of the road."

He concluded: "There is nothing I can add. What I saw was neither aerolite, nor shooting star, nor anything of that kind. It could only be some machine, the product of human brains."

Precisely what kind of "human brains" had the ability to create such astonishing craft way back in 1952 is anyone's guess!

NOVEMBER 27, 1951

TWINKLE, TWINKLE, LITTLE STAR
WRIGHT-PATTERSON AIR FORCE BASE, DAYTON, OHIO

A fascinating document was prepared by the US Air Force's Atmospheric Physics Laboratory. It was the final report on something known as Project Twinkle – a secret program created to investigate sightings of strange "green fireballs" in the southwest skies. According to the report...

"Early in 1950 the Geophysics Research Division received a directive to investigate peculiar light phenomena that had been observed in the skies of the southwestern United States. Project Twinkle was established to check into these phenomena and their explanation.

"The gist of the findings is essentially negative. The period of observations covers a little over a year. Some unusual phenomena were observed during that period, most of them, can be attributed to such man-made objects as airplanes, balloons, or rockets, among other things.Others can be attributed to natural phenomena such as flying birds, small clouds, and meteorites. There has been no indication that even the somewhat strange observations often called 'Green Fireballs' are anything but natural phenomena."

AN ATTACK BY HAIRY ETS

CARACAS, VENEZUELA

Shortly after the witching-hour, Jose Ponce and Gustavo Gonzalez had a nightmarish encounter on the outskirts of Caracas, Venezuela. As they drove, the dark road was suddenly lit up by what the astonished pair could only describe as a bright ball of light, with a circumference of around three feet. It swayed slightly in the air, not unlike a small boat bobbing along on the water.

The two slowed down their vehicle as they approached it, eventually coming to a complete halt. It was then, suddenly, that astonishment was replaced by outright terror. While Ponce stayed inside the van, Gonzalez cautiously exited the vehicle; he began to slowly and tentatively walk towards the hovering globe. Suddenly, Gonzalez found himself thrown to the ground by an unseen force. The reason why the attacker was unseen - for a few seconds, at least – was because of its size. Or, rather, its profound lack of size. Gonzalez, to his shock and fear, was finally able to see what had assaulted him: a small, hair-covered creature that was built like a man, but which was only around three feet in height. Acting on impulse and adrenalin, Gonzalez attempted to plunge his knife into the body of the creature, only for the knife to bounce off it.

In mere seconds, another hairy dwarf was on the scene, and temporarily blinded Gonzalez with a bright light that emitted from a powerful, flashlight-type device. Shocked to the core, Ponce gathered his wits together and jumped out of the van to help his friend, who was stumbling around, his eyesight still affected by the powerful beam that hit him with full force. To Ponce's growing concern, two more of the hairy creatures surfaced out of the shadows, and both making their way towards the men – and armed, no less, with large rocks.

Although the presence of the rocks suggested to the men that the hairy things were ready to kill them, with hindsight it seems they were only a defensive measure, in the event a last resort-style situation developed. Fortunately, it did not. The small things raced to the ball of light and, somehow, launched themselves inside it, despite its equally small size and vanished in the blink of an eye.

NOVEMBER 29, 1980

A POLICEMAN ENCOUNTERS AN ALIEN
TODMORDEN, YORKSHIRE

Back in November 1980, a then-serving English policeman named Alan Godfrey had a profound UFO encounter in Todmorden, Yorkshire – a pleasant locale that has its origins in the 17th century. Godfrey's encounter came just five months after he was involved in the investigation of a curious death in town. The victim was a man named Zigmund Adamski. As most people will know, the not exactly common name of Adamski is a very famous one in

Ufology. It was just one of those strange synchronicities that pro-liferate when the UFO phenomenon looms large.

As for Godfrey's UFO encounter, it occurred under cover of darkness, in the pre-dawn morning of November 29, 1980, while he was out on patrol in his police car. As he drove along one par-ticular stretch of road, Godfrey was amazed by the sight of what he first thought was a bus positioned oddly in the road. As Godfrey got closer, however, he could see it was something else entirely. It was actually nothing less than a somewhat egg-shaped UFO.

There then followed an experience that contained certain, key elements of the UFO phenomenon, such as missing-time, and recollections of being taken on-board a craft. However, the entity Godfrey was confronted by on the craft was not the typ-ical black-eyed, dwarfish "Gray." Rather, it was a human-looking figure dressed in a long gown and sporting a beard. In that sense, there was more of a "Contactee"-style component to the incident. But, there was even more to the affair, too. And this is where things become intertwined with matters of the paranormal kind.

While undergoing hypnotic regression, Godfrey said that also aboard the UFO was a large black dog. This was not the first encounter Godfrey had with an anomalous hound. Years earlier, he had seen a ghostly Labrador. There was also an odd occasion – in the 1960s, and near Todmorden – when what seemed to be a woman with a large black dog stepped out in front of Godfrey's vehicle, causing him to slam the brakes on. Both the woman and the dog vanished. It just so happens that Todmorden has in its midst centuries-old legends of what are known as the "Gabriel Hounds." They are akin to the UK's wider, ancient, phenome-non of so-called "Phantom Black Dogs" of the kind that inspired Sir Arthur Conan Doyle to pen the Sherlock Holmes novel, *The*

Hound of the Baskervilles. One of the strangest of all UFO encounters ever reported? No doubt!

LIVING FOREVER, AND ALL THANKS TO ALIENS!
BAGHDAD, IRAQ

A very strange story was told to me on this date, a story which revolves around the significant matter of immortality. It was all focused on a hush-hush program that was run out of a particular facility in Utah. It was a program that allegedly began in 2003 and which was prompted by the discovery of certain, unspecified, ancient "things" in Baghdad, after the invasion of Iraq began. The project had at its heart something both amazing and controversial. It all revolved around nothing less than attempts to bring the human aging process to a halt – and maybe, even…*to reverse it*. This was, however, a very unusual program, in the sense that it didn't just rely on modern day technology and medicine.

Yes, the program had a number of brilliant scientists attached to it, but it was also populated by theologians, historians, and archaeologists – who were quietly contracted and hired and subjected to grim non-disclosure agreements. The quest for the truth of immortality was, to a very significant degree, not based around the present or the future, but on the distant past. Much time was spent digging into accounts of none other than "Manna from Heaven," and the controversies surrounding what has become known as "White Powder Gold," the "Bread of Presence," and "Amrita," all of which the group concluded, were the creations of ancient aliens.

Deep underground, scientists who had spent much of their

working lives striving to understand why, exactly, the aging process occurs as it does, were sat next to biblical experts who were deciphering and interpreting ancient texts on the aforementioned life-extending, digestible substances. Military personnel, who were dutifully ensuring the program ran under the strictest levels of security and safety, rubbed shoulders with modern day alchemists, who were striving to crack the White Powder Gold conundrum. And learned souls in the fields of none other than "ancient astronauts," and the Bible's legendary "men of renown," crossed paths with demonologists.

The story continued that at least as late as 2010, absolutely no progress had been made, beyond adding to the lore and legend that surrounds tales of immortality and massive lifespans in times long gone. Rather ironically, the fact that I was told the project was a one hundred percent failure added credibility to the story – for me, at least, it did.

DECEMBER

THE SMALLEST UFO OF ALL?

SOUTH WALES

A small village in South Wales briefly became the target of extra-terrestrials, according to Alan Williams. Now in his seventies, Williams recalls that, as a young man, he overheard his parents talking about a UFO encounter that his uncle had experienced the day before. Williams is sure of the dates, as his birthday is December 2. So, he says, it was easy for him to remember the chain of events, time-wise. So the story went, the witness – as he was about to head off to work in the early hours of the morning – saw a very small UFO as he walked down the drive of his home and towards his car, which was parked in the street.

As he was about to unlock the car-door, Williams' uncle saw a roughly-golf-ball-sized UFO appear before him and which "traveled around the car for a bit" before "jetting off" into the skies above.

A SECRET UFO PANEL

WASHINGTON, D.C.

The CIA's Assistant Director H. Marshall Chadwell noted, in a classified report on UFO activity in American airspace: "Sightings of unexplained objects at great altitudes and traveling at high speeds in the vicinity of major U.S. defense installations are of such nature that they are not attributable to natural phenomena or known types of aerial vehicles."

Believing that something really might be afoot in the skies of

America, Chadwell prepared a list of saucer-themed recommendations for the National Security Council (QUOTE BEGINS):

1. The Director of Central Intelligence shall formulate and carry out a program of intelligence and research activities as required to solve the problem of instant positive identification of unidentified flying objects.

2. Upon call of the Director of Central Intelligence, Government departments and agencies shall provide assistance in this program of intelligence and research to the extent of their capacity provided, however, that the DCI shall avoid duplication of activities presently directed toward the solution of this problem.

3. This effort shall be coordinated with the military services and the Research and Development Board of the Department of Defense, with the Psychological Board and other Governmental agencies as appropriate.

4. The Director of Central Intelligence shall disseminate information concerning the program of intelligence and research activities in this field to the various departments and agencies which have authorized interest therein." (END OF QUOTE)

The overall conclusion of the Robertson Panel was that while UFOs did not appear to have a bearing on national security or on the defense of the United States, the way in which the subject could be used by unfriendly forces to manipulate the public mindset and disrupt the U.S. military infrastructure *did* have a bearing – and a major one, too – on matters of a security nature. According to the panel's members:

"Although evidence of any direct threat from these sightings was wholly lacking, related dangers might well exist resulting from: A. Misidentification of actual enemy artifacts by defense personnel. B. Overloading of emergency reporting channels with 'false' information. C. Subjectivity of public to mass hysteria and greater vulnerability to possible enemy psychological warfare."

DECEMBER 3, 1967

POLICING A UFO

ASHLAND, NEBRASKA

During the early hours of December 3, 1967, police officer Herbert Schirmer was on duty in the town of Ashland, Nebraska. "On-duty" meant that he was patrolling the neighborhood, ensuring all was normal. It transpired, however, that things were most definitely not normal. As he turned onto one particular road, Schirmer saw what he first thought was a truck, stuck at the side of the road. It was no truck. As Schirmer got closer, he could see that it was actually an egg-shaped craft, hovering eight or nine feet off the ground, with interior lighting of a bright red color. Then things became fuzzy and confused. The next he knew, Schirmer was heading back to the police station to make a report.

When he began to be troubled by bad dreams, Schirmer elected to be placed under hypnosis to determine if there was more to the encounter than met the eye. There was. And then some. Schirmer recalled being approached by a trio of approximately 5-foot-tall aliens. One – who Schirmer took to be in charge – asked the shocked officer: "Are you the watchman of this place?" To which Schrimer replied, "Sure." With intergalactic pleasantries out of the way, the aliens invited Schirmer to take a tour of their craft, which he accepted. He noted that all of the crew wore tight-fitting outfits, emblazoned with the image of a winged serpent.

Before the aliens returned amazed Schirmer to his car, the "leader" made an odd but intriguing statement: "We want you to believe in us, but not too much."

DECEMBER 4, 1967

UFOLOGICAL NOISE

ITHACA, NEW YORK

On this particular evening, Mrs. Rita Maley was driving along Route 34 to Ithaca, New York, when she became aware of an unidentified red light that seemed to be following her. Glancing out of the window, she was shocked to see an illuminated object that was maneuvering near a row of power lines: "It made a humming sound, something like the vibration of a television antenna in the wind," she later stated.

Notably, Mrs. Maley reported that she felt the humming sound was taking away her self-will – and she also found that her car would not respond properly. Interestingly, she added that her son – who was in the car with her – "was in some kind of trance" during the time that the UFO was in view.

DECEMBER 5, 1950

A UFO CRASHES IN MEXICO

MEXICO, SOUTH OF LAREDO, TEXAS

The FBI Office at Richmond issued the following, *Urgent* Teletype message to Bureau Headquarters at Washington, D.C.: "Re

Flying Saucers. This Office very confidentially advised by Army Intelligence, Richmond, that they have been put on immediate high alert for any data whatsoever concerning flying saucers. CIC here states background of instructions not available from Air Force Intelligence, who are not aware of reason for alert locally, but any information whatsoever must be telephoned by them immediately to Air Force Intelligence. CIC advises data strictly confidential and should not be disseminated."

Precisely what led to the issuing of this "high alert" remains unknown. Unofficially and according to whistleblower testimony and documentation, however, the alert followed the crash and subsequent retrieval of a UFO in Mexico in the same time frame.

For example, in an affidavit originally filed with the National Investigations Committee on Aerial Phenomena (NICAP) that is now housed in the archives of the Center for UFO Studies (CUFOS), retired Air Force Colonel Robert Willingham confirmed his knowledge of the detection on radar and subsequent crash of an object of unknown origin "south of Laredo, Texas" at the time in question.

According to Willingham, he and a co-pilot were able to fly a light aircraft to the crash site that was already secured by "armed guards" before being waived off. Although Willingham did not see the crashed object itself, he did retrieve a piece of metal from the site that "looked like a magnesium steel... I tried to heat it... it just wouldn't melt."

Then, Willingham said, he took the debris to a Marine Corps metallurgy laboratory inHagerstown Maryland, where the debris mysteriously vanished and the trail went cold.

Researcher Bruce Maccabee states: "[The investigator] Todd Zechel...investigated Willingham's story...It was Zechel's opinion…that the crash occurred on December 5, the recovery occurred on December 6, a general alert to counterintelligence was sent out on December 7, and the FBI learned about it on December 8."

DECEMBER 6, 1954

"AIRCRAFT DESIGNERS MAY BE APPROACHING THE ERA OF THE EARTH-BUILT FLYING SAUCER"

WASHINGTON, D.C.

As most people with an interest in the subject of UFOs will be aware, pretty much since the term "Flying Saucer" was coined in the summer of 1947 rumors have circulated to the effect that some UFOs are secret, military hardware. We're talking about man-made UFOs. Of course, those who roll their eyes at such possibilities very often bring up the matter of the decidedly ill-fated "Avrocar." It was a saucer-shaped vehicle that promised a great deal but ultimately turned out to be a disaster. It's intriguing to note, however, that in the 1950s – when UFOs were at their height, so to speak – a great deal of enthusiasm for saucer-shaped craft was exhibited by the US military.

A perfect example of this enthusiasm can be found in the pages of the Air Intelligence Digest, Volume 7, Issue 12, dated December 6, 1954. It states, under the "Editor's Notes" section: "We have not joined the ranks of publications that print speculative stories of strange flying contraptions, nor have we had any polka-dotted strangers from outer space visiting our office. This is for real. A new aircraft configuration with a circular platform is taking shape on the drawing boards of Western aircraft designers that may well be the beginning of a new era of flight."

We are then told: "New type of jet aircraft, powered by a turbine larger than any now in use, is expected to take off, land vertically, and be able to hover. It may cruise at 1,500 knots and have a range of 15,000 nautical miles. Aircraft designers may be approaching the era of the Earth-built flying saucer. Latest information indicates that a turbine-powered, circular-shaped jet aircraft – literally a flying turbojet engine – will be in existence in the West just 5 years from now. No such aircraft have yet flown, but an experimental project is actively under way in the Western Hemisphere. Such a machine may turn out to be a formidable weapon capable of traveling so fast and so high that it will be virtually immune from attack by present-day defense systems."

That's all very impressive, as is the following from the Digest: "If the developments now under way culminate in successful flight – and the chances are considered good that they will – the disc-shaped aircraft is expected to be able to take off and land vertically, to be able to hover, and to travel at speeds and altitudes than those possible to attain now with conventional wing-and-fuselage jet aircraft. In addition, the range of a disc-type bomber may be greater than that of present-day bombers."

DECEMBER 7, 2015

"IT APPEARED TO HAVE THREE CIRCLES IN A TRIANGLE SHAPE"

EDINBURG, TEXAS

Roger Marsh, the editor of the *MUFON UFO Journal*, says:

"A Texas witness at Edinburg reported watching a triangle-shaped UFO with 'circle-like' neon lights at each of the three points that hovered momentarily and moved quickly away, according to testimony in Case 73039 from the Mutual UFO Network (MUFON) witness reporting database."

According to the witness: "It appeared to have three circles in a triangle shape emitting an orange light from each circle-like bright neon light. The night sky was very clear and the shape of the object appeared to be a triangle or V-shaped. It traveled faster than a jet, but slower than a falling star. Its path was straight."

DECEMBER 8, 1974

PENETRATING AN ALIEN BASE

MOUNT HAYES, ANCHORAGE, ALASKA

In his 1997 book *Remote Viewers*, Jim Schnabel told the story of the U.S. Intelligence community's involvement in the controversial issue of psychic spying that largely began in the early-to-mid 1970s. Commenting on the skills of a talented remote-viewer in relation to matters of a UFO nature, one Pat Price, Schnabel noted Price was of the opinion that "...Alaska's Mount Hayes, the jewel of a glacial range northeast of Anchorage, housed one of the aliens' largest bases."

According to Pat Price, and based on his psychic penetration of the mountain on November 24, the aliens that lived deep inside Mount Hayes were very human looking, differing only in their heart, lungs, blood, and eyes. Ominously, he added that the aliens use "thought transfer for motor control of us." Price added: "The site has also been responsible for strange activity and malfunction of U.S. and Soviet space objects."

A CRASHED UFO? NASA SAYS "NO!"

KECKSBURG, PENNSYLVANIA

In the late afternoon of December 9, 1965, some form of object crashed to earth near the small town of Kecksburg, Pennsylvania, after having initially been observed in the sky as a fireball that hurtled across several US states and parts of Canada.

At the scene, officials and some onlookers believed that a meteor had fallen; however, the next day both local authorities and the US Government declared strongly that nothing had fallen that night and that, as a result, nothing of any substance was found. Nevertheless, independent witnesses have provided intriguing testimony, strongly suggesting that the official explanation is far from being the correct one, and that a device of unknown origin (at least, unknown to the public and the media) was located within the woods at Kecksburg by the military, who promptly removed the mysterious device from the area.

Firefighters, newspaper reporters and a radio news director at WHJB Radio described seeing a military presence at the scene. One particular area was cordoned off. Some also reported having witnessed the recovery of an acorn-shaped object at the crash site that was loaded aboard a military transporter.

Project Blue Book, the official US Air Force investigation into UFOs that was terminated in 1969, asserted that no space debris entered American airspace on the day in question. Data provided by the US Space Command and the Russian Space Agency indicated that whatever came down, it was not a Russian satellite or space probe, as skeptics had suggested - despite the fact that, according to NASA, a failed Russian Venus probe called Cosmos

96 did reenter the Earth's atmosphere over Canada at about 3:18 a.m. on December 9, far from Pennsylvania. Moreover, Blue Book records assert that nothing more substantial than a three-person team was dispatched to the area by the Air Force in a vain attempt to locate whatever it was that had reportedly crashed at Kecksburg. This is very much at odds with the testimony of numerous locals who reported a heavy military presence in the vicinity of Kecksburg.

DECEMBER 10, 1967
AN UNDERGROUND ALIEN BASE AND A NUCLEAR DETONATION
DULCE, NEW MEXICO

Longstanding rumors suggest that a vast underground alien base exists within, and below, a massive mesa at Dulce, Rio Arriba County, New Mexico. Interestingly, we can prove there has been a wealth of weird activity in the area. For example, the FBI has officially declassified a large file on cattle-mutilations in and around Dulce, spanning the mid to late 1970s. And, on December 10, 1967, the Atomic Energy Commission (AEC) detonated a 29-kiloton-yield nuclear device 4,240 feet below ground in an attempt to provoke the release and, as a direct consequence, production of natural gas.

Thus was born Gasbuggy: a program of an overall project known as Operation Plowshare, which, ostensibly, was designed to explore the peaceful uses of atomic energy. Notably, the location of the Gasbuggy test – that covered an area of 640 acres – was New Mexico's Carson National Forest, which just happens to be situated only twelve-miles from the town of Dulce.

Today, people are forbidden from digging underground in that very area – which is very interesting in view of the underground base allegations.

Within conspiracy-based research circles, it has been suggested that the nuclear detonation had a very different goal; namely, to destroy the aforementioned alien base and wipe the deadly, hostile ETs. Certainly, it's a strange and foreboding story. And there are no shortages of accounts suggesting that such a base existed (and may still exist), and in which freakish monsters were being created by the alien entities. As one example of many, we have the following, from someone we might justifiably call a ufological whistleblower / Edward Snowden:

"Sir, first off, if you want the full story let me know. But this will explain how Mothman came about. U.S. Energy Secretary John Herrington named the Lawrence Berkeley Laboratory and New Mexico's Los Alamos National Laboratory to house advanced genetic research centers as part of a project to decipher the human genome. The genome holds the genetically coded instructions that guide the transformation of a single cell, a fertilized egg, into a biological organism.

"'The Human Genome Project may well have the greatest direct impact on humanity of any scientific initiative before us today,' said David Shirley, Director of the Berkeley Laboratory. Covertly, this research has been going on for years at the Dulce bio-genetics labs. Level 6 is hauntingly known by employees as 'Nightmare Hall.' It holds the genetic labs at Dulce. Reports from workers who have seen bizarre experimentation, are as follows:

"I have seen multi-legged 'humans' that look like half-human/half-octopus. Also reptilian-humans, and furry creatures that have hands like humans and cries like a baby, it mimics human words. Also, huge mixtures of lizard-humans in cages. There are fish, seals, birds and mice that can barely be considered those species. There are several cages (and vats) of winged-humanoids, grotesque bat-like creatures, but 3 1/2 to 7 feet tall. Gargoyle-like beings and Draco-Reptoids.

"Level 7 is worse, row after row of thousands of humans and human mixtures in cold storage. Here too are embryo storage vats of humanoids in various stages of development. I frequently encountered humans in cages, usually dazed or drugged, but sometimes they cried and begged for help. We were told they were hopelessly insane, and involved in high risk drug tests to cure insanity. We were told to never try to speak to them at all. At the beginning we believed that story. Finally in 1978 a small group of workers discovered the truth."

DECEMBER 11, 1963

A UFO LANDS AND A FILE IS OPENED
WOLVERHAMPTON, ENGLAND

Shortly after midnight, at a British military base called Royal Air Force Cosford, a UFO was seen to land by a pair of young personnel. Today, the Royal Air Force facility at Cosford, near Wolverhampton, is probably best known for its huge museum, which is home to an impressive collection of vintage military and civil aircraft. More than thirty years ago, however, Cosford became briefly famous for an entirely different reason. On the night in question, a dome-shaped UFO touched down on the base, bathed the surrounding area in a beam of green light, and was seen at close quarters by at least two RAF apprentices, before making its escape. The case became the subject of an extensive file; a file which has now been declassified under the terms of the Freedom of Information Act. Unfortunately, it sheds very little light on what the young men briefly saw.

DECEMBER 12, 1910

GLOWING ENTITIES IN IRELAND

LISTOWEL, COUNTY KERRY, IRELAND

W.Y. Evans-Wentz was born in Trenton, New Jersey in 1878 and developed a deep interest in the world of the paranormal at a young age. It was an interest that he never lost. Indeed, it stayed with him until his death in 1965. As well as being a respected anthropologist, Evans-Wentz was someone who was also fascinated by Buddhist teachings and beliefs.

Evans-Wentz was a prestigious writer and publisher, having published, in 1927, an English version of widely acclaimed and still extensively read, *The Tibetan Book of the Dead*. As for his own books, they were as notable as they were varied, one of the most revered being *The Fairy-Faith in Celtic Countries*. It's a book which is packed with fascinating accounts of old, supernatural encounters between the people of Ireland, Wales, Scotland, the Isle of Man, and Brittany, and magical entities that have variously been referred to as elementals, fairies, goblins, sprites, and the "wee folk." One story collected by Evans-Wentz stands out.

The story was personally shared with Evans-Wentz by a colleague at England's Jesus College at Oxford University – a university which Evans-Wentz studied at as a young man. The story told to Evans-Wentz was as bizarre as it was undeniably sensational. The man in question was Irish and a former resident of County Kerry, one who had chosen Oxford University as his place of education. According to the curious story told to Evans-Wentz, it was in the first week of December 1910 that the man and a friend were heading home from a night out in the Irish city of Limerick. Given that it was a fair distance away, and darkness was already on the land when they went out - never mind during their return - they chose to travel on horseback, something which would make the journey to Limerick, and home again, an easy one. It turned out, however, that for these two twenty-three-year-olds, fate had other things in store. Very strange and unforgettable things.

It was as they approached Listowel — a 14th century market town in County Kerry — that the pair couldn't fail to see a powerful, brilliant light at a distance of around half a mile from them. Suddenly, the light was joined by another one that was practically identical in appearance, and also in size, which was somewhere in the order of around six feet in height. As the two men sat on their horses, and stared in amazement at these curious displays of light, they saw something incredible happen: within the flames that were contained within the two lights, they could see a pair of what were described as radiant beings with "human form;" the flames having transformed into the entities. The lights then moved towards each other and unified as one. The figures within, Evans-Wentz was told, then strode out of the lights and towards the two men. Incredibly, they seemed to be glowing. In other words, the brilliance they gave off was not a reflection from the balls of light that surrounded them. No, they were radiating the glowing eeriness themselves.

Such was the brightness, the two friends were unable to make out if their visitors of the night were male or female, or one of each. But, they were clearly humanoid and had noticeable halos around their heads. Not surprisingly, they quickly headed home, their galloping horses getting them there in a timely fashion.

A UFO CULT IS BORN

AVERGNE, FRANCE

On December 13, and for no logical reason at all, a French man named Calude Maurice Marcel Vorilhon felt compelled to take a drive to Puy de Lasollas, which is situated near the capital of Avergne, and the site of a dormant volcano. UFO researcher Dr. Jacques Vallee outlines what happened next: "The weather was foggy, overcast. He suddenly saw a blinking red light, and something like a helicopter came down and hovered two yards above the ground. It was the size of a small bus, conical on top. A stairway appeared, and a child-like occupant came out, smiling with a glow around his body."

The very human-looking extraterrestrial gave its name as Yahweh – also the name of the God of Israel - and entered into extensive dialog with the amazed and astonished Vorilhon. The aliens were known as the Elohim, so Rael was advised. Or, those who came from the sky.

During the early, burgeoning years of human development, the Elohim – Vorilhon was told - sent a number of ambassadors to our planet, chiefly as a means to try and ensure that early man lived a good and peaceful life. Among those ambassadors were such luminaries as Buddha, Jesus, and Moses. And, those same Elohim had a firm plan in mind for Rael – a plan which has, ever since, pretty much dominated the rest of his life.

One day, Rael was told, the Elohim will return to the Earth and finally show themselves – and on a planet-wide scale, no less. And Rael was specifically selected as their number-one on Earth to pave the way for the return of the ancient alien race. The first thing Rael was asked to do was to build an embassy for the aliens, and also to create a group to which others of a like-mind could gravitate. Its name, The Movement for Welcoming the Elohim, Creators of Humanity – Madech, in abbreviated form.

It was in September 1974 that things exploded big time for Rael. That was the month in which he held a major conference in the city of Paris, at which he told the story of his by now extensive encounters, and of the alien Elohim, and their mission on Earth. It was a phenomenally successful conference which attracted more than 2,000 curious and excited attendees. Madech soon became the International Raelian Movement, and, in no time, the group went global. The rest, as the old saying goes, is history. The Raelians continue to thrive, and even to attract worldwide attention.

DECEMBER 14, 1981

A FLYING EXTRATERRESTRIAL
SAN ANTONIO, TEXAS

What can only be described as a Mothman-like "flying humanoid" was seen late at night on the fringes of the city of San Antonio, Texas. According to the witness, an Australian woman named Mavis, who moved to the United States in 1971, it was while she was hanging out washing to dry in the early afternoon that she saw a large shadow pass by, and, on looking up, saw a large, human figure gliding through the sky at a height of little more than twenty feet and at a fast rate.

Mavis, terrified, instinctively ducked, even though the fearsome flier was already by now a few hundred yards away. She had no idea what it was she encountered; except that it was human-like, flew the air "like Superman," and was gone in an instant or several.

DECEMBER 15, 1992

"A BRIGHT GOLD COLORED LIGHT"

NORTHVIEW, MISSOURI

From the UFO Hunters, there is this, from a firsthand witness: "I was followed by an oval shaped object for several miles and it took off rapidly after I shined a spotlight on it. On the night of December 15, 1992, I left Marshfield, MO and was going to visit a friend who lived just outside Elkland, MO. As I was crossing the I-44 overpass at Exit 100, I noticed a bright gold colored light to my left. It appeared to be no more than 100 feet off the ground and less than a mile west of me. Hundreds of people reported sightings of mysterious lights in the nighttime sky in the vicinity of Northview, MO (I-44 exit 96) in 1992, and I personally saw lights from a distance many times myself, and spoke to others who saw things up close, but this was by far the closest I had ever been to it."

DECEMBER 16, 1956

AN E.T. IN THE PENTAGON

WASHINGTON, D.C.

On November 21, 2008, UFO researcher-author Greg Bishop wrote: "The Reverend Frank Stranges, author of such contactee classics as *Stranger at the Pentagon* and *Flying Saucerama*, has returned to his permanent home with the space brothers, according to an email today from Tim 'Mr. UFO' Beckley. Stranges founded the National Investigations Committee on Unidentified Flying Objects (NICUFO) in 1967, apparently in homage to NICAP [the National Investigations Committee on Aerial Phenomena], the original civilian UFO group founded in 1956. He may have been piggybacking on NICAP's strong public image, but we can of course forgive him for that. Stranges most lasting legacy may be his narrative in Stranger at the Pentagon, the story of Venusian Captain 'Valiant Thor.'"

Bishop continued: "According to Stranges, After Val had met with the president and members of the Joint Chiefs, he had a meeting with Stranges at the Pentagon. Val Thor sounded (and looked) like Michael Rennie's portrayal of the ufonaut Klaatu in [the 1950 movie] *The Day The Earth Stood Still*" (Ibid.).

In relation to that alleged meeting with Thor in the Pentagon, Stranges, himself, offered the following: "Being a minister of the Gospel of Jesus Christ, as well as a student of the Bible for many years, coupled with my experience as an special investigator, I felt as though my senses were functioning properly and that I knew exactly what I was about to do. I was on my guard for fakes and frauds. In walked a man, about six feet tall, perhaps 185 pounds, brown wavy hair, brown eyes."

"His complexion appeared normal and slightly tanned. As I approached him and he looked at me it was as though he looked straight through me. With a warm smile and extending his hand, he greeted me by name. His genuineness astonished me, but quickly I understood. As I gripped his hand, I was somewhat surprised to feel the soft texture of his skin, like that of a baby but with the strength of a man that silently testified to his power and intensity."

As for why, precisely, Thor had made it his business to visit the Earth, Stranges informed his followers: "He told me that his purpose in coming was to help mankind return to the Lord. He spoke in positive terms...always with a smile on his face. He said that man was further away from *God* than ever before, but there was still a good chance if man looks in the right place. He told me he had been here nearly three years and would depart in just a few months."

"Claiming that he would not use force to speak with men in authority in America, he was happy to consult with them at their invitation. He further stated that thus far only a few men in Washington knew of his existence in the Pentagon."

DECEMBER 17, 1965

"OBVIOUSLY HIGHLY SENSITIVE"

LONDON, ENGLAND

Stamped *Priority*, this brief but potentially important report was quietly declassified by the UK Ministry of Defense in 1996, having originated with its Defense Intelligence Staff: "17 Dec 1965. Sighting of unusual phenomena between Ruthin and Mold on A494 map reference 172584, Mr. Kenneth William Reece saw a white light descend into valley where it exploded and disintegrated on the ground at position reference 196526 Llandegla."

An attempt to secure further data from the MoD brought forth the following response from the Government Services Department: "The registered files of the Defense Intelligence Staff which have been selected for permanent preservation have been assigned to a Public Record Office class (reference DEFE31). All of them were retained by the Ministry of Defense. These records were retained because they contain information relating to the security and intelligence services and are obviously highly sensitive."

In other words, go away!

DANGER IN THE WOODS

SLITTING MILL, STAFFORDSHIRE, ENGLAND

It was in the early hours of a winter's morning in 1975 when Barry and Elaine, a married couple then in their late twenties and with two small children, were driving towards their then-Slitting Mill, Staffordshire, England home after attending an early Christmas party in the nearby town of Penkridge. As the pair headed towards the small village (its population today, four centuries after its initial foundations were laid, is still less than three hundred), their car's engine began to splutter and, to their consternation and concern, completely died. Having managed to carefully coast the car to the side of the road, Barry proceeded to quickly open the hood and took a look at the engine – "even though I'm mainly useless at mechanical stuff," he states.

According to Barry, Elaine let out a loud scream, terrified by the sight of a small figure that ran across the road in front of them at a high rate of speed. She explains: "I just about saw it at the last second, and then another one followed it, and then a third one. The best way I can describe them to you is like a hairy troll or something like that. We had some moonlight and they were like little men, but with hunchbacks and big, hooked noses and not a stitch on them at all. Not a stitch, at all; just hair all over them. I'd say they were all four-feet-tallish, and when the third one crossed by us, you could see them at the edge of the trees – wary, or something, anyway.

"Things became very hazy indeed, says Barry: "We both know from memory that they came forwards, towards us, very slowly to us, and I've thought since that they were interested in us or wanted to know who we were. They came very slowly, and it was a bit like we were being hunted, to me. Elaine was hysterical; and with the kids with us, I wasn't far-off, either.

"But that's all we remember. The next, it's all gone; nothing. Neither of us remembers seeing them go, and the next thing it was about two o'clock and the car started fine, then. It felt like something had happened to us, but I couldn't quite put my finger on, you know what I mean? But the memory thing is the biggest problem, even now. What was it? I *did* have a dream later about them surrounding the car, but that's it, really."

Real trolls? Probably more likely, alien abductors.

DECEMBER 19, 1973

"THE BEING CARRIED A DEVICE WITH A LONG HANDLE"
VILVOORDE, BELGIUM

On This Day says: "A famous well-investigated close encounter of the third kind report occurred on this night in Vilvoorde, Belgium. A 28-year-old man awoke at 2:00 a.m. and saw in the yard behind his house a short entity about 1.1 meters tall dressed in a luminous green space suit and helmet. The being carried a device with a long handle and a base that looked similar to a vacuum cleaner. He walked up the side of a wall. The domed disc UFO was about six meters in diameter, and had an insignia shaped like a black circle with a diagonal lightening flash through it."

DECEMBER 20, 1948

"THE OBJECT LOOKED LIKE A V-1'S EXHAUST"

LOS ALAMOS, NEW MEXICO

UFO authority Joel Carpenter says:

"11:35 PM - A Los Alamos patrol reports a greenish-white light moving toward them in an arc from a great distance. It grows to 1/4 full Moon size, in a 20 deg glide, then its path flattens out until parallel with the ground. It does not fall, but continues in level flight until disappearing. Two other observers make simultaneous observations: George Skipper of the Security Division and Lt Clifford Strang of AESS. Strang had seen a German V-1 cruise missile during the 'Blitz' in England and thinks that the object looked like a V-1's exhaust. Skipper thinks it was a vehicle's exhaust too."

DECEMBER 21, 1955

"THE EXPERIENCE MADE HER FEEL NAUSEOUS"

WASHBURN, MAINE

Also from On This Day: "From her bedroom window in Washburn, Maine, Mrs. Jacobs watched a reddish-orange glare resolve into a golden domed elliptical saucer at eleven o'clock at night. In the lower part of the dome she could see figures moving about, like people 'walking in front of a light.' The experience made her feel nauseous, and at the same time she had a definite feeling of being watched.

DECEMBER 22, 1967

"STOP PRINTING UFO STORIES"
POINT PLEASANT, WEST VIRIGINA

Men in Black authority, Gareth Medway, says: "Mary Hyre, news-woman of Point Pleasant, West Virginia, was visited by two men in black overcoats who asked her: 'What would you do if someone did order you to stop writing about flying saucers?' Later the same day, 'Jack Brown', who like the other two looked oriental, came and asked her: 'What – would – what would you do – if someone ordered – ordered you to stop - to stop printing UFO stories?'"

To her credit, Hyre said she would tell them to go to hell.

DECEMBER 23, 2012

A VIOLENT INTRUDER
CORPUS CHRISTI, TEXAS

Of the many and varied shapeshifters that have plagued and ter-rified people for countless centuries, there are very few which are more frightening than bedroom-invading monsters known as Incubus and Succubus; male and female monsters that, in numer-ous are perceived as having outright demonic origins. They are terrifying things that have a long history of diabolical interaction with the human race. As evidence of this, reports of these evil things date back not just decades or centuries, but millennia too. All of which brings us to the most important question of all: what are they? For some, Incubus and Succubus are actually aliens, per-ceived by the ancients as demons. One of those is Michelle of Corpus Christi, Texas.

Imagine the scene: it's around 3:00 a.m. and you're fast asleep when, suddenly, you find yourself in a semi-awake state. Confusion and terror quickly overwhelm you, as you realize you are unable to move. Even worse, you sense that something dangerous and malevolent is walking, or crawling, towards the bedroom. You struggle to move, but it's all to no avail. The thing then enters the room and you see its hideous form. It looms over you, like a monstrous sword of Damocles. Your heart pounds and your breathing becomes shallow as the nightmarish beast jumps onto the bed, straddles you, and forcibly pins you down. The creature screams at the top of its voice, and in a wailing, banshee-like style, and proceeds to have violent sex with you – against your will. You try and fight it off, but your arms and legs are like lead-weights. And, then, as suddenly as the horrifying encounter began, it's all over. The oppressive atmosphere is gone, the evil entity has vanished too, and you find yourself shaking, and in a cold sweat, as you wonder if what just happened was the result of a bad dream or something worse: violation at the claws of a supernatural monster.

Encounters of the kind I just described extend back to the earliest years of human civilization. Indeed, the term, Incubus, is taken from an ancient, Latin word, "incubare," which means "to lie upon," which is a most apt description. As for their appearances, Incubus and Succubus can take on multiple forms. There are forms which range from beautiful women to hideous monsters – hence the shapeshifting connection.

For Michelle, however, they are ETs that can take on multiple forms.

DECEMBER 24, 1971

THE LITTLE MEN OF THE WOODS

TREMPEALEAU MOUNTAIN, WISCONSIN

Frank Banner's family tells of the time that Frank, in 1971, encountered a group of around fifteen strange, diminutive beings in the vast woods surrounding Trempealeau Mountain, Wisconsin, as he took a stroll with the family dog. According to Banner, as he walked along one particular track he suddenly developed a sense of being watched. He was. Within seconds, a group of very human looking, but only about two-feet-tall, creatures came out of the woods in front of him. Curiously, the dog did not act in a hostile fashion, but wagged its tail vigorously, as if it was greeting a bunch of old friends Banner, however, was terrified by the sight of this strange band of mini-people – all of who were dressed in what Banner described as "primitive clothing." The group did nothing more than smile at Banner, wave, and then continue on their way, into the woods on the other side of the track.

Despite the fact that the family made jokes about Frank having met a tribe of pixies, until his dying day banner believed he had encounter an extraterrestrial race of very human-like – albeit small – proportions.

DECEMBER 25, 1985

THE DREAM INVADER

STONEHENGE, WILTSHIRE, ENGLAND

Only hours after briefly seeing a cigar-shaped UFO hovering near Stonehenge, Wiltshire, England, Sandra Green – who was driving home after a late night Christmas Eve party, in the English city of

Bath – had a bizarre dream in which three Men in Black warned her to keep her nose out of UFOs. That the dream was so graphic led Sandra to believe that the MIB had the ability to literally get inside her dreams, manipulate those very same dreams, and issue a bone-chilling warning – one she has not forgotten.

DECEMBER 26, 1978

THE LIZARD MAN
BIG THICKET, TEXAS

Some might say that the following case falls into the domain of cryptozoology. Maybe so. Granted, no UFO was seen. But, the affair definitely has UFO overtones attached to it. Alan Briggs was driving through Texas' Big Thicket on a weekday afternoon when he saw race across the road what he described as "a large lizard running upright." Most bizarre of all, the lizard-man – who stood around eight-feet in height and whose skin was bright green – was wearing a bright blue outfit, not unlike that of a fighter pilot in style. Briggs stared in awe and shock as the thing charged across in front of him – never to be seen again.

DECEMBER 27, 1980

A UFO LANDING IN THE UK
SUFFOLK, ENGLAND

Just two days after Christmas 1980, one of the most significant of all UFO encounters occurred in Rendlesham Forest, Suffolk, England – adjacent to the twin-Royal Air Force Bases, Wood-bridge and Bentwaters. A memo prepared the Deputy Base Commander, Lieutenant Charles Halt reveals the astonishing facts:

"Early in the morning of 27 Dec 80 (approximately 0300L) two USAF security police patrolmen saw unusual lights outside the back gate at RAF Woodbridge. Thinking an aircraft might have crashed or been forced down, they called for permission to go outside the gate to investigate. The on–duty flight chief responded and allowed three patrolmen to proceed on foot.

"The individuals reported seeing a strange glowing object in the forest. The object was described as being metallic in appearance and triangular in shape, approximately two to three meters across the base and approximately two meters high. It illuminated the entire forest with a white light. The object itself had a pulsing red light on top and a bank(s) of blue lights underneath. The object was hovering or on legs.

"As the patrolmen approached the object, it maneuvered through the trees and disappeared. At this time, the animals on a nearby farm went into a frenzy. The object was briefly sighted approximately an hour later near the back gate."

The notable encounter remains unresolved to this day.

DECEMBER 28, 1980

FACE TO FACE WITH ET

RENDLESHAM FOREST, ENGLAND

One day after the events described by Lt. Col. Charles Halt in the section directly above, there was yet another close encounter in Rendlesham Forest. The account comes from an airman named Larry Warren.

Along with a number of his comrades, Warren was ordered to make his way into the woods. The scene was as amazing as it was surreal: When the group arrived at a clearing, they could see that the immediate vicinity was lit up by an eerie mist. Tensions were high. Wild rabbits and deer were seen fleeing the area, as if for their very lives. Dozens of people were swarming around, some with camera equipment, and others with Geiger-counters. Something weird was going down. Something *very* weird.

Out of the blue, a small ball of light headed towards the mist, then came to a sudden halt, hanging directly over it. In seconds, and amid a powerful flash, the light was gone. In its place was a not particularly large object that was pyramid-like in shape.

It wasn't long before something incredible happened: a large ball of gold/blue light surfaced from the side of the craft, maneuvered slowly, and came to a halt about three or so meters before the military personnel. Contained within the ball were a trio of small creatures. They were clearly not human. That much was made obvious by their large heads and cat-like eyes. Warren recalls some kind of dialog occurring between the entities and a military officer – following which Warren and his comrades were told to return to the truck in which they had arrived.

Warren, the next night, was rendered into a drugged-like state and taken to a below-level part of the base, where he encountered what may have been some kind of extraterrestrial. Or, perhaps, his superiors were intent on scrambling Warren's mind to the point where he was unsure what the truth of the situation was.

UFO TERROR

HUFFMAN, TEXAS

When, shortly before 9:00 p.m., Vickie Landrum, her grandson, Colby, and Betty Cash exited the restaurant where they had just eaten a fine Texan dinner, they couldn't imagine what was just around the corner. As they headed towards the town of Huffman, they were terrified by the sudden sight of an unknown object in the sky. Worse, it was descending on a flight-path guaranteed to ensure it landed on the road they were on.

As they got closer, they could see the aerial thing appeared to be in flames and shaped not unlike a diamond. It reached a perilously low level of around twenty-five feet, something which ensured a screeching of brakes and the car brought to a shuddering standstill. The interior temperature of the car suddenly reached intolerable levels. The three jumped out of the vehicle and could only stare in awe and fear. Then, out of the blue, around two dozen, double-rotor helicopters were on the scene, clearly intent on caroling the UFO. Or, perhaps they were escorting it. Cash was sure they were Boeing CH-47 Chinooks. They watched as both the UFO and the helicopters left the area and were finally lost from sight.

Within days, all three fell sick: nausea and vomiting were at the forefront. Betty Cash was the one affected most of all – which may be explainable by the fact that she was the one member of the group who got closest to the object. Her hair started to fall out, her skin was covered with pustules and blisters, and the nausea got worse.

Despite attempts to force the US Government to come clean on what went down, there was nothing but denial after denial from the authorities. The case is a puzzling one, with some UFO researchers believing the three encountered a real UFO, while others suspect they were unfortunate enough to cross paths with a top secret, nuclear-powered, prototype aircraft that was in deep trouble.

DECEMBER 30, 1947
"SOME TYPE OF FLYING OBJECT HAS BEEN OBSERVED"
UNITED STATES

A November 3, 1947 U.S. Air Force document, titled "Flying Object Incidents in the United States," reveals…

"By letter dated 30 December 1947 from the Director of Research and Development, Headquarters USAF, your Headquarters was required to establish Project 'SIGN.' The conclusion appears inescapable that some type of flying object has been observed. Identification and the origin of these objects is not discernible to this Headquarters. It is imperative, therefore, that efforts to determine whether these objects are of domestic or foreign origin must be increased until conclusive evidence is obtained. The needs of national defense require such evidence in order that appropriate countermeasures may be taken."

DECEMBER 31, 2009
FROM HOLIDAY TO UFO
SAN JUAN, PUERTO RICO

While vacationing on Puerto Rico with her boyfriend – and while sat on a stretch of San Juan beach that overlooked the ocean around 11:00 p.m., and as a new year was about to dawn – Christina was amazed to see a large, white-colored, triangular-shaped UFO rise out of the sea. It did so in completely silence and in a very slow fashion. As the pair stared at the massive craft, in awe, it suddenly shot into the heavens above, and vanished. Both estimated the object to have been a couple of hundred feet in length. They were unable to explain what it was they saw; however, they seriously doubt it was anything built on Earth.

ACKNOWLEDGMENTS

I would like to offer my very sincere thanks to all of the following: my literary agent, publisher and friend, Lisa Hagan; my editor and co-publisher, Beth Wareham, book-designer, Simon Hartshorne, and everyone who generously shared their UFO-themed experiences with me.

ABOUT NICK REDFERN

Nick Redfern is the author of 40 books on UFOs, lake-monsters, the Roswell UFO crash, zombies, and Hollywood scandal, including *Men in Black*; *Chupacabra Road Trip*; *The Bigfoot Book*; and *Close Encounters of the Fatal Kind*. Nick has appeared on many TV shows, including: Fox News; the BBC's *Out of This World*; the SyFy Channel's *Proof Positive*; the History Channel's *Monster Quest*, *America's Book of Secrets*, *Ancient Aliens* and *UFO Hunters*; the National Geographic Channel's *Paranatural*; and MSNBC's *Countdown* with Keith Olbermann. He can be contacted at: http://nickredfernfortean.blogspot.com

BIBLIOGRAPHY

Adamski, George. *Behind the Flying Saucer Mystery*. NY: Paperback Library, Inc., 1967.

Andrews, George C. *Extra-Terrestrials Among Us*. Woodbury, MN: Llewellyn Publications, 1986.

Angelucci, Orfeo. *Son of the Sun*. New Brunswick, NJ: Global Communications, 2008.

Barker, Gray. *They Knew Too Much about Flying Saucers*. Clarksburg, WV: Saucerian Press, Inc., 1975.

Beckley, Timothy Green. *The UFO Silencers*. New Brunswick, NJ: Inner Light Publications, 1990.

Bender, Albert K. *Flying Saucers and the Three Men*. NY: Paperback Library, Inc., 1968.

Bennett, Colin. *Looking for Orthon*. NY: Paraview Press, 2001.

Bethurum, Truman. *Aboard a Flying Saucer*. Los Angeles, CA: DeVorss & Co., 1955.

Bishop, Greg. *Project Beta*. NY: Paraview–Pocket Books, 2005.

Bowen, Charles (editor). *The Humanoids*. Chicago, IL: Henry Regnery Company, 1969.

"Burn marks and holes found after UFO seen close to ground." http://www.ufoevidence.org/cases/case578.htm.

Butler, Brenda, Street, Dot & Randles, Jenny. *Sky Crash*. London, U.K.: Grafton Books, 1986.

Carpenter, Joel, "Green Fireball Chronology"

Central Intelligence Agency (CIA) documents on UFOs declassified under the terms of the Freedom of Information Act.

Chapman, Robert. *Unidentified Flying Objects*. Aylesbury, U.K.: Mayflower Paperbacks, 1970.

Cherry, Ken. *Marc Slade Investigates: The Stephenville UFO*. Hamburg, NJ: Glannant Ty Publishing, 2015.

Civil Aviation Authority (CAA) documents on UFOs declassified under the terms of the Freedom of Information Act.

Clarke, David & Roberts, Andy. *Out of the Shadows*. London, U.K.: Piatkus, 2002.

Coleman, Loren. "Space Pancakes…A Fortean Breakfast Story." http://www.anomalist.com/reports/pancakes.html.

Colvin, Andrew B. *The Mothman Speaks*. Seattle, WA: Metadisc Books, 2010.

Colvin Andrew B. *The Mothman's Photographer*. Seattle, WA: Metadisc Books, 2007.

Computer UFO Network. http://www.cufon.org/.

Corso, Philip J. & Birnes, William J. The Day After Roswell. NY: Simon & Schuster, 1997.

David, Jay. *The Flying Saucer Reader*. NY: Signet Books, 1967.

Defense Intelligence Agency (DIA) documents on UFOs declassified under the terms of the Freedom of Information Act.

Derenberger, Woody. *Visitors from Lanulos*. Point Pleasant, WV: New Saucerian Press, 2014.

Didymus, John Thomas. "NASA Allegedly Sent Human Astronauts to an Alien Planet in 1965." http://www.inquisitr.com/23323 24/nasa-allegedly-sent-human-astronauts-to-an-alien-planet- in-1965/. August 13, 2011.

Dolan, Richard M. *UFOs and the National Security State, the Cover-Up Exposed, 1973-1991*.

Rochester, NY: Keyhole Publishing Company, 2009.

Downes, Jonathan. *The Owlman and Others.* Woolsery, U.K.: CFZ Press, 2006.

Downes, Jonathan & Wright, Nigel. *The Rising of the Moon.* Corby, U.K.: Domra Publications, 1999.

Edwards, Frank. *Flying Saucers – Serious Business.* NY: Lyle Stuart, 1966.

Emenegger, Robert. *UFO's, Past, Present & Future.* NY: Ballantine Books, 1974.

"Endangered Species (1982)." http://www.imdb.com/title/tt0083885/.

Evans-Wentz, W.Y. *The Fairy-Faith in Celtic Countries.* Wayne, NJ: New Page Books, 2004.

Fawcett, Lawrence & Greenwood, Barry. *Clear Intent.* Englewood Cliffs, NJ: Prentice-Hall, Inc., 1984.

Federal Bureau of Investigation (FBI) documents on cattle mutilations declassified under the terms of the Freedom of Information Act.

Federal Bureau of Investigation (FBI) documents on the 1986 Space Shuttle *Challenger* explosion declassified under the terms of the Freedom of Information Act.

Federal Bureau of Investigation (FBI) documents on UFOs declassified under the terms of the Freedom of Information Act.

Feschino, Jr., Frank. *The Braxton County Monster.* Lulu, 2012.

Flammonde, Paris. *UFO Exist!* NY: Ballantine Books, 1976.

Fowler, Raymond. *UFOs: Interplanetary Visitors.* NY: Bantam Books, 1979.

Fuller, John G. *The Interrupted Journey*. NY: Dial Press, 1966.

Gerhard, Ken. *Encounters with Flying Humanoids*. Woodbury, MN: Llewellyn Publications, 2013.

Gibbons, Gavin. Secaucus, NJ: *They Rode in Space Ships*. Citadel Press, 1957.

Girvan, Waveney. *Flying Saucers and Common Sense*. London, U.K.: Frederick Muller, Ltd., 1955.

Good, Timothy. *Above Top Secret*. London, U.K.: Sidgwick & Jackson, 1987.

Good, Timothy. *Alien Base*. London, U.K.: Arrow Books Ltd., 1999.

Good, Timothy. *Alien Liaison*. London, U.K.: Century, 1991.

Gordon, Stan. *Silent Invasion*. Greensburg, PA: self-published, 2010.

Guieu, Jimmy. *Flying Saucers Come from Another World*. London, U.K.: Hutchinson, 1956.

Hanks, Micah. *The Ghost Rockets*. Rocketeer Press, 2013.

Hickson, Charles & Mendez, William. *UFO Contact at Pascagoula*. Tucson, AZ: Wendelle C. Stevens Publishing.

Hidell, Alec. "Tracks in the Desert." *Wake Up Down There!* Edited by Greg Bishop. Kempton, IL: Adventures Unlimited Press, 2000.

Holledge, James. *Flying Saucers Over Australia*. Melbourne, Australia: Horowitz Publications, Inc., 1965.

Holzer, Hans. *The Ufonauts*. St. Albans, U.K.: Granada Publishing Ltd., 1979.

Hynek, J. Allen. *The UFO Experience.*
NY: Ballantine Books, 1974.

Hynek, J. Allen, Imbrogno, Philip J. & Pratt, Bob. *Night Siege.* Woodbury, MN: Llewellyn Publications, 1998.

Icke, David. "Reptilian Agenda." https://www.davidicke.com/category/271/reptilian-agenda.

Jessup, Morris K. *The UFO Annual.* NY: The Citadel Press, 1956.

Keel, John. *The Mothman Prophecies.* NY: Tor Books, 1991.

Keith, Jim. *Black Helicopters II.* Lilburn,
GA: IllumiNet Press, 1997.

Keith, Jim. *Black Helicopters Over America.*
Lilburn, GA: IllumiNet Press, 1994.

Keyhoe, Donald E. *Aliens from Space.*
NY: Doubleday & Co., 1973.

Keyhoe, Donald E. *Flying Saucers: Top Secret.*
NY: G.P, Putnam's Sons, 1960.

Keyhoe, Donald E. *The Flying Saucers Are
Real.* NY: Fawcett Publications, 1950.

"Listing of Australian Crash Retrieval Stories." http://www.ufoevidence.org/documents/doc1600.htm.

Lorenzen, Coral & Lorenzen, Jim. *Encounters with UFO Occupants.* NY: Berkeley Publishing Corporation, 1976.

Lorenzen, Coral & Lorenzen, Jim. *Flying Saucer Occupants.* NY: Signet Books, 1967.

Mack, John E. *Passport to the Cosmos.* NY:
Three Rivers Press, 1999.

Marsh, Roger. "Texas Triangle UFO Emits Orange Color From Three Lights." http://www.openminds. tv/texas-triangle-ufo-emits-orange-color-from-three-lights/35892. December 16, 2015.

Marsh, Roger. "Utah witness recounts UFO encounter near military base." http://www.openminds.tv/utah-witness-recounts-ufo-encounter-near-military-base/37178. May 5, 2016.

Medway, Gareth J. "Men in Black Encounters, a Short Catalogue." http://pelicanist.blogspot. com/p/mib-encounters.html.

Meehan, Paul. "Phantom Clowns, Bogus Social Workers, and Men in Black." http://www.theofantastique. com/2011/11/30/phantom-clowns- bogus-social-workers-and-men- in-black/. November 30, 2011.

MI5 documents on Crop Circles declassified under the terms of the Freedom of Information Act.

Michel, Aime. *The Truth about Flying Saucers*. NY: Pyramid Books, 1967.

Ministry of Defense (MoD) documents on UFOs declassified under the terms of the Freedom of Information Act.

National Security Agency (NSA) documents on UFOs declassified under the terms of the Freedom of Information Act.

O'Brien, Christopher. *Stalking the Herd*. Kempton, IL: Adventures Unlimited Press, 2014.

"On This Day." http://www.ufoinfo. com/onthisday/calendar.html.

Palmer, Raymond A. *The Real UFO Invasion*. San Diego, CA: Greenleaf Classics, Inc., 1967.

Project Moon Dust documents declassified under the terms of the Freedom of Information Act.

Rael. *The Message Given to Me by Extra-Terrestrials*. Japan: AOM Corporation, 1986.

Ramsey, Scott, Ramsey, Suzanne & Thayer, Frank. *The Aztec UFO Incident*. Wayne, NJ: New Page Books, 2016.

Randle, Kevin D. & Schmitt, Donald R. *UFO Crash at Roswell*. NY: Avon Books, 1991.

Randles, Jenny. *The Pennine UFO Mystery*. St. Albans, U.K.: Granada Publishing, Ltd., 1983.

Randles. Jenny. *The Truth Behind Men in Black*. NY: St. Martin's Paperbacks, 1997.

Redfern, Nick. *A Covert Agenda*. London, U.K.: Simon & Schuster, 1997.

Redfern, Nick. *Chupacabra Road Trip*. Woodbury, MN: Llewellyn Publications, 2015.

Redfern, Nick. *Close Encounters of the Fatal Kind*. Wayne, NJ: New Page Books, 2014.

Redfern, Nick. *Cosmic Crashes*. London, U.K.: Simon & Schuster, 1999.

Redfern, Nick. *Final Events*. San Antonio, TX: Anomalist Books, 2010.

Redfern, Nick. *Men in Black*. Bracey, VA: Lisa Hagan Books, 2015.

Redfern, Nick. *Nessie*. Woodbury, MN: Llewellyn Publications, 2016.

Redfern, Nick. *The FBI Files*. London, U.K.: Simon & Schuster, 1998.

Redfern, Nick. *The Monster Book*. Canton, MI:Visible Ink Press, 2016.

Redfern, Nick. *The Strange Story of the UFO on the Moors*. http://mysteriousuniverse.org/2016/11/the-strange-story-of-the-ufo-on-the-moors/. November 22, 2016.

Redfern, Nick. "UFOs: Manipulating & Destabilizing." http://mysteriousuniverse.org/2014/05/ufos-manipulating-destabilizing/. May 6, 2014.

Redfern, Nick. *Women in Black*. Bracey, VA: Lisa Hagan Books, 2016.

Riggs, Rob. *In the Big Thicket*. NY: Paraview Press, 2001.

Roberts, Andy. *UFO Down?* Woolsery, U.K.: CFZ Press, 2010.

Royal Air Force (RAF) documents on UFOs declassified under the terms of the Freedom of Information Act.

Ruppelt, Edward J. *The Report on Unidentified Flying Objects*. NY: Ace Books, Inc., 1956.

Sagan, Carl & Page, Thornton (editors). *UFO's – A Scientific Debate*. London, U.K.: Cornell University Press, 1972.

Salisbury, Frank B. *The Utah UFO Display*. Old Greenwich, CT: Devin-Adair Company, 1974.

Sanderson, Ivan. *Invisible Residents*. NY: Avon Books, 1973.

Schnabel, Jim. *Remote Viewers*. NY: Dell Publishing, 1997.

Schuessler, John F. *The Cash-Landrum UFO Incident*. CreateSpace, 2016.

Scully, Frank. *Behind the Flying Saucers*. NY: Henry Holt & Co., Inc., 1950.

Staff of the *New York Post. Heaven's Gate.*
NY: Harper Paperbacks, 1997.

Stanford, Ray. *Socorro "Saucer" in a Pentagon Pantry.*
Austin, TX: Blueapple Books, 1976.

Steiger, Brad. *Flying Saucers are Hostile.* NY: Award Books, 1967.

Steiger, Brad. *Project Blue Book.* NY: Ballantine Books, 1976.

Stevens, Wendelle. *UFOs Over China.* Tucson,
AZ: Wendelle C. Stevens Publishing.

Stranges, Frank E. *Stranger at the Pentagon.* New
Brunswick, NJ: Inner Light Publications, 1991.

Stringfield, Leonard H. *Situation Red: The UFO
Siege.* London, U.K.: Sphere Books, Ltd., 1977.

Stringfield, Leonard H. *The Fatal Encounter at
Ft. Dix-McGuire.* Self-published, 1985.

Stringfield, Leonard H. *The UFO Crash/Retrieval Syndrome.*
Seguin, TX: Mutual UFO Network, Inc., 1980.

Stringfield, Leonard H. *UFO Crash/Retrievals: Amassing
the Evidence.* Cincinnati, OH: self-published, 1982.

Stringfield, Leonard H. *UFO Crash/Retrievals: Is the
Cover-Up Lifting?* Cincinnati, OH, self-published, 1989.

Stringfield, Leonard H. *UFO Crash/Retrievals: The Inner
Sanctum.* Cincinnati, OH, self-published, 1991.

Swann, Ingo. *Penetration.* Rapid City,
SD: Ingo Swann Books, 1998.

"The Invaders (1967–1968), Panic." http://
www.imdb.com/title/tt0611985/.

"The Man in Black." https://en.wikipedia.
org/wiki/The_Man_in_Black_(film).

Thomas, Kenn. *Maury Island UFO*. Lilburn,
GA: IllumiNet Press, 1999.

Thull, R.E. *The UFO Connection*. Self-published, 2000.

Torres, Noe. *Mexico's Roswell*. College Station,
TX:VBW Publishing, 2007.

Vallee, Jacques. *Anatomy of a Phenomenon*. Chicago,
IL: Henry Regnery Company, 1965.

Vallee, Jacques. *Passport to Magonia*. Chcago,
IL: Contemporary Books, Inc., 1993.

"Visitors from Lanulos." https://www.amazon.com/
Visitors-Lanulos-Contact-Indrid-Illustrated/dp/1499307039.

Warren, Larry & Robbins, Peter. *Left at
East Gate*. NY: Cosimo, 2005.

Weatherly, David. *The Black Eyed Children*.
AZ: Leprechaun Press, 2012.

Wilkins, Harold T. *Flying Saucers on the
Attack*. NY: Ace Books, Inc., 1967.

Wilkins, Harold T. *Flying Saucers Uncensored*.
NY: Citadel Press, 1955.

Wood, Robert M. & Redfern, Nick. *Alien Viruses*.
Rochester, NY: Richard Dolan Press, 2013.

Wood, Ryan S. *Majic Eyes Only*. Broomfield,
CO:Wood Enterprises, 2005.

Printed in Great Britain
by Amazon